An Inimitable Example

An Inimitable Example

THE CASE FOR
THE PRINCESSE DE CLÈVES

EDITED BY PATRICK HENRY,
Professor of French, Whitman College
Walla Walla, Washington

The Catholic University of America Press
Washington, D.C.

Copyright © 1992
The Catholic University of America Press
All rights reserved
Printed and bound in Canada.

The paper used in this publication meets the minimum
requirements of American National Standards for Information
Science—Permanence of Paper for Printed Library materials,
ANSI Z39.48-1984.
∞

Library of Congress Cataloging-in-Publication Data
An Inimitable example : The case for the Princesse de Clèves /
    edited by Patrick Henry.
        p. cm.
    Includes bibliographical references and index.
        1. La Fayette, Madame de (Marie-Madeleine Pioche de la
    Vergne), 1634–1693. Princesse de Clèves. 2. Feminism and
    literature—France—History—17th century. 3. Women and
    literature—France—History—17th century. I. Henry,
    Patrick (Patrick Gerard)
    PQ1805.L5A757   1993
    843'.4—dc20
    92-5968
    ISBN 0-8132-0765-7 (alk. paper)

In memory of my father, Thomas Joseph Henry (1896–1975), and with love and gratitude to my mother, Jeannette Elizabeth Henry, on her 80th birthday. Her life, like the princess's, has provided "inimitable examples of virtue."

Contents

Foreword

I would like to thank all the contributors for their willingness to participate in this scholarly project, particularly John Lyons, who contributed far more than the epilogue. I would certainly be remiss if I failed to thank Jane Baffney and especially Sally Hooker for their patience and good humor while preparing the manuscript. At The Catholic University of America Press, I am particularly indebted to David McGonagle and Susan Needham, who both helped me over rough spots along the way, and to Philip Holthaus, for a superb job of copyediting. Finally, as always, my greatest debt is to Mary Anne and Anne, who have helped me in every imaginable way and without whom the project would never have been realized.

Acknowledgments

The editor would like to thank the following journals and publishers for permission to reprint articles originally published elsewhere: *Papers on French Seventeenth-Century Literature,* of Paris, Seattle, and Tübingen, for permission to reprint an English translation of Wolfgang Leiner's "La Princesse et le directeur de conscience: Création romanesque et prédication," first published in *La Pensée religieuse dans la littérature et civilisation du XVIIème siècle en France: Actes du Colloque de Bamberg 1983,* edited by Manfred Tietz and Volker Kapp (1984).

PMLA, for permission to reprint Joan DeJean's "Lafayette's Ellipses: The Privileges of Anonymity" (99 [1984]: 884–902), and Nancy Miller's "Emphasis Added: Plots and Plausibilities in Women's Fiction" (96 [1981]: 36–48).

Summa Publications, of Birmingham, Alabama, for permission to reprint Patrick Henry's *"La Princesse de Clèves* and *L'Introduction à la vie dévote,"* first published in *French Studies in Honor of Philip A. Wadsworth,* edited by D. W. Tappan and W. A. Mould (1985).

Introduction

PATRICK HENRY

ORTY years after the quarrel over *Le Cid,* Mme de Lafayette started another literary battle when she published *La Princesse de Clèves* anonymously in March 1678. Rarely is literature taken so seriously. Letters passed back and forth discussing the work; a newspaper took a poll concerning the behavior of the heroine; books of criticism appeared within only months of publication critiquing various aspects of the work and its characters. On April 13, 1678, the author wrote to Lescheraine, "On est partagé sur ce livre-là, à se manger; les uns en condamnent ce que les autres en admirent."[1]

The debate, in fact, started before the book was published. Word had spread, as Mme de Scudéry tells Count Bussy-Rabutin in December 1677, that "Monsieur de la Rochefoucault et madame de la Fayette ont fait un roman des galanteries de la cour de Henry second."[2] It had become known too that in this work a woman would confess to her husband that she was in love with another man. Two months before the book was published, an unsigned short story entitled "La Vertu malheureuse" appeared in the January 1678 issue of Donneau de Visé's *Mercure galant.* The tale contained the salient points of the unpublished narrative: the confession followed by the husband's death and the widow's refusal to marry her loved one. With such prepublication publicity, the public devoured the work immediately upon

1. Mme de Lafayette, *Correspondance,* 2 vols., ed. André Beaunier (Paris: Gallimard, 1942), 2:63; hereafter cited parenthetically in the text.

2. Roger de Bussy-Rabutin, *Correspondance,* 6 vols., ed. Ludovic Lalanne (Paris: Charpentier, 1858), 3:431–32; hereafter cited parenthetically in the text.

publication. A month later the same *Mercure galant* polled its readers regarding the wisdom of the heroine's confession to her husband. The next three issues reported the results of the referendum. The overwhelming majority of the responses, most of which came from the provinces, condemned the princess's behavior, often, ironically in retrospect, for having destroyed "domestic repose." A highly original voice in the survey was that of the famous geometrician Fontenelle who, although he objected to the "digressions" and the long introduction, admired the work for its psychological finesse and the confession in particular: "Qu'on raisonne tant qu'on voudra là-dessus, je trouve le trait admirable et très bien préparé . . . je ne vois rien à cela que de beau et d'héroïque."[3]

At the same time, in April 1678, Mme de Lafayette denied authorship—"je vous asseure que je n'y en ay aucune [part] et que M. de la Rochefoucauld, à qui on l'a voulu donner aussi, y en a aussi peu que moy"—but praised the book for its "parfaite imitation du monde de la cour et de la manière dont on y vit." It is not therefore "un roman" [a romance], she wrote, "c'est proprement des mémoires" (2:62–63). This is not, however, how Bussy-Rabutin evaluated the text which, he claimed, "sent le roman." In his famous letter of June 29, 1678, to Mme de Sévigné, he deems the confession "extravagant" and enumerates several episodes that he finds "invraisemblables" (4:141).

The first full-length major criticism of *La Princesse de Clèves* appeared anonymously in June 1678. Although originally attributed to Bouhours, *Lettres à Mme la Marquise * * * sur le sujet de "La Princesse de Clèves"* came from the insightful and witty pen of Jean-Baptiste Valincour, the twenty-five-year-old friend of Boileau and Racine and protégé of Bossuet. It consists of three long letters that deal with the action, characters, style, and language of the work. Central to the entire text is the concept of *vraisemblance* (plausibility/verisimilitude) which the author applies to both events and psychology. The opening historical tableau and the "digressions" are but a series of hors-d'oeuvre, while, for example, the vidame's lost letter, the unaccom-

3. Fontenelle's letter is reproduced in its entirety in Alain Niderst, *"La Princesse de Clèves" de Mme de Lafayette* (Paris: Nizet, 1977), 204–5. See too Maurice Laugaa, *Lectures de Mme de Lafayette* (Paris: Armand Colin, 1971), 22–25.

panied princess in the jewelry shop, the presence of Nemours at the confession scene, and the death of the Prince de Clèves are all in the work "aux dépens du vray-semblable."[4] At the psychological level, none of the main characters seems plausible. The Prince de Clèves dies like a fool "sans vouloir être éclairci" (76) and Nemours, who knows he is loved and is the greatest seducer at court, "n'en sçait pas profiter" (171). But it is the princess who really baffles Valincour. Her passion is too sudden; she doesn't speak enough; her simplicity is "extraordinaire" (126). In his bewilderment, he ends up comparing her to Agnès in *L'Ecole des femmes*. Once more, neither her confession to her husband nor her renunciation of Nemours is *vraisemblable*. "C'est une femme incompréhensible que Madame de Clèves," he concludes, "c'est la prude la plus coquette et la coquette la plus prude que l'on ait jamais veûë" (272–73).

Equally important in Valincour's critique is the idea of genre. In his text *un homme savant* defines two types of fiction. In the first type an author is permitted to "suivre son imagination en toutes choses, sans avoir aucun égard à la vérité" (93). It doesn't matter whether events in this type of fiction have actually happened, only that they could have happened (94). In the second type of fiction, subjects are drawn from history and authors are consequently not entirely masters of their inventions. One can add and subtract, "mais ce ne doit estre que dans les circonstances" (95). The foundation must be built upon historical truth. As John Lyons has pointed out, Valincour is distinguishing between "romance" and "novella" even though he never uses these terms.[5] In each case, Mme de Lafayette's text is found wanting. Hardly romance in that it is set in the court of Henri II and contains historical characters, it is not a novella because it introduces fictional characters (La Princesse de Clèves and Mme de Chartres) into a precise historical setting and changes the status—there never was a married Duc de Clèves at Henri's court—of real historical figures. As such, it is not a faithful representation of the history it purports to relate.

4. Jean-Baptiste Valincour, *Lettres à Mme la Marquise * * * sur le sujet de "La Princesse de Clèves"* (Paris: Sébastien Mabre-Cramoisy, 1678), 50; hereafter cited parenthetically in the text.

5. John Lyons, in his illuminating "Marie de Lafayette: From Image to Act," in *Exemplum: The Rhetoric of Example in Early Modern France and Italy* (Princeton: Princeton University Press, 1989), 196–236.

Neither fish nor fowl, romance nor novella, *La Princesse de Clèves* is a text without a genre.

Eleven months later, in May 1679, a reply to Valincour appeared entitled *Conversations sur la critique de "La Princesse de Clèves."* It was written by Jean-Antoine de Charnes, the author of a life of Tasso and a translation of *Lazarillo de Tormes.* Composed of four long conversations that continue Valincour's fictional "salon" setting, Charnes's work nonetheless lacks the wit and verve of Valincour's. His defense of the "digressions" is weak and his point-by-point analysis of the criticisms raised by Valincour is heavy-handed and pedantic. Worse still are the substitutions of insults for arguments and the doubly irrelevant ad hominem attacks against Bouhours who Charnes thought had authored the work written by Valincour. But Charnes's book does have two strengths: its well-developed theory of the novella and its defense of the verisimilitude of the characters. In addition, Charnes responds well to Valincour's insinuation that Mme de Lafayette took the idea of the confession from Mme de Villedieu's *Les Désordres de l'amour,* a novel published in 1675. He argues convincingly that *La Princesse de Clèves* had been completed before the publication of Mme de Villedieu's novel and that the confession was more likely inspired by Pauline in Corneille's *Polyeucte,* "car du moins les caractères en sont bien plus semblables."[6] Finally, the fact that Charnes refers to the original draft of the novel given to the printer, thereby blaming him for some of the grammatical and stylistic infelicities underscored by Valincour, suggests that Mme de Lafayette may have played some role in the composition of this response to *Lettres à Mme la Marquise * * * sur le sujet de "La Princesse de Clèves."*

Notwithstanding certain exceptions, the seventeenth century viewed *La Princesse de Clèves* from the outside. The *aveu* ("confession" but also "proof of fidelity"), for example, is never considered as it functions in the psychology of the protagonist and in the world of the novel. The inside of the novel is judged by criteria that exist outside of it; in other words, *vraisemblance* (plausibility/verisimilitude) is predicated upon *bienséance* (propriety/decorum). Only what is socially acceptable can

6. Jean-Antoine de Charnes, *Conversations sur la critique de "La Princesse de Clèves"* (Paris: Claude Barbin, 1679), 234. See the excellent introduction to the edition of Charnes's work published by the "groupe d'étude du XVIIe siècle de l'Université François Rabelais (Tours, France: Université de Tours, 1972), i–xxviii.

be credible in fiction. The confession is therefore *invraisemblable*, not because it is inconsistent with the psychology of the princess, but because it does not conform to seventeenth-century French standards of behavior for wives. *La Princesse de Clèves* triggered a literary debate regarding the role of verisimilitude and history in prose narrative fiction. It mirrored the quarrel over *Le Cid* in that it too dealt, in large measure, with the *vraisemblance*, that is the appropriateness, of the behavior of the central female character. Once more, each work marked a profound rethinking of a set of aesthetic assumptions at the heart of a literary genre. Oddly enough, in the case of *La Princesse de Clèves*, it is only now, at the end of the twentieth century, as several of the chapters in this collection will demonstrate, that we are finally coming to terms with the significance of the earliest written criticism of the novel.

If the seventeenth century was above all struck by the implausibility of *La Princesse de Clèves*, the eighteenth century was charmed by the work's graceful style and, indeed, its triumph over earlier improbable romances. In 1751, in the supplement to his *Siècle de Louis XIV*, Voltaire praised the style and defended the *vraisemblance* of the novel: "[*La*] *Princesse de Clèves* et . . . *Zayde* furent les premiers romans où l'on vit les moeurs des honnêtes gens, et des aventures naturelles décrites avec grâce. Avant [Mme de Lafayette], on écrivait d'un style ampoulé des choses peu vraisemblables."[7] It was Voltaire too, eighteen years earlier in his *Temple du Goût*, who definitively rendered unto Mme de Lafayette what was hers. Responding indirectly to the continued assertions that her novels were composed by La Rochefoucauld, Segrais, and herself, Voltaire writes sardonically: "Segrais voulut un jour entrer dans le sanctuaire, en récitant ce vers de Despréaux: *Que Segrais dans l'églogue en charme les forêts*; mais la critique ayant lu, par malheur pour lui, quelques pages de son *Énéide* en vers français, le renvoya assez durement, et laissa venir à sa place Mme de La Fayette qui avait mis sous le nom de Segrais le roman admirable de *Zaïde* et celui de *la Princesse de Clèves*."[8]

Criticisms formulated against the novel during this period were constructed upon criteria significantly different from those established by the first readers of the text. The issue now became whether *La*

---

7. Voltaire, *Le Siècle de Louis XIV*, in *Oeuvres historiques* (Paris: Gallimard, 1957), 1170.
8. Voltaire, *Le Temple du Goût*, in *Mélanges* (Paris: Gallimard, 1961), 147–48.

Princesse de Clèves was a dangerous book to read or an exemplary work of fiction. The more common view was that the novel is better than most in this respect. As the Abbé de Bellegarde writes in his *Lettres curieuses de littérature et de morale,* "vous pouvez lire quelquefois des Romans sérieux, quand ils ne blessent point les bienséances, et les bonnes moeurs, tels que sont ceux que l'on a attribuez à Monsieur de la Rochefoucault, et à Madame de la Fayette."[9] Nonetheless, a group of eighteenth-century moralists condemned *La Princesse de Clèves* along with all other examples of the genre. Much more interesting is Marmontel's analysis in his *Essai sur les Romans,* an analysis that epitomizes a very real ambivalence that would nevertheless lead to condemnation. On the one hand, unlike the host of novels currently in vogue where he finds "le vice coloré en vertu," *La Princesse de Clèves* takes its readers along the path "du devoir et de la vertu." On the other hand, however, as Marmontel notes, that path is slippery and perilous: "Toute jeune femme sensible, prise d'une passion qui ne lui est pas permise, dira aussi qu'elle est involontaire, s'en accusera doucement, se flattera de ne pas s'y livrer, s'avancera au bord du précipice; et la nature faisant un pas de plus que le roman, l'innocence trop rassurée ne s'apercevra du péril qu'après qu'elle y aura succombé" (Laugaa, 144). Irony of ironies, the princess is now an example of virtue, but the novel is deemed dangerous because it is an inimitable one.

Outside the moralist milieu, *La Princesse de Clèves* enjoyed high esteem throughout the eighteenth century, and perhaps even more so after the translations of Richardson's novels and the veritable birth of "les âmes sensibles" with a decided taste for emotion and virtue. Rousseau states proudly that because of "les finesses de coeur" that one finds in his *Nouvelle Héloïse,* he would place "sans crainte sa quatrième partie à côté de la *Princesse de Clèves.*"[10] Rousseau claimed too in his *Confessions* that it would be impossible to appreciate *La Nouvelle Héloïse* "sans avoir ce sixième sens, ce sens moral" (646), which accounts, perhaps, for La Harpe's appreciation of *La Princesse de Clevès* at the

---

9. Quoted in Laugaa, *Lectures de Mme de Lafayette,* 137. All Lafayette scholars are indebted to Laugaa for having collected and published relatively inaccessible but significant texts of criticism on the novel. Henceforth I will cite his book parenthetically in the text.

10. Jean-Jacques Rousseau, *Les Confessions,* ed. J. Voisine (Paris: Garnier Frères, 1964), 642–43; hereafter cited parenthetically in the text.

very end of the century: "Jamais l'amour combattu par le devoir n'a été peint avec plus de délicatesse."[11]

As we would expect, each new century does not produce a completely original reading of the novel. Accordingly, the years 1800 to 1930 attest to both continuity and change in the reception of Mme de Lafayette's masterpiece. At the same time that its description of the passions was deeply admired, charges of the novel's immorality were again heard. Although she deems *La Princesse de Clèves* "un ouvrage sans modèle et tout à fait original," Mme de Genlis, in her *De l'Influence des femmes sur la littérature*, recalls the eighteenth-century moralists by denouncing the work's pernicious influence on youth (Laugaa, 164–67). This criticism is echoed later in the century when Saint-Marc Girardin affirms that, with *La Princesse de Clèves*, the novel is on the slope that leads to the corrupt sophisms of *La Nouvelle Héloïse* (Laugaa, 184).

Now that, by and large, Mme de Lafayette was recognized as the author of *La Princesse de Clèves*, we find a good deal of biographical criticism in which the heroine is often identified with the author, sometimes contrasted with the author, but almost always compared to her. While biographical criticism is commonplace during this historical period, it is a form of criticism particularly associated with female authors. From Mme de Lafayette to Simone de Beauvoir, the history of the criticism of women's writing is disproportionately the reduction of the fictional text to a biographical commentary. Rather than an analysis of the work per se, a study of the characters as imaginative creations, and an elucidation of the philosophy and aesthetics of the narrative, we all too often discover an extratextual intrusion into the character, private life, and personal morality of the author. Sainte-Beuve, for one, insists on the intimate relationship between the psychology of the author and that of the princess: "Mme de Clèves, en un mot, maladive et légèrement attristée, à côté de M. de Nemours vieilli et auteur des *Maximes*: telle est la vie de Mme de La Fayette et le rapport exact de sa personne à son roman. . . . Le désabusement de toutes choses se montre dans cette crainte que [Mme de Lafayette] prête à Mme de Clèves, que le mariage ne soit le tombeau de l'amour du prince, et n'ouvre la porte aux jalousies" (Laugaa, 171–72, 175).

---

11. Jean-François de la Harpe, *Cours de littérature* (Paris: Firmin-Didot, 1851), 2:70.

Stendhal, who admired the novel and, like Rousseau, compared one of his, *Armance,* to it, also alludes to the private life of the author, but to differentiate it from that of her fictional heroine: "Je crois que si Mme de Clèves fût arrivée à la vieillesse à cette époque où l'on juge la vie, et où les jouissances d'orgueil paraissent dans toute leur misère, elle se fût repentie. Elle aurait voulu avoir vécu comme Mme de la Fayette" (Laugaa, 181). This personal criticism continues throughout the period and, indeed, is taken to new excesses, as Laugaa has shown (214–22), in the work of Emile Magne where the textual and the biographical uneasily fuse.

Because each new work of literature creates its predecessors and transforms them, *La Princesse de Clèves,* in the age of Balzac, Flaubert, and Stendhal, was analyzed through the lens of great realist fiction. Thus it was now seen by d'Haussonville as the first novel whose sub-title could have been "roman d'une femme mariée." The same critic sees M. de Clèves as "le premier type du mari sympathique" and compares him favorably to M. de Wolmar, "un Prince de Clèves pédant, gourmé et jouant à tout prendre un rôle assez ridicule" (Laugaa, 202). Fittingly too, the critics of the nineteenth century continued to discuss the historicity of the novel. In an age deeply interested in history, Stendhal wrote on the difference between the historical novel à la Scott and Mme de Lafayette's masterpiece, while other critics, praising the use of local color and the general depiction of the court in a debate that has lasted well into the twentieth century, argued that the court depicted is that of Louis XIV and not Henri II (Laugaa, 181, 224).

Finally, one cannot peruse the criticism of this period without noting, particularly during the positivist era, the frequent insistence on the secular nature of Mme de Lafayette's oeuvre. Speaking of *La Princesse de Clèves,* Pierre Laffitte, for example, underscores "l'absence complète de toute considération surnaturelle; le nom de Dieu n'y est pas même prononcé" (Laugaa, 198). This so-called absence of God was often cited and in turn denounced by some (Laugaa, 185, 204) and admired by others, notably Auguste Comte who esteemed above all "cette femme tendrement éprise qui trouve la force de rester pure; qui la trouve, non dans des circonstances d'un ordre surnaturel, dans la crainte des châtiments du ciel, mais dans la droiture de son coeur, dans le simple sentiment de ses devoirs" (Laugaa, 188).

The reverberations of the post-1950 critical explosion have certainly been felt in the scholarly work done on *La Princesse de Clèves*. A good number of essential studies have been recorded in James Scott's very useful *Madame de Lafayette: A Selective Critical Bibliography*. New critical methods have been applied to the novel which now has its structuralist, poststructuralist, Freudian, narratological, and semiotical readings. At the same time, in this age of theory, a number of more traditional readings, both ideological and formalist, have appeared.[12] Much of this work has been historical; the novel continues to be read as a mirror of its author's time rather than the moment of time depicted within the novel. Even this historical moment, however, must be subdivided. On the one hand, we have studies that link the work to the age of Louis XIII (Corneille, Descartes, neostoicism) providing both optimistic—Lanson—and pessimistic—Allentuch—readings of the novel.[13] On the other hand, and far more numerous, are those critical analyses that depict the novel emerging from the Pascalian, La Rochefoucauldian, Racinian, and Jansenistic pessimism of the age of Louis XIV. Here one might cite, for example, Bernard Pingaud and the much more recent study of David Shaw who sees the novel as "perhaps the most disturbingly pessimistic work of fiction of the age."[14] Finally, Claude Vigée sees the insoluble problem of the novel emanating precisely from the conflict of values between the two generations, while Serge Doubrovsky, rejecting the thesis that the conflict in the novel is between its Corneilian characters and its Racinian passion, attempts to define the specificity of Mme de Lafayette's novelistic universe.[15]

12. In addition to Laugaa, I have profited from Marie-Odile Sweetser's insightful and useful "*La Princesse de Clèves* devant la critique contemporaine," *Studi francesi* 52 (1974): 13–29; hereafter cited parenthetically in the text.

13. Gustave Lanson, *Histoire de la littérature française* (Paris: Hachette, 1909), 490; hereafter cited parenthetically in the text. Harriet Allentuch, "Pauline and the Princesse de Clèves," *Modern Language Quarterly* 30 (1969): 171–82; hereafter cited parenthetically in the text.

14. Bernard Pingaud, *Madame de La Fayette par elle-même* (Paris: Seuil, 1959), 62; hereafter cited parenthetically in the text. David Shaw, "*La Princesse de Clèves* and Classical Pessimism," *Modern Languages* 63 (1982): 231; hereafter cited parenthetically in the text.

15. Claude Vigée, "*La Princesse de Clèves* et la tradition du refus," *Critique* 159–60 (1960): 723–54; hereafter cited parenthetically in the text. Serge Doubrovsky, "*La Princesse*

Three critics above all have insisted upon the formalistic originality of the novel. Jean Fabre, whose penetrating *L'Art de l'analyse dans "La Princesse de Clèves"* appeared in 1946, shows convincingly that Mme de Lafayette created a new form. Even though psychological analysis existed in prose narrative beforehand, only with *La Princesse de Clèves* does the unraveling of the plot depend solely upon it.[16] Jean Rousset's analysis also depicts the formal originality of the novel and highlights the balance in the technique that alternately portrays the heroine "sous le regard d'autrui" and alone in moments of solitude and reflection where she is able to "se regarder et se reconnaître."[17] Finally, Gérard Genette, whose brilliant reflections on the novel have had perhaps the most widespread influence, shows how the author, working on the narratological principle that the end justifies the means, simultaneously appeals to internal *vraisemblance* and rejects verisimilitude.[18] Marie-Odile Sweetser has shown how this technique approaches the aesthetics of Corneille, Mme de Lafayette having thus realized for the novel what the great French tragedian had accomplished for the theater (24).

More modern studies that, to a large degree, detach the work from its historical moment have also proliferated. Albert Camus, for example, sees the novel in the framework of the injustice of the human condition, "une revanche, une façon de surmonter un sort difficile en lui imposant une forme" and Mme de Lafayette, more than the most audacious romantic, painting with intensity the ravages of passion. It is therefore in order to establish psychological order, to "preserver son être," that the princess, "par un mouvement étonnant de pessimisme," renounces Nemours.[19] Georges Poulet too insists upon the destructive power of the passions—"L'amour apparaît comme une

de Clèves: Une Interprétation existentielle," *La Table ronde* 138 (1959): 36–51; hereafter cited parenthetically in the text.

16. Jean Fabre, "L'Art de l'analyse dans 'La Princesse de Clèves,'" in *Travaux de la Faculté des Lettres de l'Université de Strasbourg* (Paris: Les Belles-Lettres, 1946), 261–306.

17. Jean Rousset, "La Princesse de Clèves," in *Forme et signification* (Paris: José Corti, 1962), 20–21; hereafter cited parenthetically in the text.

18. Gérard Genette, "Vraisemblance et motivation," in *Figures II* (Paris: Seuil, 1969), 71–99.

19. Albert Camus, "L'Intelligence et l'échafaud," in *Théâtre, récits, nouvelles* (Paris: Gallimard, 1962), 1893, 1891.

force explosive qui rompt la continuité de l'être"[20]—and the princess's need for continuity. Her ultimate choice is that of permanence over the radical discontinuity of her being. Finally, Serge Doubrovsky, in a powerful existential reading of the text, discovers a "drame de la liberté" at the center of the novel: "Le fond du problème, c'est un choix de valeurs, un choix déchirant entre les valeurs délibérément choisies d'un code aristocratique et les valeurs spontanément élues de la passion. Tout le drame est dans ce conflit" (45–46).

What remains constant in the diverse mass of post-1950 critical commentary is the tendency to denigrate the heroine. If the seventeenth century was obsessed by the princess's confession to her husband, the twentieth has been preoccupied with her final renunciation of Nemours. It is precisely for her renunciation that she has sustained a barrage of charges most of which are variations on the themes of egoism and lack of authenticity. Doubrovsky speaks of her "égoïsme total" (48), Vigée "de sa prodigieuse préoccupation avec sa propre personne" (740), and Allentuch echoes the popular view that the princess rejects Nemours egoistically in order to preserve her passion in its idealized state: "Le trait de caractère fondamental de la princesse est l'égoïsme, le désir de posséder l'être aimé de façon permanente" (175). In the same vein, Sylvère Lotringer notes that "la princesse ne quittera pas la cour pour fuir la passion, mais pour la conserver,"[21] which recalls Hipp's archetypal study according to which an obstacle is sought so as to eternalize one's love. Here the princess is guided by "cette recherche à la fois inconsciente et délibérée de l'obstacle, fondement de la conception occidentale de l'amour."[22]

If not seen as concerned only with her own person, the princess is normally charged with not being her own person. Martin Turnell defines her virtue and that of her mother as "little more than keeping up appearances,"[23] while Doubrovsky speaks of the heroine's "mauvaise foi" (42, 46), and Janine Kreiter underscores her desire to

---

20. Georges Poulet, "Mme de Lafayette," *Etudes sur le temps humain* (Paris: Plon, 1950), 125; hereafter cited parenthetically in the text.

21. Sylvère Lotringer, "La Structuration romanesque," *Critique* 26 (1970): 517.

22. Marie-Thérèse Hipp, "Le Mythe de Tristan et Iseut et *La Princesse de Clèves*," *Revue d'histoire littéraire de la France* 65 (1965): 414.

23. Martin Turnell, *The Novel in France* (New York: Vintage, 1958), 39.

"sauvegarder son paraître."[24] Jean Fabre too sees her rejection of Nemours as the triumph of "la bienséance," the acceptance of the prefabricated social values of her age.[25] Typical of the "marionette-of-her-mother" criticism is Marianne Hirsch's remark that the princess "exists only in relation to her mother's advice and admonitions" which trap her "in a structure of repetitions which ultimately preclude development and progression."[26]

Such negative interpretations, of course, lead to a dismal reading of the novel's ending which is often judged claustrophobic, "une sorte de fixité sans désir," according to Georges Poulet (132). Doubrovsky too insists upon its suffocating nature: "S'il n'y a aucune transcendance vers un avenir humain, il n'y a pas davantage de transcendance vers le Divin" (50). Numerous are the critics who view the ending as a product of the princess's weakness: "a case of 'opting out,'" writes David Shaw, "a negative, inconclusive process which again underlines her weakness rather than her strength" (229). For Pingaud, it is a "mort volontaire" (104); for Rousset, "une extinction" (24); for Doubrovsky, "le suicide" (49).

Thus the history of the reception of *La Princesse de Clèves* has been a checkered one. While certain uncontestably brilliant aspects of the novel have been noted and praised, from Valincour to the present the heroine has been either ridiculed or attacked. The novel, however, can never be fully understood until the situation of its protagonist has been adequately assessed. The chapters in this collection will reexamine the situation of the Princesse de Clèves. Feminist, sociocritical, ethical, religious, psychological, and narrative arguments will be advanced to defend her against many of the charges made over the centuries, to rehabilitate her reputation, as it were, and to depict her authenticity as a fictional character.

24. Janine Kreiter, *Le Problème du paraître dans l'oeuvre de Mme de Lafayette* (Paris: Nizet, 1977), 183n.

25. Jean Fabre, "Bienséance et sentiment chez Mme de Lafayette," *Cahiers de l'Association internationale des études françaises* 11 (1959): 54–55.

26. Marianne Hirsch, "A Mother's Discourse: Incorporation and Repetition in *La Princesse de Clèves*," *Yale French Studies* 62 (1981): 78, 73.

PART I Feminist Readings

1 Emphasis Added

Plots and Plausibilities in Women's Fiction

NANCY K. MILLER

Nothing came down the street; nobody passed. A single leaf detached itself from the plane tree at the end of the street, and in that pause and suspension fell. Somehow it was like a signal falling, a signal pointing to a force in things which one had overlooked.

    —VIRGINIA WOOLF, A Room of One's Own[1]

I F WE take *La Princesse de Clèves* as the first text of women's fiction in France, then we may observe that French women's fiction has from its beginnings been *discredited*.[2] By this I mean literally and literarily denied credibility: "Mme de Clèves's confession to her husband," writes Bussy-Rabutin to his cousin Mme de Sévigné, "is extravagant, and can only happen [*se dire*] in a true story; but when one is inventing a story for its own sake [*à plaisir*], it is ridiculous to ascribe such extraordinary feelings to one's heroine. The author in so

    1. Although what is being pointed to ultimately is an "elsewhere" under the sign of an androgyny I resist, I respond here to the implicit invitation to look again. The quotation should be replaced both in its original context and within Carolyn Heilbrun's concluding argument in *Toward a Recognition of Androgyny* (New York: Knopf, 1973), 167–72, which is where I (re)found it.

    2. If one must have a less arbitrary origin—and why not?—the properly inaugural fiction would be Hélisenne de Crenne's *Les Angoysses douloureuses qui procèdent d'amours*, of 1538. But *La Princesse de Clèves* has this critical advantage: it also marks the beginning of the modern French novel.

doing was more concerned about not resembling other novels than obeying common sense."[3] Without dwelling on the local fact that a similarly "singular" confession had appeared in Mme de Villedieu's *Les Désordres de l'amour* some three years before the publication of Mme de Lafayette's novel, and bracketing the more general fact that the novel as a genre has from its beginnings labored under charges of *invraisemblance*,[4] let us reread Bussy-Rabutin's complaint. In a true story, as in "true confessions," the avowal would be believable because in life, unlike art, anything can happen; hence the constraints of likeliness do not apply. In a made-up story, however, the confession offends because it violates our readerly expectations about fiction. In other words, art should not imitate life but *re*inscribe received ideas about the representation of life in art. To depart from the limits of common sense (tautologically, to be extravagant) is to risk exclusion from the canon.[5] Because—as Genette, glossing this same document in "Vraisemblance et motivation," puts it—*"extravagance is a privilege of the real,"*[6] to produce a work not like other novels, an original rather than a copy, means paradoxically that its literariness will be sniffed out: "The first adventure of the Coulommiers gardens is not plausible," Bussy-Rabutin observes later in his letter, "and reeks of fiction [*sent le roman*]."

Genette begins his essay with an analysis of contemporary reactions

3. Bussy-Rabutin's oft-cited remarks on the novel are easily found in Maurice Laugaa's excellent volume of critical responses, *Lectures de Mme de Lafayette* (Paris: Armand Colin, 1971), 18–19. The translation is mine, as are all other translations from the French, unless otherwise indicated.

4. On the function and status of the confession in Mme de Villedieu's novel and on the problems of predecession, see Micheline Cuénin's introduction to her critical edition of *Les Désordres de l'amour* (Geneva: Droz, 1970). The best account of the attack on the novel remains Georges May's *Le Dilemme du roman au XVIII* siècle (New Haven: Yale University Press, 1963), especially his first chapter.

5. I allude here (speciously) to the first definition of "extravagant" in *Le Petit Robert* (Paris: Société du Nouveau Littré, 1967), 668: "S'est dit de textes non incorporés dans les recueils canoniques" [Used to refer to texts not included in the canon].

6. I refer here, as I indicate below, to Gérard Genette's "Vraisemblance et motivation," included in his *Figures II* (Paris: Seuil, 1969), 74. In my translation-adaptation of Genette's analysis, I have chosen to render *vraisemblance* by "plausibility," a term with a richer semantic field of connotations than "verisimilitude." Page references to Genette's essay hereafter appear parenthetically in the text.

to *La Princesse de Clèves*. Reviewing the writings of seventeenth-century poeticians, Genette shows that *vraisemblance* and *bienséance,* "plausibility" and "propriety," are wedded to each other; and the precondition of plausibility is the stamp of approval affixed by public *opinion*: "Real or assumed, this 'opinion' is quite close to what today would be called ideology, that is, a body of maxims and prejudices which constitute both a vision of the world and a system of values" (73). What this statement means is that the critical reaction to any given text is hermeneutically bound to another and preexistent text: the *doxa* of socialities. Plausibility, then, is an effect of reading through a grid of concordance: "What defines plausibility is the formal principle of respect for the norm, that is, the existence of a relation of implication between the particular conduct attributed to a given character, and a given, general, received and implicit maxim. . . . To understand the behavior of a character (for example), is to be able to refer it back to an approved maxim, and this reference is perceived as a demonstration of cause and effect" (174–75). If no maxim is available to account for a particular piece of behavior, that behavior is read as unmotivated and unconvincing. Mme de Clèves's confession makes no sense in the seventeenth-century sociolect because it is, Genette underlines, *"an action without a maxim"* (75). A heroine without a maxim, like a rebel without a cause, is destined to be misunderstood. And she is.

To build a narrative around a character whose behavior is deliberately idiopathic, however, is not merely to create a puzzling fiction but to fly in the face of a certain ideology (of the text and its context), to violate a grammar of motives that describes while prescribing, in this instance, what wives, not to say women, should or should not do. The question one might then ask is whether this crucial barbarism is in any way connected to the gender of its author. If we were to uncover a feminine "tradition"—diachronic recurrences—of such ungrammaticalities, would we have the basis for a poetics of women's fiction? And what do I mean by women's fiction?

Working backward, I should say first that I do not mean what is designated in France these days as *écriture féminine,* which can be described roughly as a process or a practice by which the female *body,* with its peculiar drives and rhythms, inscribes itself as text.[7] "Fem-

7. For an overview of the current discussion about women's writing in France, see Elaine Marks's fine piece "Women and Literature in France," *Signs* 3 (1978): 832–42.

inine writing" is an important theoretical formulation; but it privileges a textuality of the avant-garde, a literary production of the late twentieth century, and it is therefore fundamentally a hope, if not a blueprint, for the future. In what is perhaps the best-known statement of contemporary French feminist thinking about women's writing, "The Laugh of the Medusa," Hélène Cixous states that, "with a few rare exceptions, there has not yet been any writing that inscribes femininity." On the contrary, what she finds historically in the texts of the "immense majority" of female writers is "workmanship [which is] . . . in no way different from male writing, and which either obscures women or reproduces the classic representations of women (as sensitive—intuitive—dreamy, etc.)."[8] I think this assertion is both true and untrue. It is true if one is looking for a radical difference in women's writing and locates that difference in an insurgence of the body, in what Julia Kristeva has called the irruption of the semiotic.[9] And it is true again if difference is sought on the level of the sentence, or in what might be thought of as the biofeedback of the text. If, however, we situate difference in the insistence of a certain thematic structuration, in the form of content, then it is not true that women's writing has been in no way different from male writing. I consider the "demaximization" wrought by Mme de Lafayette to be one example of how difference can be read.

Before I proceed to other manifestations of difference, let me make a few general remarks about the status of women's literature—about its existence, in my view, as a viable corpus for critical inquiry. Whether one believes, as does Cixous, that there is "male writing," "*marked* writing . . . run by a libidinal and cultural—hence political—typically masculine economy," or that (great) literature has no sex because a "great mind must be androgynous," literary *history* remains a male preserve, a history of writing by men.[10] In England the history of the novel admits the names of Jane Austen, the Brontës, George Eliot, and Virginia Woolf. In France it includes Mme de La-

---

8. Hélène Cixous, "The Laugh of the Medusa," trans. Keith Cohen and Paula Cohen, *Signs* 1 (1976): 878.

9. For a statement of Kristeva's position on a possible specificity to women's writing, see "Questions à Julia Kristeva," *Revue des sciences humaines* 168 (1977): 495–501.

10. Cixous, "Medusa," 879. The opposition between these positions is more rhetorical than actual, as Woolf's gloss on Coleridge in *A Room of One's Own* shows.

fayette, although only for *La Princesse de Clèves* and always with the nagging insinuation that La Rochefoucauld had a hand in that. Mme de Staël, George Sand, and Colette figure in the national record, although mainly as the scandalous heroines of their times. Nevertheless, there have always been women writing. What is one to do with them? One can leave them where they are, like so many sleeping dogs, and mention them only in passing as epiphenomena in every period, despite the incontrovertible evidence that most were successful and even literarily influential in their day. One can continue, then, a politics of benign neglect that reads difference, not to say popularity, as inferiority. Or one can perform two simultaneous and compensatory gestures: the archaeological and rehabilitative act of discovering and recovering "lost" women writers and the reconstructive and reevaluative act of establishing a parallel literary tradition, as Elaine Showalter has done in *A Literature of Their Own* and Ellen Moers in *Literary Women*. [11] The advantage of these moves is that they make visible an otherwise invisible intertext: a reconstituted record of predecession and prefiguration, debts acknowledged and unacknowledged, anxieties, and enthusiasms.

Elizabeth Janeway, by way of T. S. Eliot, has suggested another way of thinking about women's literature. She cites the evolution in Eliot's attitude toward that body of texts we know as American literature. At first he held, as many critics have about women's literature, that it does not exist: "There can only be one English literature. . . . There cannot be British or American literature." Later, however, he was to acknowledge "what has never, I think, been found before, two literatures in the same language." [12] That reformulation, as Janeway

11. Elaine Showalter, *A Literature of Their Own* (Princeton: Princeton University Press, 1977); Ellen Moers, *Literary Women* (New York: Doubleday, 1976). I understate the stakes of recognizing and responding to an apparently passive indifference. As Edward Said has written in another context, "Any philosophy or critical theory exists and is maintained in order not merely *to be there, passively around everyone and everything,* but in order to be taught and diffused, to be absorbed decisively into the institutions of society or to be instrumental in maintaining or changing or perhaps upsetting these institutions and that society" ("The Problem of Textuality," *Critical Inquiry* 4 [1978]: 682).

12. As quoted by Elizabeth Janeway in her insightful essay on women's writing in postwar America, "Women's Literature," in *Harvard Guide to Contemporary American Writing,* ed. Daniel Hoffman (Cambridge: Harvard University Press, 1979), 344.

adapts it to delineate the continent of women's literature, is useful because it locates the problem of identity and difference not on the level of the sentence—not as a question of another language—but on the level of the text in all its complexities: a culturally bound and, I would even say, culturally overdetermined production. This new mapping of a parallel geography does not, of course, resolve the oxymoron of marginality: how is it that women, a statistical majority in our culture, perform as a "literary subculture"?[13] But it does provide a body of writing from which to begin to identify specificities in women's relation to writing and the specificities that derive from that relation. Because women are both of the culture and out of it (or under it), written by it and remaining a largely silent though literate majority, to look for *uniquely* "feminine" textual indexes that can be deciphered in "blind" readings is pointless. (Documentation concerning the critical reception of *Jane Eyre* and *Adam Bede,* for example, has shown how silly such pretensions can be.)[14] There are no infallible signs, no fail-safe techniques by which to determine the gender of an author. But that is not the point of the *post*compensatory gesture that follows what I call the new literary history. At stake instead is a reading that *consciously* re-creates the object it describes, attentive always to a difference—what T. S. Eliot calls "strong local flavor" not dependent on the discovery of an exclusive alterity.

The difficulty of the reading comes from the irreducibly complicated relationship women have historically had to the language of the dominant culture, a "flirtatious" relationship that Luce Irigaray has called mimetic:

To play with mimesis is . . . for a woman to try to recover the place of her exploitation by language, without allowing herself to be simply reduced to it. It is to resubmit herself . . . to ideas—notably about her—elaborated in and through a masculine logic, but to "bring out" by an effect of playful repetition what was to remain hidden: the recovery of a possible operation of the feminine in language. It is also to unveil the fact that if women mime so well they are not simply reabsorbed in this function. *They also remain elsewhere.*[15]

13. See in particular Showalter's first chapter, "The Female Tradition," *A Literature of Their Own,* 3–36.

14. See Showalter's chapter "The Double Critical Standard and the Feminine Novel," *Literature of Their Own,* 73–99.

15. Luce Irigaray, *Ce sexe qui n'en est pas un* (Paris: Minuit, 1977), 74.

This "elsewhere"—which, needless to say, is not so easily pin-pointed—is, she adds, an insistence of "matter" and "sexual pleasure" ("jouissance"). I prefer to think of the insistence Irigaray posits as a form of emphasis: an italicized version of what passes for the neutral or standard face. Spoken or written, italics are a modality of intensity and stress, a way of marking what has always already been said, of making a common text one's own. Italics are also a form of intonation, "the tunes," Sally McConnell-Ginet writes, "to which we set the text of our talk." "Intonation," she continues, "serves to underscore the gender identification of the participants in certain contexts of com-munication," and because of differences in intonation, "women's tunes will be interpreted and evaluated from an androcentric perspective."[16] When I speak of italics, then, I mean the emphasis added by regis-tering a certain quality of voice. And this expanded metaphor brings me back to my point of departure.

Genette codes the perception of plausibility in terms of silence: "The relationship between a plausible narrative and the system of plausibility to which it subjects itself is . . . essentially mute: the conventions of genre function like a system of natural forces and con-straints which the narrative obeys as if without noticing them, and *a fortiori* without naming them" (76). By fulfilling the "tacit contract between a work and its public" (77), this silence both gives pleasure and signifies conformity with the dominant ideology. The text eman-cipated from this collusion, however, is also silent, in that it refuses to justify its infractions, the "motives and maxims of the actions" (78). Here Genette cites the silence surrounding Julien Sorel's at-tempted murder of Mme de Rênal and the confession of Mme de Clèves. In the first instance, the ideologically complicitous text, the silence is a function of what Genette calls "plausible narrative"; in the second, it is a function of "arbitrary narrative" (79). And the *sounds* of silence? They are heard in a third type of narrative, one with a motivated and *"artificial plausibility"* (79): this literature, exemplified by the "endless chatting" of a Balzacian novel, we might call "other-directed," for here authorial commentary justifies its story to society by providing the missing maxims, or by inventing them. In the ar-bitrary narrative Genette sees a rejection of the ideology of a certain

16. Sally McConnell-Ginet, "Intonation in a Man's World," *Signs* 3 (1978): 542.

plausibility—an ideology, let us say, of accountability. This "inner-directed" posture would proclaim instead "that rugged individuality which makes for the unpredictability of great actions—and great works" (77).

Two remarks are in order here. Arbitrariness can be taken as an ideology in itself, that is, as the irreducible freedom and originality of the author (Bussy-Rabutin's complaint, *en somme*). But more specifically, the refusal of the demands of one economy may mask the inscription of another. This inscription may seem silent, or *unarticulated* in/as *authorial commentary (discours)*, without being absent. (It may simply be inaudible to the dominant mode of reception.) In *La Princesse de Clèves*, for example, "extravagance" is in fact accounted for, I would argue, both by maxims and by a decipherable effect of italicization. The maxims I refer to are not direct commentary; and it is true, as Genette writes, that "nothing is more foreign to the style [of the novel] than sententious epiphrasis: as if the actions were always either beyond or beneath all commentary" (78). It is also true that within the narrative the characters do comment on the actions; and although Genette does not "count" such comments as "chatting," I would suggest that they constitute an internally motivating discourse: an artificial plausibility *en abyme*. This intratext is maternal discourse; and its *performance* through the "extraordinary feelings" of Mme de Clèves is an instance of italicization. The confession, to state the obvious, makes perfect sense in terms of the idiolect spoken by Mme de Chartres: "Be brave and strong, my daughter; withdraw from the court, force your husband to take you away; do not fear the most brutal and difficult measures; however awful they may seem at first, in the end they will be milder in their effects than the misery of a love affair" (68). [17] Moreover, the confession qua confession is set up by *reference* to a "real-life" precedent and is presented by the prince himself as a model of desirable behavior: "Sincerity is so important to me that I think that if my mistress, and even my wife, confessed to me that she was attracted by another . . . I would cast off the role of lover or husband to advise and sympathize with her" (76). Seen from this

17. My translations from *La Princesse de Clèves* are deliberately literal; page references to the French are from the readily available Garnier-Flammarion text edited by Antoine Adam (Paris: 1966) and are incorporated within the text.

perspective the behavior of the princess is both *motivated* within the narration and supplied with a pre*text*: the conditions of *imitation*. But the confession, which I may already have overemphasized, is not an isolated extravagance in the novel. It is a link in the chain of events that lead to Mme de Clèves's decision not to marry Nemours, even though in *this* instance, the maxims of the sociolect might support, even expect, the marriage. As Bussy-Rabutin again observes, "And if, against all appearances and custom, this combat between love and virtue were to last in her heart until the death of her husband, then she would be delighted to be able to bring love and virtue together by marrying a man of quality, the finest and most handsome gentleman of his time." Mme de Lafayette clearly rejects this delightful dénouement. Now, Stendhal has speculated that if Mme de Clèves had lived a long life she would have regretted her decision and would have wanted to live like Mme de Lafayette.[18] We shall never know, of course, but his comment raises an interesting question: why did Mme de Lafayette keep Mme de Clèves from living in fiction the life she herself had led? The answer to that question would be an essay in itself, but let us tackle the question here from another angle: what do Mme de Clèves's "renunciation" and, before that, her confession tell us about the relation of women writers to fiction, to the heroines of their fiction? Should the heroine's so-called refusal of love be read as a defeat and an end to passion—a "suicide," or "the delirium of a *précieuse*"?[19] Or is it, rather, a *bypassing* of the dialectics of desire, and, in that sense, a peculiarly feminine "act of victory"?[20] To understand the refusal as a victory and as, I believe, a rewriting of eroticism (an

18. Stendhal, "Du Courage des femmes," *De L'Amour* (Paris: Editions de Cluny, 1938), chapter 29, p. 111.

19. Serge Doubrovsky, *"La Princesse de Clèves: Une Interprétation existentielle,"* *La Table ronde* 138 (1959): 48. Jean Rousset, *Forme et signification* (Paris: José Corti, 1962), 25.

20. A. Kibédi Varga, "Romans d'amour, romans de femmes à l'époque classique," *Revue des sciences humaines* 168 (1977): 524. Jules Brody, in *"La Princesse de Clèves* and the Myth of Courtly Love," *University of Toronto Quarterly* 38 (1969): 105–35, esp. 131–34, and Domna C. Stanton, "The Ideal of *Repos* in Seventeenth-Century French Literature," *L'Esprit créateur* 15 (1975): 79–104, esp. 95–96, 99, 101–2, also interpret the princess's final refusal of Nemours (and her renunciation) as heroic and self-preserving actions within a certain seventeenth-century discourse.

emphasis placed "elsewhere"—as Irigaray and, curiously, Woolf say), from which we might generalize about the economy of representation regulating the heroine and her authors, let us shift critical gear for a while.

Claudine Herrmann describes the princess as a heroine "written in a language of dream, dreamt by Mme de Lafayette."[21] What is the language of that dream, and what is the dream of that language? In the essay called "The Relation of the Poet to Daydreaming" (1908), Freud wonders how that "strange being, the poet, comes by his material."[22] He goes on to answer his question by considering the processes at work in children's play and then moves to daydreams and fantasies in adults. When he begins to describe the characteristics of this mode of creativity, he makes a blanket generalization about its impulses that should immediately make clear the usefulness of his essay for our purposes: "Unsatisfied wishes are the driving power behind phantasies; every separate phantasy contains the fulfillment of a wish, and improves upon unsatisfactory reality" (47). What, then, is the nature of these wishes and, more to our point, does the sex of the dreamer affect the shaping of the daydream's text? Here, as might be expected, Freud does not disappoint:

The impelling wishes vary according to the sex, character and circumstances of the creator; they may easily be divided, however, into two principal groups. Either they are ambitious wishes, serving to exalt the person creating them, or they are erotic. In young women erotic wishes dominate the phantasies *almost exclusively,* for their ambition is *generally comprised* in their erotic longings; in young men egoistic and ambitious wishes assert themselves plainly enough alongside their erotic desires. (47–48; emphasis added)

Here we see that the either/or antinomy, ambitious/erotic, is immediately collapsed to make coexistence possible in masculine fantasies: "in the greater number of ambitious daydreams . . . we can discover a woman in some corner, for whom the dreamer performs all his heroic deeds and at whose feet all his triumphs are to be laid" (48).

But is this observation reversible? If, to make the logical extrapo-

21. Claudine Herrmann, *Les Voleuses de langue* (Paris: Editions des Femmes, 1976), 77.
22. Sigmund Freud, *On Creativity and the Unconscious,* trans. I. F. Grant Duff (New York: Harper, 1958), 44; hereafter cited parenthetically in the text.

lation, romance dominates the female daydream and constitutes its primary heroine-ism, is there a *place* in which the ambitious wish of a young woman asserts itself? Has she an egoistic desire to be discovered "in some corner"? Freud elides the issue—while leaving the door open (for us) by his modifiers, "almost exclusively" and "generally comprised"—presumably because he is on his way to establishing the relationship between daydreaming and literary creation. The pertinence of difference there is moot, of course, because he conjures up only a male creator: not the great poet, however, but "the less pretentious writers of romances, novels and stories, who are read all the same by the widest circles of men and women" (50). Freud then proceeds to identify the key "marked characteristic" of these fictions: "They all have a hero who is the centre of interest for whom the author tries to win our sympathy by every possible means, and whom he places under the protection of a special providence" (50). The hero in this literature is continually exposed to danger, but we follow his perilous adventures with a sense of security, because we know that at each turn he will triumph. According to Freud, the basis for this armchair security, for our tranquil contemplation, is the hero's own conviction of invincibility, best rendered by the expression "Nothing can happen to me!" And Freud comments, "It seems to me . . . that this significant mark of invulnerability very clearly betrays—His Majesty the Ego, the hero of *all daydreams* and *all novels*" (51; emphasis added). Now, if the plots of male fiction chart the daydreams of an ego that would be invulnerable, what do the plots of female fiction reveal? Among French women writers, it would seem at first blush to be the obverse negative of "Nothing can happen to me." The phrase that characterizes the heroine's posture might well be a variant of Murphy's law: If anything can go wrong, it will. And the reader's sense of security, itself dependent on the heroine's, comes from feeling not that the heroine will triumph in some *conventionally* positive way but that she will transcend the perils of plot with a self-exalting dignity. Here national constraints on the imagination, or what in this essay Freud calls "racial psychology," do seem to matter: the second-chance rerouting of disaster typical of Jane Austen's fiction, for example, is exceedingly rare in France. To the extent that we can speak of a triumph of Her Majesty the Ego in France, it lies in being beyond vulnerability, indeed beyond it all. On the whole, French women writers prefer what Peter Brooks has described as "the melodramatic imagination," a dreamlike and metaphorical drama of the "moral occult."[23] There are recurrent melodramatic plots about women unhappy in love because men are men and women are women. As I said earlier, however, the suffering seems to have its own rewards in the economy of the female unconscious. The heroine proves to be better than her victimizers; and perhaps this ultimate superiority, which is to be read in the choice to go beyond love, beyond "erotic longings," is the figure that the "ambitious wishes" of women writers (dreamers) takes.

In the economy of Freud's plot, as we all know, fantasy scenarios are generated by consciously repressed content; and so he naturally assumes a motive for the "concealment" of "ambitious wishes": "the overweening self-regard" that a young man "acquires in the indulgent atmosphere surrounding his childhood" must be suppressed "so that he may find his proper place in a society that is full of other persons making similar claims" (48)—hence the daydreams in which the hero conquers all to occupy center stage victoriously. The content that a young woman represses comes out in erotic daydreams because "a well-brought-up woman is, indeed, credited with only a minimum of erotic desire" (48). Indeed. Now, there is a class of novels by women that "maximizes" that minimum, a type of fiction that George Eliot attacks as "Silly Novels by Lady Novelists": "The heroine is usually an heiress . . . with perhaps a vicious baronet, an amiable duke, and an irresistible younger son of a marquis as lovers in the foreground, a clergyman and a poet sighing for her in the middle distance, and a crowd of undefined adorers dimly indicated beyond."[24] After sketching out the variations of plot that punctuate the heroine's " 'starring' expedition through life" (302), Eliot comments on the security with which we await the inevitably happy end: "Before matters arrive at this desirable issue our feelings are tried by seeing the noble, lovely and gifted heroine pass through many *mauvais moments*, but we have the satisfaction of knowing that her sorrows are wept into embroidered pocket-handkerchiefs . . . and that whatever vicissitudes she may

23. Peter Brooks, *The Melodramatic Imagination* (New Haven: Yale University Press, 1976), 20.

24. George Eliot, *The Essays of George Eliot*, ed. Thomas Pinney (London: Routledge and Kegan Paul, 1963), 301–2; hereafter cited parenthetically in the text.

undergo . . . she comes out of them all with a complexion more blooming and locks more redundant than ever" (303). The plots of these "silly novels" bring grist to Freud's mill—that is, the grist I bring to his mill—in an almost uncanny way; and they would seem to undermine the argument I am on the verge of elaborating. But as Eliot says, "Happily, we are not dependent on argument to prove that Fiction is a department of literature in which women can, after their kind, fully equal men. A cluster of great names, both living and dead, rush to our memories in evidence that women can produce novels not only fine, but among the very finest;—novels too, that have a precious speciality, lying quite apart from masculine aptitudes and experience" (324). (Let me work through her essay to my own.) What Eliot is attacking here is not only the relationship of certain women writers to literature but the critical reception given women's fiction. We might also say that she is attacking, the better to separate herself from those women writers whose language is structured exactly like the unconscious that Freud has assigned to them, those writers (and their heroines) whose ambitious wishes are contained *entirely* in their erotic longings. And she is attacking these novelists, the better to defend, *not* those women who write *like* men (for she posits a "precious speciality" to women's production), but those women who write in their own way, "after their kind," and implicitly about something else. Silly novels are that popular artifact that has always been and still is known as "women's literature"—a term, I should add, applied to such fiction by those who do not read it.[25]

Women writers, then, in contrast to lady novelists, are writers whose texts would be "among the finest" (to stay with Eliot's terminology) and for whom the "ambitious wish" (to stay with Freud's) manifests itself as fantasy within another economy. In this economy, egoistic desires would assert themselves paratactically alongside erotic ones. The repressed content, I think, would be, not erotic impulses, but an impulse to power: a fantasy of power that would revise the social grammar in which women are never defined as subjects; a fantasy of power that disdains a sexual exchange in which women can

<hr/>

25. On the content of popular women's literature and its relationship to high culture, see Lillian Robinson, "On Reading Trash," in *Sex, Class and Culture* (Bloomington: Indiana University Press, 1978), 200–222.

participate only as objects of circulation. The daydreams or fictions of women writers would then, like those of men, say, "Nothing can happen to me!" But the modalities of that invulnerability would be marked in an essentially different way. I am talking, of course, about the power of the weak. The inscription of this power is not always easy to decipher, because, as has been noted, "the most essential form of accommodation for the weak is to conceal what power they do have."[26] Moreover, to pick up a lost thread, when these modalities of difference are perceived, they are generally called implausibilities. They are not perceived, or are misperceived, because the scripting of this fantasy does not bring the aesthetic "forepleasure" Freud says fantasy scenarios inevitably bring: pleasure bound to recognition and *identification* (54), the "agrément" Genette assigns to plausible narrative. (Perhaps we shall not have a poetics of women's literature until we have more weak readers.)

In *Les Voleuses de langue*, Claudine Herrmann takes up what I call the politics of dreams, or the ideology of daydreaming, in *La Princesse de Clèves*:

A daydream is perpetuated when it loses all chance of coming true, when the woman dreaming [la rêveuse] cannot make it pass into reality. If women did not generally experience the love they desire as a repeated impossibility, they would dream about it less. They would dream of other, perhaps more interesting, things. Nevertheless, written in a language of dream, dreamt by Mme de Lafayette, the Princesse de Clèves never dreams . . . for she knows that *love as she imagines it* is not realizable. What is realizable is a counterfeit she does not want. Her education permits her to glimpse this fact: men and women exchange feelings that are not equivalent. . . . Woman's "daydreaming" is a function of a world in which nothing comes true on her terms. (77–79)

"Men and women exchange feelings that are not equivalent." Mme de Clèves's brief experience of the court confirms the principle of difference at the heart of her mother's maxims. Mme de Clèves's rejection of Nemours on his terms, however, derives its necessity not only from the logic of maternal discourse (Nemours's love, like his name, is negative and plural: *ne/amours*), but also from the demands of Mme

---

26. Barbara Bellow Watson, "On Power and the Literary Text," *Signs* 1 (1975): 113. Watson suggests that we look instead for "expressive symbolic structures."

de Lafayette's dream. In this dream nothing can happen to the heroine, because she understands that the power and pleasure of the weak derive from circumventing the laws of contingency and circulation. She withdraws then and confesses, not merely to resist possession, as her mother would have wished, but to improve on it: to *rescript* possession.

The plausibility of this novel lies in the structuration of its fantasy. For if, to continue spinning out Herrmann's metaphor, the heroine does not dream, she does daydream. And perhaps the most significant confession in the novel is neither the first (to her husband, that she is vulnerable to desire) nor the third (to Nemours, that she desires him) but the second, which is silent and entirely telling: I refer, of course, to her nocturnal *rêverie* at Coulommiers. Although all three confessions prefigure by their extravagance the heroine's retreat from the eyes of the world, it is this dreamlike event that is least ambiguous in underlining the erotic valence of the ambitious scenario.

At Coulommiers, her country retreat, Mme de Clèves sits one warm evening, secretly observed by Nemours, winding ribbons of his colors around an India cane. (I take her surreptitious acquisition of his cane to be the counterpart of his theft of her miniature, in this crisscrossing of desires by metonymy.) As Michel Butor observes in his seductive reading of this scene, "the mind of the princess is operating at this moment in a zone obscure to herself; it is as if she is knotting the ribbons around the cane in a dream, and her dream becomes clear little by little; the one she is thinking of begins to take on a face, and she goes to look for it."[27] Thus, having finished her handiwork, she places herself in front of a painting, a historical tableau of members of the court that she has had transported to her retreat, a painting including a likeness of Nemours: "She sat down and began to look at this portrait with an intensity and dreaminess [*rêverie*] that only passion can inspire" (155). And Butor comments, "One hardly needs a diploma in psychoanalysis to detect and appreciate the symbolism of this whole scene" (76). Indeed, it is quite clear that the princess is seen here in a moment of solitary pleasure, in a daydream of "feti-

---

27. Michel Butor, "Sur *La Princesse de Clèves*," in *Répertoire* (Paris: Minuit, 1960), 76–77; hereafter cited parenthetically in the text.

chistic sublimation." This autoeroticism would seem to be the only sexual performance she can afford in an economy regulated by dispossession.[28]

Her retreat to Coulommiers, though, must be thought of not as a flight from sexuality but as a movement *into* it. As Sylvère Lotringer has observed, Mme de Clèves leaves the court not to flee passion but to preserve it. To preserve it, however, on her own terms. Unlike Nemours—who is not content to possess the object of his desire in representation (the purloined portrait) and who pleads silently after this scene, "Only look at me the way I saw you look at my portrait tonight; how could you look so gently at my portrait and then so cruelly fly from my presence?" (157)—the princess chooses "the duke of the portrait, not the man who seeks to step out of the frame."[29] Here she differs from Austen's heroine Elizabeth Bennet, who stands gazing before her lover's portrait and feels "a more gentle sensation towards the original than she had ever felt in the height of their acquaintance."[30] Elizabeth can accept the hand of the man who steps out of the frame; the princess cannot. For if, in the world of *Pride and Prejudice,* "between the picture's eyes and Elizabeth's hangs what will be given shape when the marriage of the lovers is formalized," in the world of the court the princess's response to Nemours must remain specular. Her desire cannot be framed by marriage—*à l'anglaise.* If, however, as I believe, the withdrawal to Coulommiers is homologous to the *final* withdrawal, then there is no reason to imagine that at a remove from the world—or, rather, in the company of the world contained by representation in painting—the princess does not continue to experience her "erotic longings." But the fulfillment of the wish is to be realized in the daydream itself.

The daydream, then, is both the stuff of fairy tales ("Someday my prince will come") and their rewriting ("Someday my prince will come, but we will not live happily ever after"). The princess refuses to marry the duke, however, not because she does not want to live

28. David Grossvogel, *Limits of the Novel* (Ithaca: Cornell University Press, 1971), 134. In Doubrovsky's terms, love in this universe means "being dispossessed of oneself and bound to the incoercible spontaneity of another" (47).

29. Sylvère Lotringer, "La Structuration romanesque," *Critique* 26 (1970): 517, 519.

30. The importance of this scene from Austen is underscored by Rachel Mayer Brownstein in *Becoming a Heroine* (New York: Viking, 1982).

happily ever after, but because she does. And by choosing not to act on that desire but to preserve it in and as fantasy, she both performs maternal discourse and italicizes it as repossession. Her choice is therefore not the simple reinscription of the seventeenth-century convention of female renunciation, dependent on the logic of either/or, but the sign of both-and, concretized by her final dual residence: in the convent *and* at home. "Perverted convention," as Peggy Kamuf names it, writing of another literary fetichist (Saint-Preux in Julie's closet): "The scene of optimal pleasure is within the prohibition which forms the walls of the house. Just on this side of the transgressive act, the fetichist's pleasure . . . is still in the closet."[31] This form of possession by metonymy both acknowledges the law and short-circuits it. Nobody, least of all the Duc de Nemours, believes in her renunciation (just as her husband never fully believed her confession): "Do you think that your resolutions can hold against a man who adores you and who is fortunate enough to attract you? It is more difficult than you think, Madame, to resist the attractions of love. You have done it *by an austere virtue which has almost no example*; but that virtue is no longer opposed to your feelings and I hope that you will follow them despite yourself" (174–75; emphasis added). Mme de Clèves will not be deterred by sheer difficulty, by mere plausibility, by Nemours's *maxims*. She knows herself to be without a text. "No woman but you in the world," she has been told earlier in the novel, "would confide everything she knows in her husband" (116). "The singularity of such a confession," the narrator comments after the fait accompli, "for which she could find no example, made her see all the danger of it" (125). The danger of singularity precisely is sociolinguistic: the attempt to *communicate* in a language, an idiolect, that would nonetheless break with the coded rules of communication. An impossibility, as Roman Jakobson has seen: "Private property, in the domain of language, does not exist: everything is socialized. The verbal exchange, like every form of human relation, requires at least two interlocutors; an idiolect, in the final analysis, therefore can only be a *slightly perverse fiction*."[32] Thus in the end Mme de Clèves herself becomes both the

---

31. Peggy Kamuf, "Inside Julie's Closet," *Romanic Review* 69 (1978): 303–4.

32. Roman Jakobson, *Essais de linguistique générale* (Paris: Minuit, 1963), 33; quoted in S. Lotringer, "Vice de forme," *Critique* 27 (1971): 203; my italics.

impossibility of an example for others "in life" and its possibility in fiction. "Her life," the last line of the novel tells us, which "was rather short, left inimitable examples of virtue" (180). The last word in French is the challenge to reiteration—*inimitables,* the mark of the writer's ambitious wish.

I hope it is understood that I am not suggesting we read a heroine as the clone of her author—a reductionist strategy that has passed for literary criticism on women's writing from the beginning. Rather, I am arguing that the peculiar shape of a heroine's destiny in novels by women, the implausible twists of plot so common in these novels, is a form of insistence about the relation of women to writing: a comment on the stakes of difference within the theoretical indifference of literature itself.

Woolf begins her essay on Eliot in the *Common Reader* by saying, "To read George Eliot attentively is to become aware how little one knows about her." But then, a few pages later, she comments:

For long she preferred not to think of herself at all. Then, when the first flush of creative energy was exhausted and self-confidence had come to her, she wrote more and more from the personal standpoint, but she did so without the unhesitating abandonment of the young. *Her self-consciousness is always marked when her heroines say what she herself would have said.* . . . The disconcerting and stimulating fact remained that she was compelled by the very power of her genius to step forth in person upon the quiet bucolic scene.[33]

What interests me here is the "marking" Woolf identifies, an underlining of what she later describes as Eliot's heroines' "demand for something—they scarcely know what—for something that is perhaps incompatible with the facts of human existence" (175). This demand of the heroine for something else is in part what I mean by "italicization": the extravagant wish for a *story* that would turn out differently.

In the fourth chapter of book 5 of *The Mill on the Floss* Maggie Tulliver, talking with Philip Wakem in the "Red Deeps," returns a novel he has lent her:

33. Virginia Woolf, *The Common Reader* (New York: Harcourt, 1953), 116, 173; emphasis added.

"Take back your *Corinne*," said Maggie . . . "You were right in telling me she would do me no good, but you were wrong in thinking I should wish to be like her."

"Wouldn't you really like to be a tenth muse, then, Maggie?"

"Not at all," said Maggie laughing. "The muses were uncomfortable goddesses, I think—obliged always to carry rolls and musical instruments about with them. . . ."

"You agree with me in not liking Corinne, then?"

"I didn't finish the book," said Maggie. "As soon as I came to the blond-haired young lady reading in the park, I shut it up and determined to read no further. I foresaw that that light-complexioned girl would win away all the love from Corinne and make her miserable. I'm determined to read no more books where the blond-haired women carry away all the happiness. I should begin to have a prejudice against them. If you could give me some story, now, where the dark woman triumphs, it would restore the balance. I want to avenge Rebecca, and Flora MacIvor, and Minna, and all the rest of the dark unhappy ones. . . ."

"Well, perhaps you will avenge the dark women in your own person and carry away all the love from your cousin Lucy. She is sure to have some handsome young man of St. Ogg's at her feet now, and you have only to shine upon him—your fair little cousin will be quite quenched in your beams."

"Philip, that is not pretty of you, to apply my nonsense to anything real," said Maggie looking hurt.[34]

Maggie's literary instincts are correct. True to the laws of genre, Corinne—despite, that is, because of, her genius and exceptionality—is made miserable and the blond Lucile, her half sister, carries the day, although she is deprived of a perfectly happy end. But whatever Eliot's, or Maggie's, "prejudices" against the destinies of Scott's heroines, Maggie no more than Corinne avenges the dark woman in her own person. Even though, as Philip predicts, Maggie's inner radiance momentarily quenches her fair-haired cousin, Lucy, "reality"—that is to say, Eliot's novel—proves as hard on dark-haired women as literature is. What is important in this deliberate intertextuality, which has not gone unnoted,[35] is that both heroines revolt against the text of a certain "happily ever after." As Madelyn Gut-

34. George Eliot, *The Mill on the Floss* (New York: NAL, 1965), 348–49; hereafter cited parenthetically in the text.

35. Moers, *Literary Women*, 174.

wirth observes in her book on Mme de Staël, Corinne prefers "her genius to the . . . bonds of marriage, but that is not to say she thereby renounces happiness. On the contrary, it is her wish to be happy, that is to be herself *and* to love, that kills her."[36] Maggie Tulliver too would be herself and love, but the price for *that* unscriptable wish proves again to be the deferral of conventional erotic longings, what Maggie calls "earthly happiness." Almost two hundred years after the challenge to the maxim wrought by the blond (as it turns out) Princesse de Clèves, George Eliot, through the scenario of definitive postponement, "imitates" Mme de Lafayette.

The last two books of *The Mill on the Floss* are called, respectively, "The Great Temptation" and "The Final Rescue." As the plot moves toward closure, the chapter headings of these books—"First Impressions," "Illustrating the Laws of Attraction," "Borne Along by the Tide," "Waking," "St. Ogg's Passes Judgment," "The Last Conflict"—further emphasize the sexual struggle at the heart of the novel. For, as Philip had anticipated, Maggie dazzles blond Lucy's fiancé, Stephen Guest, in "First Impressions," but then, surely what Philip had not dreamt of, the pair is swept away. Maggie, previously unawakened by her fiancé, Wakem, awakens both to her desire and to what she calls her duty, only to fulfill both by drowning, attaining at last that "wondrous happiness that is one with pain" (545). Though I do great violence to the scope of Eliot's narrative by carving a novel out of a novel, the last two books taken together as they chart the culmination of a heroine's erotic destiny have a plot of their own— a plot, moreover, with elective affinities to the conclusion of *La Princesse de Clèves,* and to the conclusion of my argument.

Like Mme de Clèves after her husband's death, Maggie knows herself to be technically free to marry her lover but feels bound, though not for the same reasons, to another script. And Stephen Guest, who like Nemours does not believe in "mere resolution" (499), finds Maggie's refusal to follow her passions "unnatural" and "horrible": "If you loved me as I love you, we should throw everything else to the winds for the sake of belonging to each other" (470). Maggie does love him,

36. Madelyn Gutwirth, *Madame de Staël, Novelist: The Emergence of the Artist as Woman* (Urbana: University of Illinois Press, 1978), 255.

just as the princess loves the duke, passionately; and she is tempted: part of her longs to be transported by the exquisite currents of desire. But her awakening, like that of the princess, though again not for the same reasons, is double. She falls asleep on the boat ride down the river. When she awakens and disentangles her mind "from the confused web of dreams" (494), like Mme de Clèves after her own brush with death, Maggie pulls away from the man who has briefly but deeply tempted her. She will not build her happiness on the unhappiness of others: "It is not the force that ought to rule us—this that we feel for each other; it would rend me away from all that my past life has made dear and holy to me. I can't set out on a fresh life and forget that; I must go back to it, and cling to it, else I shall feel as if there were nothing firm beneath my feet" (502). What is the content of this sacred past? Earlier, before the waking on the river, when Maggie was tempted only by the "fantasy" of a "life filled with all luxuries, with daily incense of adoration near and distant, and with all possibilities of culture at her command," the narrator had commented on the pull of that erotic scenario: "But there were things in her stronger than vanity—passion, and affection, and long deep memories of early discipline and effort, of early claims on her love and pity; and the stream of vanity was soon swept along and mingled imperceptibly with that wider current which was at its highest force today" (457). Maggie's renunciation of Stephen Guest, then, is not so simple as I have made it out to be, for the text of these "early claims," this archaic wish, has a power both erotic and ambitious in its own right. That "wider current" is, of course, the broken bond with her brother. And the epigraph to the novel, "In their death they were not divided," is the telos toward which the novel tends; for it is also the last line of the novel, the epitaph on the tombstone of the brother and sister who drown in each other's arms.

Maggie, obeying what Stephen called her "perverted notion of right," her passion for a "mere idea" (538), drowns finally in an implausible flood. Maggie, no more than Mme de Clèves, could be *persuaded* (to invoke Jane Austen's last novel); for neither regarded a second chance as an alternative to be embraced. Maggie's return home sans husband is not understood by the community. And the narrator explains that "public opinion in these cases is always of the feminine gender—not the world, but the world's wife" (512–13). Despite the phrase, Eliot does not locate the inadequacy of received social ideas in gender per se; her attack on the notion of a "master-key that will fit all cases" is in fact directed at the "men of maxims": "The mysterious complexity of our life is not to be embraced by maxims" (521). This commentary seeks to justify Maggie's choice, her turning away from the maxim, and thus inscribes an internal "artificial plausibility": the text within the text, as we saw that function in *La Princesse de Clèves*. The commentary constitutes another *reading*, "a reading by reference," as Eliot puts it, to the "special circumstances that mark the individual lot" (521). Like Mme de Clèves, Maggie has been given extraordinary feelings, and those feelings en*gender* another and extravagant narrative logic.

There is a feminist criticism today that laments Eliot's ultimate refusal to satisfy her heroine's longing for that "something . . . incompatible with the facts of human existence":

Sadly, and it is a radical criticism of George Eliot, she does not commit herself fully to the energies and aspirations she lets loose in these women. Does she not cheat them, and cheat us, ultimately, in allowing them so little? Does she not excite our interest through the breadth and the challenge of the implications of her fiction, and then deftly dam up and fence round the momentum she has so powerfully created? She diagnoses so brilliantly "the common yearning of womanhood," and then cures it, sometimes drastically, as if it were indeed a disease.[37]

It is as though these critics, somewhat like Stendhal disbelieving the conviction of Mme de Clèves, would have Maggie live George Eliot's life. The point is, it seems to me, that the plots of women's literature are not about "life" and solutions in any therapeutic sense, nor should they be. They are about the plots of literature itself, about the constraints the maxim places on rendering a female life in fiction. Mme de Lafayette quietly, George Eliot less silently, both italicize by the demaximization of their heroines' texts the difficulty of curing plot of life, and life of certain plots.[38]

Lynn Sukenick, in her essay "On Women and Fiction," describes

37. Jenni Calder, for example, in *Women and Marriage in Victorian Fiction* (New York: Oxford University Press, 1976), 158.

38. I echo here, with some distortion, the terms of Peter Brooks's analysis of the relations between "plot" and "life" in his illuminating essay "Freud's Masterplot," *Yale French Studies* 55–56 (1977): 280–300, esp. 298.

the uncomfortable posture of all women writers in our culture, within and without the text: what I would call a posture of imposture. And she says of the role of gender in relation to the literary project: "Like the minority writer, the female writer exists within an inescapable condition of identity which distances her from the mainstream of the culture and forces her either to stress her separation from the masculine literary tradition or to pursue her resemblance to it." Were she to forget her double bind, the "phallic critics" (as Mary Ellman describes them) would remind her that she is dreaming: "Lady novelists," Hugh Kenner wrote not so long ago, "have always claimed the privilege of transcending *mere plausibilities*. It's up to men to arrange such things. . . . Your bag is sensitivity, which means knowing what to put into this year's novels" (emphasis added).[39] And a recent reviewer of a woman's novel in a popular magazine complains: "Like most feminist novels [this one] represents a triumph of sensibility over plot. Why a strong, credible narrative line that leads to a satisfactory resolution of conflicts should visit these stories so infrequently, I do not know. Because the ability to tell a good story is unrelated to gender, I sometimes suspect that the authors of these novels are simply indifferent to the rigors of narrative."[40] The second gentleman is slightly more generous than the first. He at least thinks women capable of telling a good—that is, credible—story. The fault lies in their *in*difference. I would not have descended to the evidence of the middlebrow mainstream if it did not, with curious persistence, echo the objections of Bussy-Rabutin.

The attack on female plots and plausibilities assumes that women writers cannot or will not obey the rules of fiction. It also assumes that the truth devolving from *veri*similitude is male. For sensibility, sensitivity, "extravagance"—so many code words for feminine in our culture that the attack is in fact tautological—are taken to be not merely inferior modalities of production but deviations from some obvious truth. The blind spot here is both political (or philosophical) and literary. It does not see, nor does it want to, that the fictions of

39. Lynn Sukenick's essay is quoted from *The Authority of Experience: Essays in Feminist Criticism,* ed. Arlyn Diamond and Lee R. Edwards (Amherst: University of Massachusetts Press, 1977), 28; Kenner's observation is quoted in the same essay, 30. Mary Ellman's term is taken from *Thinking about Women* (New York: Harcourt, 1968), 28–54.

40. Peter Prescott, *Newsweek,* 16 October 1978, p. 112.

desire behind the desiderata of fiction are masculine and not universal
constructs. It does not see that the maxims that pass for the truth of
human experience, and the encoding of that experience in literature,
are organizations, when they are not fantasies, of the dominant culture. To read women's literature is to see and hear repeatedly a chafing
against the "unsatisfactory reality" contained in the maxim. Everywhere in *The Mill on the Floss* one can read a protest against the division
of labor that grants men the world and women love. Saying no to
Philip Wakem and then to Stephen Guest, Maggie refuses the hos-
pitality of the happy end: "But I begin to think there can never come
much happiness to me from loving; I have always had so much pain
mingled with it. I wish I could make myself a world outside it, as
men do" (430). But as in so much women's fiction a world outside
love proves to be out of the world altogether. The protest against that
topographical imperative is more or less muted from novel to novel.
Still, the emphasis is always there to be read, and it points to another
text. To continue to deny the credibility of women's literature is to
adopt the posture of the philosopher of phallogocentrism's "credulous
man who, in support of his testimony, offers truth and his phallus as
his own proper credentials."[41] Those credentials are more than suspect.

41. Jacques Derrida, "Becoming Woman," trans. Barbara Harlow, *Semiotext(e)* 3
(1978): 133.

2 Lafayette's Ellipses

The Privileges of Anonymity

JOAN DEJEAN

Have more than thou showest
Speak less than thou knowest,

. . . .

And thou shalt have more
Than two tens to a score.
——SHAKESPEARE, *King Lear*

WOMEN'S writing in France is often confined to a territory circumscribed in either utopian or negative terms. On the one hand, this territory is a projected new frontier, an "elsewhere" that, while still a no-woman's-land, will be claimed by women authors when they forge a writing that, in Hélène Cixous's phrase, "inscribes femininity."[1] On the other hand, the accomplishments of women writers in France are described in terms of absence and effacement, as though writing "otherwise" had thus far only been writing against (dominant masculine discourse), a type of *écriture blanche* or nonwriting, a negative discourse, and therefore invisible and indescribable. Claudine Herrmann's *Les Voleuses de langue* stands as eloquent testimony to this view of women's writing as a camouflaged, self-effacing, fearful, derivative (because stolen) medium.[2]

1. Hélène Cixous, "The Laugh of the Medusa," trans. Keith Cohen and Paula Cohen, *Signs* 1 (1976): 878.
2. Claudine Herrmann, *Les Voleuses de langue* (Paris: Editions des Femmes, 1976); hereafter cited parenthetically in the text.

It may be impossible to delimit the female literary estate more concretely and more optimistically as long as theory attempts to account for the entire history of women's writing, as though occurrences at different periods could always be understood in the same way, as though similarities should be pointed out, even at the price of an awareness of diachronic change. We should not minimize the significance of striking ahistorical resemblances made apparent by synchronic comparisons such as the one Herrmann draws between a tenth-century Japanese writer, Lady Murasaki, and her counterpart in seventeenth-century France, the Comtesse de Lafayette (34–48). However, unless we also interpret women's writing in the historical context in which it was created, we run the risk of reading assertion as effacement, of dismissing demonstrable gains as unreadable blanks. Writing "otherwise" always takes place somewhere. For the authors who concern me here, seventeenth-century French women writers and Lafayette in particular, that somewhere is no uncharted utopian space but a territory clearly and self-consciously defined by its creators.

Only in the very recent past have historians and cultural historians—Ian Maclean, Dorothy Backer, and Carolyn Lougee, to name but the most eminent specialists—laid the groundwork for a significant revision of seventeenth-century French history by giving new and detailed evidence of the extent and the force of women's political and social influence during what is arguably the century that set the standards for modern French literature.[3] Their conclusions apply as well in the literary domain. All too often women's literary achievements are discussed as though English literature constituted a generally valid model. In France, however, women's writing acquired a history and a tradition long before it did in England. In the seventeenth century, the modern French novel came into existence, and, as has often been true in the history of this genre, women writers played a decisive role in its development. Though by no means the first writer to forge the association between women and the novel, Marie-Madeleine Pioche de la Vergne, Comtesse de Lafayette, is the best known. Remarkably, although she composed her novels just after an age when women were,

3. Ian Maclean, *Woman Triumphant* (Oxford: Clarendon Press, 1977); Dorothy Backer, *Precious Women* (New York: Basic Books, 1974); Carolyn Lougee, *Le Paradis des femmes* (Princeton: Princeton University Press, 1976).

in Maclean's characterization, "triumphant," Lafayette published either under the name of a male writer and friend (Segrais signed *Zayde*) or resorted to anonymity (as she did for her most famous fiction, *La Princesse de Clèves*).

By refusing to attach her name to her creation and thereby choosing absence over presence, silence over speech, Lafayette would seem to be writing against the grain of a tradition of women's literature already well established in France. In the twelfth century, the founding poet of this tradition, Marie de France, launched both her *Lais* and the story of French *écriture féminine* by proclaiming that "he to whom God has granted wisdom and eloquence in speech, ought not to hide these gifts in silence."[4] Among those echoing her inaugural pronouncement was Louise Labé, who in the mid-sixteenth century spoke out just as openly and with greater gender specificity against women's effacement and silence: "Because the time has come . . . when men's harsh laws no longer prevent women from devoting themselves to study, I believe that . . . if someone [quelcune] reaches the point of being able to put her conceptions in writing, she should do so wholeheartedly and without scorning glory."[5]

Most scholars interpret the anonymous publication of *La Princesse de Clèves* as the mark of the woman writer's "discretion": Herrmann points out, for example, that Lafayette did not wish to be taken for a *femme savante* (33–34). Such a reading follows the model established by Virginia Woolf, who argues, in *A Room of One's Own,* that female literary anonymity results from the internalization of a patriarchal demand for effacement.[6] But in her late essay "Anon" Woolf herself takes a far more suggestive position on anonymity, one that is inextricably bound to her remarks in a second unfinished essay, "The Reader." In the oral tradition, she maintains, storytellers and their audiences were not terribly interested in each other: on the one hand, the singer sought no recognition;[7] on the other, the audience "was so

4. Marie de France, *Lais,* trans. E. Richert (London: 1904), 6. The translation is mine, as are all translations from the French in this chapter, unless otherwise indicated. I provide my own intentionally literal translations from *La Princesse de Clèves*.

5. Louise Labé, *Oeuvres poétiques* (Paris: Club Français du Livre, 1961), 1.

6. Virginia Woolf, *A Room of One's Own* (New York: Harcourt, 1929), 52.

7. Virginia Woolf, "'Anon' and 'The Reader': Virginia Woolf's Last Essays," ed. Brenda R. Silver, *Twentieth Century Literature* 25 (1979): 391; hereafter cited parenthetically in the text.

little interested in [the singer's] name that he never thought to give it" (382). In this situation of impersonal reception, anonymity was a source of authorial power: "Anonymity was a great possession. . . . It allowed us to know nothing of the writer: and so to concentrate upon his song. Anon had great privileges. He was not responsible. He was not self conscious. He is not self conscious" (397).

For Woolf, strong anonymity cannot be gender-specific—"Anon is sometimes man, sometimes woman" (382)—because she refers only to absolute namelessness, instances when the author's identity will never be established. Furthermore, in her view this strong anonymity, this authorship beyond person, is impossible once the individual reader has replaced the plural audience (398). I would like to suggest that Lafayette anticipated Woolf's view of Anon's "privileges," that she sought both to appropriate those privileges for herself and, in so doing, to alter the relation between author and reader by returning it to the distanced, impersonal sphere described in "Anon." For Lafayette, however, authorship beyond person is clearly not writing beyond gender: she saw that the reader's invasive power over the author after the death of Anon poses a particular threat to the female writer. The complex strategy she devised to counteract that threat resulted in the creation of a double signature. In the first place, she forged an external authorial signature that should not be confused with effaced, silent instances of anonymous publication. Then, in her novel, she staged woman's initiation both into writing and into the privileges of anonymity. This dramatic representation of an authorial signature climaxes in the Princesse de Clèves's own use of anonymity to protect herself against the dangers of public exposure and to gain control over her (life) story. Furthermore, the critical reception Lafayette sought was also gender-specific, for both author's and character's signatures were designed to bring about a new type of reading of women's fiction.

Anonymity, or what is usually termed anonymity, was in no way a surprising stance for a seventeenth-century French author, especially a novelist. All rejections of the signature in that period have generally been interpreted in the same way, perhaps because the standard modern definition of an "anonymous" publication, a work "bearing no author's name" (OED), refers only to the nonrelation between author and book and not to the reader's reception of a text. Yet in seventeenth-century France, the anonymity of a work depended primarily on the reader's ignorance of its author; both Richelet's (1680) and Furetière's (1689) dictionaries define an anonymous author as one "whose name is not known." Examined from this second perspective, many, if not most, of the seventeenth-century works printed with no authors' names on their title pages would not have been considered anonymous in their own time, because the authors' identities were an open secret. Thus, for example, during the eight-year period 1662–69 that forms the literary context for *La Princesse de Clèves* (1678), seventy-one original novels were published in France—including *La Princesse de Montpensier,* by Lafayette herself; *La Promenade de Versailles,* by Scudéry, her novelistic precursor; and the still controversial *Lettres portugaises.* Nineteen of those seventy-one remain unattributed today but an additional thirty-four were originally published without authors' names or with only undecipherable initials on their title pages, so that fifty-three novels (74%) would have corresponded to today's standard definition of "anonymous."[8] Many of the thirty-four, however, failed to fulfill the essential condition for textual anonymity in the seventeenth century, because their authors—like Scudéry, whose prose fiction is a clear-cut example of transparent anonymity—were known to all.

Many explanations have been advanced for the pervasive practice of anonymous publication in seventeenth-century France. Adrien Baillet, writing in 1685, listed no fewer than fourteen possible reasons for an author's refusal to accept public responsibility for his or her work. The most diachronically valid explanations concern politically dangerous works, a category that includes several of the thirty-four originally unidentified but today attributed works—for example, Bussy-Rabutin's *Histoire amoureuse des Gaules,* first published with no authorial signature. Baillet rehearses certain culturally bound reasons as well, such as those he advances for the anonymity of seventeenth-

8. I owe my statistics to Maurice Lever's excellent bibliography of seventeenth-century French prose fiction, *La Fiction narrative en prose au 17e siècle* (Paris: CNRS, 1976). Since Lever is understandably interested only in whether a work has had definite attribution, he does not always indicate that it was published anonymously if its authorship was never in doubt. Therefore my figures may not be totally accurate, but my aim is merely to suggest the extent of anonymous publication. I classify a novel as anonymous if the title page omits the author's name, thus offering readers what might be termed a "contract of anonymity," even though the name appears, as it does in several of these works, in the *privilège,* the permission to publish included on the work's last page.

century aristocrats: they would feel shame at being associated with an activity unworthy of their rank, and their modesty would make them oblivious to public recognition of their talents.[9] These have been the traditional explanations for unsigned publication by writers of aristocratic birth, or with aristocratic pretensions, when the work's content did not preclude acknowledgment. (Thus historical justifications for an author's self-effacement join recent feminist discussions of anonymity as a classic signature of the woman writer.)

It is usually impossible to test the validity of these assumptions about a well-connected writer's avoidance of public exposure, for virtually all the evidence is found in correspondence that records only the writer's self-presentation to an audience well informed about authorial secrets. Thus Scudéry sends her anonymously published works to friends, with authorial commentary, and in return accepts their epistolary praise. The example of Lafayette's close friend and literary collaborator, La Rochefoucauld, is even more revealing. Although his *Maximes* (1664) was originally published with no author's name on the title page, his correspondence testifies to a serious, prolonged, and well-publicized involvement with his text. Indeed, these anonymous publications seem to have been readily decoded by their intended audiences, for the identity of their authors has never been disputed.

In the literary annals of seventeenth-century France, however, a few anonymous works fall outside all standard patterns of both authorial intention and reader response. It is surely no accident that all the texts never completely accounted for are tales of female passion that portray the dangers of public exposure for the woman who dares to place herself in an authorial position. Furthermore, in all but one the intratextual threat was doubled by either an extratextual loss of authority or an invasion of the privacy of the woman writer responsible for the transcription of the story. One of these texts, a series of letters from a woman who loves too much, was interpreted either as a real correspondence made public by a woman indifferent to her privacy or as an early epistolary fiction; in either case, it was an anonymous text that aroused great curiosity about its author's identity. Only recently have researchers penetrated the anonymity of the so-called *Lettres et billets*

9. Adrien Baillet, *Jugemens des savants,* 5 vols. (1795; reprint, New York: Olms, 1971), 5:2.

galants (1668), revealing that the slim volume was a greater indiscretion than any of its curious readers had dared imagine. The letters are an authentic correspondence composed by one of the most talented women novelists of the day, Marie-Catherine Desjardins, but made public against her wishes by their recipient, her former lover, the Villedieu whose name she appropriated to sign most of her novelistic production. As a result of its anonymous publication, this text of a woman's passion reduced its author to another type of anonymity, a consequence she herself foresees in a letter written to the book's publisher in a futile effort to stop its publication: "Exposing" what was intended for "the eyes of love alone" to those of the general public made her story impersonal, a generalized, inauthentic fiction in the public domain. [10]

It is hardly surprising that Desjardins-Villedieu's publisher did not heed her plea for the rights to her story, for he was none other than the man Lafayette's closest confidant, the Marquise de Sévigné, referred to as "ce chien de Barbin," [11] the century's most prolific purveyor of the fictions of women seduced and abandoned. Just the year after the Villedieu correspondence appeared in print, he brought out the most elusive of the age's unsigned outpourings of female passion, the *Lettres portugaises,* a text that, because the evidence for a widely accepted recent attribution is inconclusive, remains in the same undecided generic space that both it and the Villedieu letters inhabited in the seventeenth century. Even today, some regard the "letters of a Portuguese nun" as correspondence handed over to Barbin by the writer's former lover, and others consider it a novel written by a man to exploit the public's hunger for fictions of female desire, a novel in which the absence of proper names allowed readers to appropriate the authorial right to assign identities to actors in the drama. [12] The very

10. Marie-Catherine Desjardins (Mme de Villedieu), *Lettres et billets galants,* ed. Micheline Cuénin (Paris: La Société d'Etude du XVIIe Siècle, 1975), 92–93. Cuénin recounts the story of the letters' publication and reception in the introduction to her edition.

11. Marie de Rabutin-Chantal Sévigné, *Correspondance,* 3 vols., ed. Roger Duchêne (Paris: Gallimard, 1972), 1:459; hereafter cited parenthetically in the text.

12. For evidence that the text is a real correspondence, see Yves Florenne's preface to his edition (Paris: Livre de Poche, 1979); for the case attributing the text to Guilleragues, see the preface to the Deloffre-Rougeot edition (Paris: Garnier, 1962). All editors discuss the identities that have been proposed for the nun and her lover.

presentation of the text illustrates perfectly the consequence that Villedieu foresaw would result from the woman writer's exposure. The foreword ("au lecteur") characterizes the work as an arrangement among publisher, translator, and recipient, an arrangement that denies the writer all rights to her story, eliding her scriptive authority even as it makes her betrayal public. [13]

It is impossible to know how Lafayette interpreted any of these texts or even how much any seventeenth-century reader could have known about the complexities surrounding their publication. Nevertheless, two of the key stories in *La Princesse de Clèves,* the princess's and Nemours's re-creation of the lost love letter and the oral publication of her *aveu* (confession or acknowledgment), can be seen as representations of these betrayals of the privacy of female passion, with the resultant erasure of the woman author's authority once her text passes into the public domain. Both Lafayette's authorial strategy and the controversial conduct she devises for her heroine are attempts to avoid the loss of authority that accompanies every public appropriation of fictionalized female desire and to create enigma from the protection of privacy, thus generating new privileges of anonymity. [14] Both author and character forge an *écriture féminine* that is beyond person but not beyond gender, because it focuses the reader's attention in a new way on the central problem for the woman writer in Lafayette's day—and possibly for the woman writer in any age—her signature, the trace of her authority that must simultaneously assert her power and protect her person.

The complex relation that Lafayette engineered between author and

13. "I have been able . . . to recover a faithful copy of the translation of five Portuguese letters that were written to a man of quality, stationed in Portugal. . . . I know the name neither of the man to whom they were written {celui auquel on les a écrites} nor of the individual {celui} responsible for the translation" (*Lettres portugaises,* ed. Bray and Landy-Houillon {Paris: Garnier-Flammarion, 1983}, 69). Still another anonymously published novel, from later in the century, may present a related configuration of authentic love letters made public by a former lover and read as either a novel or a real correspondence published by the woman herself. See Godenne's discussion of the third part of Anne Ferrand's 1689 *Histoire nouvelle des amours de la jeune Bélise et de Cléante,* ed. René Godenne (Geneva: Slatkine, 1980), v–vii.

14. There are several important readings of *La Princesse de Clèves* that suggest positive interpretations of the princess's final renunciation. My reading differs from them in its emphasis on authorial strategy.

text provoked a new type of reading for women's fiction and may thus have altered the course of criticism in France. On the one hand, previous commentaries on women's novels of unacknowledged authorship had been exclusively of the *à clef* variety, for readers regarded these fictions solely as literary games, whose potential was exhausted once their protagonists were identified. Works whose authors were known, on the other hand, generally suffered a related fate, though perhaps a more interesting one, when they were read as autobiographical projections—witness Donneau de Visé's *Réponse à l'impromptu de Versailles,* which devotes more pages to the possibility that Molière was himself a cuckold than to Molière's portrayal of the anxiety of cuckoldry in *L'Ecole des femmes.* The complex, perhaps unique, anonymous signature Lafayette crafted for herself precluded both these responses. When *La Princesse de Clèves* appeared with no author's name on its title page, critics were unable to view the story as an extension of Lafayette's life. Furthermore, as the following pages show, Lafayette's anonymity, unlike that of other women writers of her day, was neither transparent nor total. Her creation of extra- and intratextual authorial enigma forced critics to go beyond the issue of identity and to focus their attention on questions of strategy and motivation. Thus the earliest important readings of Lafayette's novel, Valincour's *Lettres à Madame la Marquise * * * sur le sujet de "La Princesse de Clèves"* and Charnes's *Conversations sur la critique de "La Princesse de Clèves"* are not only the first detailed considerations of the modern French novel but the first important readings of an individual literary work to focus almost exclusively on the text. Through the complex relation Lafayette maintained with her fiction, she managed to turn the absence of signature into a distinctive mark, laying claim to her fictional territory and indicating her identity as a woman writer.

THAT OBSCURE OBJECT OF DESIRE

The appearance of Lafayette's most famous novel may well signify the creation of modern techniques of book promotion. Months before the novel was put on sale, on March 17, 1678, various strategies were deployed to whet the public's literary appetite. Copies were evidently passed around in manuscript, not enough to begin to saturate the demand that was quickly created, but just enough to prompt the spread of rumors announcing the novel's impending "birth." During the winter preceding its publication, a series of letters circulated containing the same affirmation, almost identically phrased. Thus in December Georges de Scudéry's widow wrote to Bussy-Rabutin that "Monsieur de la Rochefoucauld and Madame de Lafayette have made a novel of the intrigues of Henri II's court which is said to be admirably well written."[15] At this stage, there is no question of anonymity; on the contrary, the novel, while not yet officially "born," has both a "mother" and a "father"—to borrow the terminology proposed by the correspondents. At about this time, what is undoubtedly the most remarkable publicity campaign of the century was launched in the pages of Donneau de Visé's *Mercure galant*. That journal's January issue featured an anonymous *nouvelle*, "La Vertu malheureuse," with a plot so similar to part of *La Princesse de Clèves* that its author almost certainly had access to a manuscript of Lafayette's novel. Maurice Laugaa refers to this story as an "advance reproduction of the masterpiece" and claims that publishing it a full two months before *La Princesse de Clèves* was "a veritable preconditioning of the public."[16]

By the time *La Princesse de Clèves* was put on sale, suspense had primed its potential public into a state of eager anticipation. "Never has a work made me more curious," Valincour notes. "It had been announced long before its birth; enlightened people, very capable of judging the matter, had praised it as a masterpiece. . . . One can say that there are few books which have enjoyed . . . such widespread approval . . . before they have even been seen by the public."[17] Apparently, that public was not disappointed. In March, the very month of the novel's publication, the *Mercure galant* reported, "You know for how long and with what favorable preoccupation everyone was waiting for [*La Princesse de Clèves*]. It has lived up to these expectations" (Lau-

15. Roger de Bussy-Rabutin, *Correspondance*, 6 vols., ed. Ludovic Lalanne (Paris: Charpentier, 1858), 3:431–32; hereafter cited parenthetically in the text.

16. In citing the *Mercure galant*, I quote from Maurice Laugaa's excellent anthology, *Lectures de Mme de Lafayette* (Paris: Colin, 1971), 26, 25, which contains selections from the journal's 1678 issues; hereafter cited parenthetically in the text.

17. J. B. de Valincour, *Lettres à Mme la Marquise * * * sur le sujet de "La Princesse de Clèves,"* ed. Jacques Chupeau et al. (Tours, France: Université François Rabelais, 1972), 2; hereafter cited parenthetically in the text.

gaa, 21). Parisian readers were evidently as quick to grab up copies of the new novel as the *Mercure galant* was to proclaim its success, for Sévigné, writing to her cousin Bussy-Rabutin, described it as "a little book that Barbin gave us two days ago, which seems to me one of the most charming things I've ever read" (2:602). Their less fortunate counterparts in the provinces, such as Bussy-Rabutin, had to beg for copies from their numerous correspondents who sang the new best-seller's praises. The prepublication buildup was more than matched by the clamor that surrounded the novel's first months on the literary scene. Correspondences like Sévigné's and Bussy-Rabutin's function as veritable scorecards, with these masters of the epistolary art tallying favorable and derogatory responses to the novel.

Contemporary letters record the phenomenon to which Valincour and Charnes trace the origin of their texts, what could be termed the apotheosis of *La Princesse de Clèves,* the novel's reign as chief subject for debate in Parisian salons. "Everywhere people are on the alert about this work" (Valincour, 102; see also 250, 260, 269, 365–66). When Lafayette's early critics composed studies of her novel nearly as long as the novel itself, they commemorated this debate in print and added fuel to the fire of publicity. Only a little more than a month after the novel's publication, Bussy-Rabutin was informed that "We are promised its critique" (4:98). Indeed, *La Princesse de Clèves* had been on the market barely six months when Valincour's *Lettres* provided the informal academies in the salons with both a mirror image of their debates and a new subject of controversy: who was the author of the impatiently awaited critique? and what was the value of "his" arguments? A mere five months later, Charnes's anonymous defense of the novel and his critique of Valincour's critique reenacted both controversies.

During this entire year of intense debate, the *Mercure galant* followed suit: Donneau de Visé attempted to turn his readers into small-scale Valincours and Charnes by printing a series of *questions galantes* to which readers were invited to respond. For example, in the April issue readers were asked:

whether a virtuous woman, who has all the esteem possible for her husband, the perfect *honnête homme,* and who is nonetheless combatted by a very great passion for a lover . . . does better to confide her passion to this husband than to say nothing of it, at the risk of the battles she will continually be forced to concede because of the unavoidable opportunities to see this lover, from whom she has no other means of distancing herself than the confidence in question. (Laugaa, 27)

Responses were printed in subsequent numbers, and near the end of the debate readers responded to other readers' responses to the novel, echoing Charnes's analysis of Lafayette through Valincour. As Laugaa points out, the *Mercure*'s questions universalized the novel's plot (29): readers were asked to reach a verdict on "une femme de vertu" rather than on the Princesse de Clèves. De Visé's elimination of the proper names had the same effect as Lafayette's choice of anonymity. The *Mercure*'s readers—who frequently remained anonymous themselves, thereby prompting future rounds of debate—were encouraged to put themselves in the place of Lafayette's heroine, to replace her elided name with their own names as they sat in judgment on her acts. Furthermore, they were encouraged to publish their own versions of the princess's story and thereby invite others to respond to the Ur-text only through these new versions. The story of the first year of *La Princesse de Clèves*'s life is a hall of mirrors in which one sees the same scenario reflected seemingly ad infinitum: an author refuses to accept responsibility for his or her work, creating an enigma to make the work controversial; others accept the author's invitation to evaluate the work, appropriating in the process the author's abnegated authority, becoming in turn writing subjects inviting critiques of their own anonymous texts.

Despite its complexity, the publicity campaign that attended the publication of *La Princesse de Clèves* might seem a mere literary curiosity were it not for the unsettling denial that throws new light on the entire enterprise. As I mentioned earlier, before the novel's publication the names of its reputed coauthors, Lafayette and La Rochefoucauld, are always linked to the object of desire. But during March and April 1678 hesitation creeps in, for the newborn novel now seems an orphan. "It is not, however, all that we had been promised," Mme de Scudéry informs Bussy-Rabutin, "it's an orphan [*une orpheline*] whose father and mother disown it" (Bussy-Rabutin, 4:77; see also 4:98). The novel is no sooner published than those recently rumored to have been "pregnant" with such a fiction vigorously and unequivocally deny any responsibility for its existence. Their repudiation of the text apparently leads to the final, most troubling stage in the seventeenth-century maternity trial, general silence regarding the novel's author (or authors)—witness Valincour's and Charnes's critiques. From this point on, even those close to Lafayette—Sévigné, for example—never again associate an author's name with the much-talked-about novel. The question of the contemporary public's attribution of the controversial text is ultimately undecidable. It is, however, related to a potentially more fruitful subject for inquiry: why did the author disown her most famous fiction? Sainte-Beuve, commenting on Lafayette's decisive role in the evolution from romance to novel, observes that "certainly she was aware of what she did, and she intended to do it."[18] By the same token, Lafayette's decision to sever the connection already established between her name and her fiction must be taken for nothing less than a carefully calculated strategy. To understand the terms of her calculation, let us turn to *La Princesse de Clèves* and to Valincour's and Charnes's readings of it.

THE LANGUAGE OF ANGELS

Valincour mocks Lafayette's heroine because of the princess's "innocence," her "outrageous simplicity" (129). He means, quite simply, her silence. Valincour becomes angry (150) because Mme de Clèves, in almost all the central confrontations in the novel, simply says nothing or next to nothing, failing to reward her interpreting publics with any form of expression more eloquent than a blush or a turn of the head. The novel's most dedicated early detractor was the first to understand the interpretive dilemma posed by the woman's language Lafayette developed for her heroine. When dealing with the princess, readers must read between the lines: they must interpret (verbalize) the unsaid and even the unsayable, for the language of Lafayette's heroine is a language of lack, of silence, of repression, of gaps. Valincour affirms that if Lafayette's discourse were to gain currency, "we would soon see ourselves reduced to the language of angels, or at least we would be forced to speak to each other in signs" (318). In his view the author shares in the princess's simplicity. The novel's "language of angels" is a language of lack: ellipsis and ambiguity ("équivoque")

18. Charles-Augustin Sainte-Beuve, *Portraits de femmes* (Paris: Garnier, 1876), 250.

are the rhetorical sins that Valincour notes most frequently in *La Prin-cesse de Clèves*.

To lend force to his contentions, Valincour brings in a grammarian to carry on a dialogue with the author of the *Lettres*. The unifying thread in the grammarian's arguments is his attack on forms of ellipsis in Lafayette's novel. He uses a variety of terms for this stylistic fault—ambiguity, brevity, abbreviation, laconism, and so on—but his meaning is always the same: *La Princesse de Clèves* is too elliptical. Through repeated analysis, Valincour attempts to demonstrate that the novel is often obscure because its author is driven by a rage to eliminate and abbreviate that goes beyond concision and creates a text riddled with gaps. His criticisms apply not only to individual sen-tences but to the overall construction. "At least if the author had secret reasons for not leaving out [Mme de Tournon's] story, he should have given it . . . more of a connection with the rest of his work" (159). Genette has referred to this lack of justification as narrative "mu-tism."[19] John Lyons, in a detailed and stimulating analysis of the passages criticized as digressions, has demonstrated the correctness of Valincour's perception: by the standards of her time, Lafayette was saying (too) little and shifting enormous responsibility onto her reader.[20] In characterizing her style as a poetics of lack, Valincour's grammarian prefigures the judgment of later critics. He argues that this desire to suppress is the result of a failed wager. The author of *La Princesse de Clèves* "resembles those people who, as a result of trying to say too much, say nothing" (318).

The excessiveness of Valincour's attack should not blind us to its correct evaluation of the stakes involved in Lafayette's wager. Ellipsis, as rhetoricians consistently point out, is an all-or-nothing figure, in some sense a mathematical impossibility. Thus Fontanier gives the etymology of "ellipsis" as "retrenchment, suppression: derived from . . . to lack, to be lesser." Simultaneously absence and presence, el-lipsis gives a plenitude to silence: though there is nothing on the page, the reader is made to recognize that there could have been something more, that something has been removed. Thus ellipsis has the po-

19. Gérard Genette, "Vraisemblance et motivation," in *Figures II* (Paris: Seuil, 1969), 78.

20. John Lyons, "Narrative Interpretation and Paradox: *La Princesse de Clèves,*" *Romanic Review* 72 (1981): 386, passim.

tential for unusual semantic fullness. Once again, according to Fontanier, "Ellipsis is one of the figures that express the most and provoke the most thought."[21] In other words, the elliptical lack is one of the most economically sound figures of rhetoric: for a loss that is not completely a loss, a writer has the possibility of winning, in Pascal's terms, an "infinite gain." The budget-conscious critic that Genette has shown Valincour to be was quick to note the central role of ellipsis in *La Princesse de Clèves*. The same type of economic analysis that Genette, using Valincour, applies to the example of *vraisemblance*[22] can also serve to illustrate the functioning of Lafayette's poetics of lack.

Perhaps the sin of omission for which Valincour criticizes Lafayette most frequently is the substitution of a third-person pronoun or a general noun for a proper name. He contends that antecedents and referents are often not clearly indicated. While some of his analyses stem from an overzealous critical imagination, at times he objects to sentences that are in fact difficult to interpret. One of his victories is provided by the following passage: "[Monsieur de Clèves] prévoyait de grands obstacles par le duc de Nevers, son père. Ce duc avait d'étroites liaisons avec la duchesse de Valentinois: elle était ennemie du vidame, et cette raison était suffisante pour empêcher le duc de Nevers de consentir que son fils pensât à sa nièce."[23] "Is it the niece of his son," Valincour asks, "that of the Duc de Nevers, that of the vidame, or that of the Duchesse de Valentinois? For [the possessive pronoun] could refer to any of the four" (292). Readers of the novel, as even Valincour admits, can supply the name that identifies the pronoun ("du vidame"). Yet when the sentence is taken out of context, the accusation of ambiguity no longer seems far-fetched. Valincour has once again put his finger on an obsessive trait of Lafayette's style: the elimination of proper names and their replacement with third-person pronouns that take on some of the elusiveness of free-floating signifiers. These incompletely anchored pronouns work against the prin-

21. Pierre Fontanier, *Les Figures du discours* (Paris: Flammarion, 1977), 483, 308.

22. *Vraisemblance*, a key term in the seventeenth-century reception of women's fiction, can be rendered either as "verisimilitude" or as "plausibility." For a discussion of the concept, see Gérard Genette (71–99) and Nancy K. Miller, "Emphasis Added: Plots and Plausibilities in Women's Fiction," chap. 1 of the present volume.

23. Marie-Madeleine Lafayette, *La Princesse de Clèves*, ed. Antoine Adam (Paris: Garnier-Flammarion, 1966), 44; hereafter cited parenthetically in the text.

ciple of difference, as characters seem almost interchangeable—witness the effect of "la sienne" ("hers") in the first sentence of the novel's third paragraph (35).

In *Traité des tropes*, Du Marsais refers to this sort of ambiguity as "équivoque" (Valincour's word) or as "louche" ("ambiguous" or "cross-eyed"): "*Louche* is a metaphorical term here; for just as cross-eyed people seem to be looking in one direction while they look in another, so in cross-eyed constructions, the words seem to have a certain relation to each other, while they in fact have another."[24] Du Marsais's rule of thumb is that it is best to avoid *louche* constructions if they are immediately clear only to those "who already know what they are reading" (197). Unlike Valincour, however, Du Marsais is not blind to the figure's potential for increasing a passage's semantic charge. The constructions he calls cross-eyed, like other forms of ellipsis, use elimination for the purpose of multiplication. *Louche* words have a certain relation to the context, but they appear to have a different one, or at least suggest the possibility of an alternative; in *La Princesse de Clèves,* they suggest that individuals are, grammatically if not socially, infinitely replaceable. Du Marsais's description, "cross-eyed people seem to be looking in one direction while they look in another," is particularly appropriate for the microcosm Lafayette paints in her novel of false appearances. "[C]e qui paraît n'est presque jamais la vérité" (56), according to Mme de Chartres's often-cited formula. The characters in the novel pretend to look one way while looking in another in an attempt to glimpse the truth camouflaged by a façade of codified behavior. Lafayette's *louches* and elliptical constructions identify the act of reading with her heroine's struggle to preserve her identity and to avoid the reduction to anonymity that inevitably results from being seen through.

THE WAGES OF ANONYMITY

The ultimate lack in *La Princesse de Clèves* may be the text's original ellipsis, the absence that dominated contemporary readings of the

24. César Du Marsais, *Traité des tropes* (Paris: Nouveau Commerce, 1977), 196–97; hereafter cited parenthetically in the text.

novel: the suppression of the author's name. Though insisting on all that is missing from the pages of the novel, Valincour represses its already repressed origin and makes no mention of the enigma most frequently alluded to by its first readers. Despite his apparent neutrality, however, there is evidence to suggest that the stridency of his attacks on Lafayette's language and plot reflects a fear that the work's anonymous signature was a sign of female self-assertion.

That *La Princesse de Clèves* appears with no author's name on its title page does not make it an anonymous publication according to the seventeenth-century usage of the term. Many early readers must have been privy to the rumor about Lafayette's and La Rochefoucauld's joint authorship. For them, the missing information on the title page was, like an ellipsis, simultaneously absence and presence. Because they were able to identify *La Princesse de Clèves* as the novel they had been waiting for, they could simply fill in the absent author's name, just as they filled in "du vidame" after "nièce" in the example criticized by Valincour. For them, the real enigma of the novel's title page was not the absence of *le nom d'auteur* but the denial of what Lafayette and La Rochefoucauld had presumably encouraged these readers to believe.

Even this denial follows the elliptical model Lafayette stamped on her fiction: she simultaneously suppressed and multiplied. Had she really wanted to end the association between her name and this novel, why would she have continued to praise it so lavishly, as contemporary accounts maintain that she did? "M. de la Rochefoucauld and Mme de la Fayette strongly deny being its authors, but at the same time they praise [the novel] excessively," Mme de Seneville wrote to Bussy-Rabutin on April 25, 1678 (4:98). Lafayette's often-cited letter to Lescheraine of April 13, 1678, confirms the contradictory behavior that puzzled her contemporaries. She opens the discussion of *La Princesse de Clèves* by denying that she is in any way responsible for the novel; she then proceeds, exactly like the other amateur critics of her day, to give her opinion of the work, an opinion that appears as ingenuous as it is laudatory:

Je le trouve tres agréable, bien escrit sans estre extrêmement châtié plein de choses d'une délicatesse admirable et qu'il faut mesme relire plus d'une fois. Et surtout, ce que j'y trouve, c'est une parfaite imitation du monde de la cour et de la manière dont on y vit. Il n'y a rien de romanesque et de grimpé; aussi n'est-ce pas un roman; c'est proprement des mémoires et c'estoit, à ce qu'on m'a dit, le titre du livre, mais on l'a changé.[25]

It is easy to understand why such behavior bewildered Lafayette's contemporaries. The recipients of her denials of authorship must have found the shape of those denials more confusing still. For example, her eulogy of La Princesse de Clèves to Lescheraine begins with this disavowal:

[J]e vous asseure que je n'y en ay aucune [part] et que M. de La Rochefoucauld, à qui on l'a voulu donner aussi, y en a aussi peu que moy; il en a fait tant de serments qu'il est impossible de ne le pas croire; surtout pour une chose qui peut estre avouée sans honte. Pour moy, je suis flattée que l'on me soupçonne et je croy que j'avoûrois le livre, si j'estois asseurée que l'autheur ne vînt jamais me le redemander. (2:63)

Lafayette argues that La Rochefoucauld must be taken at his word because "he has taken so many oaths to that effect." Yet nowhere in La Rochefoucauld's correspondence is there any reference to his authorship or nonauthorship of La Princesse de Clèves. He praises the work, but only Lafayette combines flattering critical commentary with repudiation of the fiction. The coy ending—she would accept the attribution if only she were sure it wouldn't be taken away from her—is a denial that opens up the possibility of an affirmation, a configuration she later puts to even more striking use in what is certainly her most bizarre denegation of authorship.

In 1691, a lifelong friend and former teacher with whom Lafayette had recently been out of touch, Ménage, begged her to confirm for him that she was in fact the author of La Princesse de Clèves. Explaining that the subject had come up in a history he was writing, he adds, "Having had the honor of knowing you since you were born, . . . I would be ashamed to have been misinformed of this circumstance, and to have misinformed the public" (Lafayette, Correspondance 2:181). Even this personal appeal is rewarded with nothing more straight-

25. Marie-Madeleine Lafayette, Correspondance, 2 vols. ed. André Beaunier (Paris: Gallimard, 1942), 2:63; hereafter cited parenthetically in the text. The letter presents one seemingly critical comment as praise: "full of things . . . that one must even reread more than once." This oblique directive to the reader reveals Lafayette's understanding of her novel's narrative complexity and her conviction that this interpretive difficulty is a source of the book's strength.

forward than a formulation so convoluted as to be nearly incomprehensible: "The people who are your friends don't admit to having a part in it; but to you what wouldn't they admit?" (2:182). The editor of Lafayette's correspondence refers to this letter as proof of Lafayette's authorship, but this sentence can be read at most as an admission wearing the mask of a denial: "What wouldn't your friends admit to you?" is prefaced and therefore silenced by "your friends will not admit having had any role in it." The phrase, far from putting an end to the question it allegedly answers, only raises additional questions. "Qui s'excuse, s'accuse." Lafayette's denegations are true denials in the psychoanalytic sense of the term: they are simultaneously affirmations and negations, simultaneously presence and absence. They function like the elliptical structures that Valincour describes as her novel's dominant stylistic trait. It seems inevitable to conclude that Lafayette struggled to establish and maintain undecidability at her most famous novel's origin because she was hoping to reap the high profits Fontanier considered the reward of ellipsis.

Lafayette's first published work is perhaps most remarkable for its title: "Portrait de Madame la Marquise de Sévigné par Madame la Comtesse de LaFayette sous le nom d'un inconnu." The title defines the fiction of the portrait: the unknown man is the "narrator" of Sévigné's charms. Read literally, however, the title illustrates the elliptical relation Lafayette maintained with her fiction throughout her career. Her strategy in this text, the only work for which she ever publicly accepted responsibility, perfectly prefigures what was to become a recurrent authorial pose. Time and again Lafayette as author hides behind a man (Ménage for *La Princesse de Monpensier,* Segrais for *Zayde,* La Rochefoucauld for *La Princesse de Clèves*). Each of these men serves as her amanuensis, her adviser, and her editorial assistant. In these strange voluntary reenactments of an age-old situation—behind every great man there is a woman—Lafayette uses the male writers as fronts for her activities. Whenever she denies her authorship and casts doubt on a work's origin, she has her name covered with "the name of an (un)known man." Both Valincour and Charnes refer to "the author of *La Princesse de Clèves*" as "he"—masculine, singular, and undefined. As we have seen, however, this disguise does not end the association of her own name with her fiction. The trace of "Madame la Comtesse de LaFayette" is tantalizingly (in)visible, as the title of the Sévigné portrait claims, behind (*sous*) the (un)defined masculine name. In the portrait, the anonymous narrator explains that the quality of the narration results from "ce privilège d'Inconnu dont je jouis auprès de vous."[26]

The "privileges of anonymity" that Lafayette sought to obtain through her signature are more clearly defined in the short text that serves as a foreword to *La Princesse de Clèves*. In this text, the only one in the margins of Lafayette's novel, the author is referred to as "he," the name of an unknown man. The foreword is devoted to this ambiguous authorial status, to the factors responsible for it, and to those that could resolve the situation:

> Quelque approbation qu'ai[t] eu[e] cette Histoire dans les lectures qu'on en a faites, l'auteur n'a pu se résoudre à se déclarer; il a craint que son nom ne diminuât le succès de son livre. Il sait par expérience que l'on condamne quelquefois les ouvrages sur la médiocre opinion qu'on a de l'auteur et il sait aussi que la réputation de l'auteur donne souvent du prix aux ouvrages. Il demeure donc dans l'obscurité où il est, pour laisser les jugements plus libres et plus équitables, et il se montrera néanmoins si cette Histoire est aussi agréable au public que je l'espère. (31)

The first sentence suggests that "the author could not make up his mind to make his identity known." In this context, however, "se déclarer" can mean literally "to endorse" (an opinion) or "to declare" (one's feelings). From the outset, the author of *La Princesse de Clèves* makes it clear that "he" is keeping his views and his feelings, as well as his name, hidden from the reader. The explanation given for this withholding reveals above all a desire for judgment. A vocabulary of debate and controversy dominates the passage, and debate and controversy are ultimately equated with literary success. The author wears "the name of an unknown," so that "debate will be freer" and so that "he" will "not diminish the success of his book" (more controversy equals greater success). The truth of this axiom is borne out both by the princess's story and by the history of that story's reception.

To begin with the reception: Mme de Scudéry was correct in calling the novel an "orphan," for when Lafayette refused to give it her name,

---

26. Marie-Madeleine Lafayette, "Portrait de Madame la Marquise de Sévigné," in *Galerie des portraits*, ed. Edouard de Barthélémy (Paris: Didier, 1860), 95.

she refused to have it received as an extension of herself. She sent it out into the world to be judged instead on its own merits. In the letter to Lescheraine, Lafayette asserts that authorship of the novel is "something that can be admitted without shame." Had she really been either a shy and retiring "lady novelist" or a discreet aristocrat anxious to protect herself from exposure to the public eye, the well-managed publicity campaign surrounding her novel's appearance could never have taken place. Yet Lafayette's wiles are still devalued today. Claudine Herrmann supports her characterization of Lafayette as an anonymous thief of knowledge by pointing out that the novelist's maiden name, La Vergne, finds its Latin equivalent in Laverna, the name of the Roman patron of thieves (34). Herrmann's insight is in fact in plain view in Lafayette's correspondence: when Ménage writes to his former student, he refers to her as "mea carissima Laverna." But Laverna, patron of thieves, is also the goddess of gain. Lafayette worked under cover of anonymity—"without being seen," in Herrmann's terms—not because she was afraid to be taken for a *femme savante,* but because her enigmatic disappearance could win her great profit. According to Segrais, the writer who took public responsibility for her *Zayde,* Lafayette understood literary suppression in terms of economic gain: "Madame de Lafayette used to say that one sentence cut from a work was worth a gold *louis,* and one word, twenty *sous.*"[27] In Lafayette's authorial strategy, the nonsaid represents not a passive blank or silence but an active suppression, a distinction Marguerite Duras maintains when she insists that the marks of the feminine in her writing should be characterized not as "blanks," "void," or "lacks" but as "suppressions."[28]

Commercial considerations, then, form the context in which Lafayette's signature must be evaluated. Neither model for anonymous publication adopted by women writers in her day can be termed economically sound. On the one hand, transparent anonymity, though it guaranteed authors the credit that was their due, brought on a concomitant loss of authority for their fictions, which were judged solely as extensions of their persons. On the other hand, absolute anonymity, while protecting works from *à clef* reception, exposed their authors to

27. J. R. de Segrais, *Segraisiana* (La Haye, 1722), 196.
28. Marguerite Duras and Xavière Gauthier, *Les Parleuses* (Paris: Minuit, 1974), 12.

a potential double loss of authority. They might never receive credit for their production, and their unclaimed texts would fall into the public domain, where they would be attributed to others, appropriated by others, and on occasion deformed by editors eager to make a profit from these explorations of the female heart. With the elliptical enigma Lafayette devised as her signature, she protected her person and her property and also increased their authority. Contemporary correspondence provides ample evidence of her work's ability to generate critical discussion, and supports the remark she made in ending her letter to Lescheraine: "On est partagé sur ce livre-là à se manger" (*Correspondance* 2:63). The commentaries of Valincour and Charnes, the founding texts in what is known today as practical criticism or textual analysis, stand as the greatest tribute to the success of her authorial strategy.

In *La Princesse de Clèves* Lafayette demonstrates that writing beyond person is not writing beyond gender. The lessons that can be learned from the history of the publication of women's writing in the seventeenth century determine the fate of the most famous early heroine in women's fiction. Like the anonymous contemporary texts of female passion discussed earlier, the princess's story is simultaneously a sentimental education and an authorial apprenticeship. In learning both to shape and to direct her story, she comes to understand the powerful narrative attraction of female passion and the difficulty of controlling the fiction-making process. Lafayette's novel contains two texts of female desire originally intended for private communication, texts that generate outbursts of interpretive and attributive curiosity when they are published anonymously. One is a written text, a woman's complaint addressed, like the Portuguese nun's, to an unfaithful lover and prudently left unsigned.[29] Following the same model—witness the foreword to the *Lettres portugaises*—the recipient arouses greater curiosity than the author. Some say that the letter was written to Nemours; others champion the cause of the vidame. For the princess the lesson of this purloined letter is double, since the incident makes her first a reader, then an "author," of women's fiction. She discovers the

29. The letter is written by Mme de Thémines to the vidame. But since its author's identity is revealed only after the contents have been discussed at length (109) and is never made public, for all intents and purposes the letter remains anonymous.

power of anonymity to awaken curiosity and provoke discussion and the eagerness of readers to transform themselves into academies, interpreting bodies thirsty for half-told tales and elliptical stories that they can complete, thereby appropriating all authorial rights.

The princess, the first to read the letter (97), also becomes the first of its indiscreet readers, for she initiates its passage from authentic amorous artifact to literary text. Like "that dog Barbin," such readers are interested more in the addressee than in the writer, whose scriptive authority is elided and whose identity is important only because of her relationship to the lover who betrayed her trust. Yet the princess responds differently than other readers, whether male or female. They allegedly want to expose the letter to public scrutiny because of its literary value. Thus the vidame brags to an assembled company of young men that he has received "the loveliest letter ever written" (101), then cannot find the document, which he intended to read aloud to justify his boast. The queen claims that she wants to see it because she has heard how "lovely" it is (116). But the voyeuristic public really covets the letter because its *écriture* (handwriting) *féminine* can, if identified, determine male guilt. The princess alone finds the letter's story of interest. Instead of trying only to determine its author's identity, she generalizes its message—just as readers of the *Mercure galant* were instructed to generalize Mme de Clèves's story—and reflects on what it tells her about the female condition, woman seduced and abandoned, a fate with which she identifies: "Elle voyait seulement que M. de Nemours ne l'aimait pas comme elle l'avait pensé et qu'il en aimait d'autres qu'il trompait comme elle" (99).

But the princess's compassionate involvement with this text is temporarily suspended when she allows herself to be turned into a poor imitation of the "Guilleragues" of her day, authors whose literary genius was measured by their ability to trick readers into accepting sometimes plagiarized fictions of female desire as genuine documents. Lafayette's heroine personally completes the erasure of female identity she had initiated when she follows the dauphine's advice and has the purloined missive rewritten "in an unknown hand" (117). Nor does she simply plagiarize the letter: by the time she and Nemours get together under her husband's surveillance, she has to reinvent it, since the original has been returned to its author. In her private space, the room of her own, the princess becomes a writer, a writer with a male collaborator, playing Lafayette to Nemours's La Rochefoucauld. With her initiation into writing, the princess makes her contribution to a major literary enterprise of her day, the trafficking of female passion as literature. The product of this collaboration represents the fate of similar anonymously published contemporary texts, for its ersatz *écriture féminine*—a text copied and reimagined after an original that has been lost, stolen, and passed around—bears little resemblance to its model in either writing or handwriting (118). Yet the afternoon the princess and Nemours devote to preparing another woman's betrayal for public consumption is also the closest they ever come to a consummation of their own passion. At the time, writing serves only to mediate their desire. The scene also performs a critique of that desire, for unlike such predecessors as Paolo and Francesca, Lafayette's lovers do not read amorous fictions together but instead share in the forgery and debasement of a true confession. The princess eventually views the scene as emblematic of the destiny of all women's stories allowed to circulate among men and realizes that in this textual economy her female authority will always be eroded.

Lafayette's heroine cannot know that the vidame would have made the letter public had others not done so for him, but the fate of her own private narrative teaches her why the recipients of such letters enter into bargains with booksellers: "J'ai eu tort de croire qu'il y eût un homme capable de cacher ce qui flatte sa gloire" (138). Her involvement with the letter leads directly to her controversial *aveu* (acknowledgment), for to avoid the anonymous woman's fate she chooses to tell the story of her love for Nemours to what she believes is a private audience (100, 119). Even the dauphine, commenting on that narrative, which she knows only as another anonymous tale of a woman in love, correctly sees that the unidentified woman recounted her story to gain control over it, to remain "maîtresse de sa passion" (132).

After the voyeuristic reception scene in which Nemours represents all the indiscreet readers of tales of female passion, he assumes the princess's authorial rights and gives an *à clef* version of her account, substituting pseudonyms ("des noms empruntés") for all proper names (126), thereby transforming her story into what an eager public can take to be an enigma in search of a solution. This transformation liberates Mme de Clèves's story for public speculation: when it finally returns to its origin, the princess finds herself in the singular position of being asked to sit in judgment on her own tale, narrated by the dauphine, who has appropriated it with all the confidence of an author. When the princess witnesses the usurpation of her right to control the transmission of her own story, or even to possess that story, her experience marks the logical conclusion of the erosion of female authorial status and female identity in narrative that has been operative throughout the novel.[30]

It is no accident that this lesson is driven home most forcefully for the princess through the appropriation of a narrative that is her attempt to break free of all those seeking to control the plot of her life—her mother, her husband, her lover—and to create a story that, because it is without precedent, is uniquely hers and incapable of being taken over by anyone else. To underscore this point, she announces to the prince that she is about to make "un aveu que l'on n'a jamais fait à son mari" (122). Immediately after the *aveu,* she reenforces her self-characterization by meditating on "la singularité d'un pareil aveu, dont elle ne trouvait point d'exemple" (126). Her initial public confirms her evaluation: Nemours calls the acknowledgment "un remède si extraordinaire" (124), and the prince refers to it as "la plus grande marque de fidélité que jamais une femme ait donnée à son mari" (123).

Aveu is usually translated "confession," although Lafayette avoids the substitution of this possible synonym, perhaps because it suggests a female revelation that is both too literal and too negative. In fact, *aveu* only came to be used in the sense of "confession" in the mid-seventeenth century, when it was first used in the legal procedure by which criminals were forced to *avouer,* or admit, their crimes. The princess, however, does not use the term in this sense, as she is careful

30. This invasion of narrative territory doubles the invasion of private spaces evident throughout the novel—see Sylvère Lotringer, "La Structuration romanesque," *Critique* 26 (1970): 506. Arnold Weinstein has characterized the novel as a "massive assault on privacy, a transformation of intimacy into public spectacle"; see his *Fictions of the Self* (Princeton: Princeton University Press, 1981), 73. In a stimulating article, Michael Danahy has analyzed the sexual politics of spatial vulnerability in the novel. He points out, for example, that in the scene in which Nemours secretly watches the princess winding ribbons on a cane, the invasion of her private space is triple, for the prince's servant, representing the husband himself, watches Nemours; see "Social, Sexual and Human Spaces in *"La Princesse de Clèves,"* French Forum* 6 (1981): 219.

to make clear: "l'innocence de ma conduite et de mes intentions m'en donne la force" (122). Rather, she is attempting to enact an *aveu* in the earlier legal sense of a loyalty oath—in her husband's words, "the greatest mark of fidelity that a woman has ever given to her husband." The word originally meant "a written declaration admitting the vassal's commitment to his lord, in exchange for the heritable estate (*fief*)" (*Le Petit Robert*). This written acknowledgment of indebtedness, the representation of future obligations, was but half of a transfer in writing: to figure the guaranty of the property and of the personal authority offered the vassal, the lord "signed" and "sealed" the charter granting the estate.

The context of the princess's *aveu* reveals an awareness of the proper format for such a declaration: her husband, as though recognizing her intention of transforming her speech into a written acknowledgment, says that she has given him a "*mark* of fidelity," a sign or signature of homage. The princess also realizes the danger of attempting a transaction in and on male terms: "the singularity of such an *aveu,* for which she could find no precedent, made her aware of its peril." Although she knows only the rudiments of this male script, she attempts to forge a legally binding contract or pledge: "elle trouvait qu'elle s'y était engagée sans en avoir presque eu le dessein" (125). In her formulation, *dessein* denotes explicitly her "intention," but it also contains "design," the equivalent of her husband's "mark," the *sein,* "sign" or "seal," that could validate such a transaction. Lafayette's heroine attempts to "pledge herself" in the male script because, to maintain her innocence, she must have access to the commodity exchanged for the pledge of fidelity, land. The princess wants to escape the temptations of life at court by remaining alone at Coulommiers, the estate that her husband inherited from his ancestors, one of whom received it in return for an oath of homage. Using the proper legal code, she asks for a male prerogative: to rule as lord over an estate.

Her plan backfires. The prince wants more information: the name of the man she loves. He attempts, as the novel's readers have done from the first, to turn her promise of future loyalty, an as yet unwritten narrative, into a confession, the completed accounting for past guilt. He wants, in other words, to have her life conform to the plot male writers of Lafayette's day were crafting for female passion. *Aveu* in the sense of "confession" enters French literature in classical theater, most famously in Racine's *Phèdre* (1677), in which it refers to the heroine's revelation of Hippolyte's name and thereby of her crime of passion. For Phèdre, the *aveu* is the text of her unraveling, the mark of the self-dispossession that leads directly to her suicide. Lafayette rejects this (male) view of female revelation as loss of self. She transforms the revelation of forbidden love from a scene of female weakness to a conquest of language (*prise de parole*) that is at the same time an initiation into writing, the act by which the princess first lays title to her own story. From her aborted scene of acknowledgment, Lafayette's heroine learns that, to gain authority, she must fashion herself according to a female script.

As the repercussions of this episode demonstrate conclusively, being "extraordinary" or "singular" does not guarantee an author control over her story and thereby protect her privacy. On the contrary, narrative originality merely fuels the public's desire to identify the woman who attempts to be unlike other women. It also increases the dangers of exposure for the princess. Although the tale of betrayal told in the anonymous letter could be applied to many women, Lafayette's heroine fears that the plot she has chosen for herself will be transparent once it has been published anonymously: "il n'y a point dans le monde une aventure pareille à la mienne; il n'y a point une autre femme capable de la même chose" (136), she protests to her husband when he assures her that she must have taken another woman's story for her own. After the dauphine relates the episode of the *aveu* to the avower herself, Mme de Clèves does not merely suffer in silence but, uncharacteristically, offers an opinion on the quality of the (her own) narrative: "cette histoire ne me paraît guère vraisemblable" (132). The princess's remark is more than a self-conscious foreshadowing of criticism of her conduct (or, rather, the refutation *avant la lettre* of criticism based on verisimilitude): her analysis demonstrates that the standards by which her story can be evaluated lie elsewhere. Her judgment also marks a reorientation of her efforts to gain control over her story. When Lafayette's heroine pronounces her own story "incredible," she expresses a desire to be outside of story, to be unnarratable. This she will achieve by rejecting Nemours and life in society, by scripting a negative plot that resists accountability. The events of the last years of her life are summed up in less than a paragraph, and the narrator's global judgment of her existence is laconic, the novel's final suppression: "sa vie,

qui fut assez courte, laissa des exemples de vertu inimitables" (180)—
"inimitable": that which cannot be repeated, in life or in fiction. The
princess comes to realize that to control her story she must suppress
it. In Lafayette's novel, we witness the struggle of a subject suspended
between two modes of its own dissolution. The princess can allow
herself to be dissolved by others' curiosity, or she can direct her story
at any price, even at the cost of making herself inimitable, literally
walking out on the story of her life. The princess is no "innocent,"
speaking the "language of angels." Her language and her story are
marked not by lack but by suppression. Lafayette's heroine knows the
power of the ultimate ellipsis, the ellipsis become ambiguity. She
creates a rupture in narrative that the reader is powerless to fill.

Throughout the long history of the novel's reception, much has
been made of its conformity or nonconformity to contemporary standards of literary verisimilitude or plausibility.[31] One of its first critics,
Bussy-Rabutin, inaugurated this interpretive tradition by characterizing both Mme de Clèves's attempts at shaping her own destiny, the
acknowledgment to her husband, and her refusal to marry Nemours,
as "incredible" (Laugaa, 18–19). Recently, Genette has attempted to
understand the terms of this judgment by explaining that Mme de
Clèves's actions were considered unbelievable because they were outside the codes governing women's conduct in her day (73–75). Both
these readings, Genette's as much as Bussy-Rabutin's, take the princess at her word in her remark to the dauphine that the story of her
confession is "hardly plausible." Yet her comment is delivered, not as
an evaluation of her conduct, but in a desperate attempt to stop the
circulation of her story. She calls the anonymous woman's behavior
"implausible" in the hope that those interested in learning her identity
will stop their efforts because they will no longer believe the story.
Her ruse is unsuccessful because, within the microcosm of the novel,
readers are asked to believe that such conduct is not only possible but
desirable. Furthermore, the context in which such actions would have
been considered plausible in Lafayette's day was far broader than a
critic relying only on Bussy-Rabutin could realize.

By situating both the princess's singular actions in the context of

31. See Nancy K. Miller (chap. 1 above, esp. 15–24), whose insightful essay convincingly situates this discussion in the broader context of women's fiction.

contemporary women's fiction, Valincour—though unaware of his insight—erodes the value of the charge of implausibility that he, too,
levels against Lafayette's story. He brings up the two comparisons allegedly to denigrate the novel. Thus he claims that the "confession"
scene is not only unbelievable but unworthy of any claim to originality
(extraordinariness) because it is plagiarized from another novel, also
by a woman, Desjardins-Villedieu's *Les Désordres de l'amour,* published
by Barbin in 1675 (215–17). Valincour uses similar reasoning to
write off the power of the princess's rejection of Nemours: this action,
too, lacks both verisimilitude and originality. On the one hand, no
real woman would refuse to marry a man to protect her "repos," and
on the other, the princess's behavior, while outlandish, is not even so
interesting as that of Scudéry's heroine, Sappho, in *Le Grand Cyrus*:
"Madame de Clèves should have, following the example of this heroine, proposed to Monsieur de Nemours to go with her to her estate
near the Pyrenees to spend the rest of his days, having first received
his word that he would never push her to marry him" (275–76). Despite the implausibility of the plot, Valincour contends, readers will
not be surprised by its twists, which they have seen before.

In his attack, Valincour accurately, though unwittingly, defines the
perimeters of the "elsewhere" in which both the princess and her creator inscribe their fictions. This perception, that women writers of
his day had carved out a special territory for their narratives, explains
the occasional violence of his commentary—for example, his concluding critique of the novel's style: "I am afraid that there may be a secret
conspiracy to force the [French] Academy to accept this sorry manner
of speech [méchante façon de parler] and that [*La Princesse de Clèves*]
may be the signal sent out to the conspirators" (339). The critic felt
intimidated by what he correctly termed a conspiracy, if by conspiracy
he meant a plot that threatened to assert the authority of women's
fiction to provide an alternative to the anonymous, stolen scripts of
female passion. Within the separate narrative space delimited by the
female conspirators, the princess's actions not only seem plausible but
constitute a "triumph"—a term I borrow from *Le Triomphe de l'indifférence,* the title of a seventeenth-century explanation of the desir-
ability of the life the princess chooses. This text, a dialogue between
two young women recounted by a third,[32] is a justification of what

32. Anonymous, *Le Triomphe de l'indifférence,* ed. André Beaunier, in *Mesures* (1937):

the interlocutors term "indifference"—what the princess calls "repos" ("peace" or "tranquillity")—the decision to live apart from all the "agitation" and the "anxieties" of the world of *galanterie* in which men control all the plots (175). Since the women realize that their relative inactivity might seem "sad" to outsiders (just as the princess's fate does to some readers), they explain what they see as its positive aspects: a loss of affective life ("the heart is almost dead or leads a listless life") in exchange for permanent control over one's actions and one's emotions (204).

Le Triomphe de l'indifférence was not made public in its day. Obvious ideological affinities led its twentieth-century editor to attribute it to Lafayette. Although this attribution seems unlikely, the text nonetheless provides significant evidence of the type of female conspiracy Valincour saw as a threat to the center of male intellectual power, the French Academy. Lafayette's fiction is inscribed into a textual tradition in which the princess's decisions are the proper responses for a woman aware of her story's commercial value. In all likelihood, that plot was far more significant—if not in life, at least in fantasy and fiction— than Valincour knew or than we will ever know. For example, the letters that Mlle de Montpensier (herself a novelist of note) and Mme de Motteville exchanged in the 1660s project a plan of action identical to the one that both Lafayette and the anonymous author of *Le Triomphe de l'indifférence* imagined for their heroines: renunciation of the world of the court, with its intrigues and its *galanterie*; rejection of marriage (though, following the Scudéry model, not necessarily of men); and the creation of "a corner of the world where women are their own mistresses [maîtresses d'elles-mêmes]."[33]

The very vocabulary with which the princess's gestures toward self-possession are characterized—"extraordinary," "singular," "inimitable," "without precedent"—signals Lafayette's fidelity to the ideals of her century's most powerful female voices. These hyperbolic affir-

---

155–206. The narrator-author remains anonymous, but the agreement of adjectives and participles reveals her to be a woman. Beaunier transcribed the text from a manuscript in the Arsenal Library. His heirs published his transcription posthumously with the note "attributed to Mme de Lafayette." In his introduction, however, Beaunier does not suggest that Lafayette wrote the text, only that she reached the same conclusions about love as did its author (153–54); hereafter cited parenthetically in the text.

33. Louise d'Orléans Montpensier, *Lettres* (Paris: Collin, 1806), 35.

mations of female superiority, of woman's advancement beyond previous norms and thereby outside narrative, are the language of *préciosité,* the exclusively female literary movement with which Lafayette was associated in her youth, whose adherents both lived apart from society and defined a separate space for *écriture féminine.*[34] Furthermore, it is the language that defined Lafayette's own superior status within that movement. When Costar collected his correspondence for publication, he noted above his first letter to Lafayette (still "carissima Laverna") in 1653, that "she was usually called 'the Incomparable.'"[35] In one of the numerous contemporary treatises affirming female superiority, *Le Mérite des dames* (1657), Saint-Gabriel calls Lafayette "la non-pareille" (Moulogneau, 11–12, 14). When she who was judged beyond comparison proclaims that the plot she devises for her heroine is similarly without precedent, Lafayette continues the type of ellipsis that characterizes her style. She creates a narrative void that is also a repartition of territory and an outpouring of women's language. At the conclusion of her masterpiece, Lafayette arrives at the paradoxical situation already reached by her precursor, Scudéry—in, for example, the conversation "De la magnificence." Both want to place their fictions in an elsewhere outside existing public scripts of female desire and to do so without further contributing to the elision of female authority that results from free circulation.

Lafayette demonstrated the value of a personal mark or signature that guarantees (female) textual authority with no risk of personal exposure. When she refused *publicly* to acknowledge her fiction (*Correspondance* 2:63, 182), she consistently used the same word, *avouer,* that her heroine uses to characterize the controversial declaration in the novel. Lafayette could "disavow" her fiction without losing her authority because she had forged a personal meaning for the ambiguous term *aveu:* "signature." The princess's *aveu* is the text of her self-

34. For an overview of *préciosité* and the *précieuses'* views of female superiority, see Dorothy Backer, passim. For a more scholarly and detailed history of the movement, consult Roger Lathuillère, *La Préciosité: Etude historique et linguistique* (Geneva: Droz, 1966). In "The Fiction of *Préciosité* and the Fear of Women," *Yale French Studies* 62 (1982):107–34, Domna Stanton analyses the image of *préciosité* created by Molière and other seventeenth-century writers.

35. See Geneviève Mouligneau, *Madame de Lafayette, romancière?* (Brussels, Belgium: Université de Bruxelles, 1980), 12; hereafter cited parenthetically in the text.

definition, the mark of her self-constitution, her signature. The princess exchanges her husband's estate for the female literary estate, a territory beyond male control. At the novel's close, Nemours admits that he cannot "la faire changer de dessein" (180)—and, as in the scene of the *aveu, dessein* signifies "plot" more than "intention." The princess, like her creator, replaced the acknowledgment in the male script (*le nom d'auteur*) with a signature in the feminine.

Bussy-Rabutin pronounced *La Princesse de Clèves* so "implausible" that it "smells of the novel" ("sent le roman"; Laugaa, 19). Though it is difficult to know what type of novel he had in mind, since he himself wrote the most blatantly voyeuristic "fiction" of his day (*L'Histoire amoureuse des Gaules*), his attack, once again inadvertently, was right on the mark. In the second half of the seventeenth century, *roman* (as opposed to *nouvelle*) was generally associated with Scudéry's literary production, precisely the type of feminocentric fiction whose odor Lafayette encoded into her own language and plot. Both Lafayette's signature as a novelist and the scenario she devised for her heroine's coming to terms with the plots of women's fiction carve out a special territory for the woman writer, a "corner of the world" in which, as "mistress of herself," she can enjoy the privileges of anonymity. The "chez elle" to which the princess withdraws is the actual as well as the utopian "elsewhere" that seventeenth-century French women novelists delimited as the estate of *écriture féminine*.

3　The Princesse de Clèves

An Inimitable Model?

DONNA KUIZENGA

INCE its appearance in 1678, controversy has always swirled around *La Princesse de Clèves*. In recent years Lafayette's readers have examined the novel's structural principles, its historical bases and their uses, and its potential religious content. Perhaps most fruitfully, *La Princesse de Clèves* has been the subject of a number of excellent readings by feminist critics. In the seventeenth century, the novel in general is associated with women and women's concerns. For feminist critics, it is essential not to forget that *La Princesse de Clèves* is a woman's novel, whether by sole authorship, or by the powerful influence of the feminine and feminizing milieu. A woman's novel in patriarchal society, feminist critics argue, is always subject to question.[1] It must be carefully examined for traces of a different vision, of a questioning of the mores and values of the dominant culture. Nor are such readings anachronistic, for salon life, preciosity, and the seventeenth-century quarrels about woman's place and function are part and parcel of the milieu from which *La Princesse de Clèves* came.

The princess's renunciation of Nemours and the novel's ending have often been called into question. For some readers, of course, the renunciation and retreat represent nothing more than the princess's inability to love, or live, as a woman "should." Mme de Clèves, scarred

---

1. Nancy Miller, "Emphasis Added: Plots and Plausibilities in Women's Fiction," chap. 1 above, 17–24.

by fear, if not frigidity, and her mother's teachings, flees a world she cannot endure. For others, the princess's renunciation and retreat constitute rather an affirmation of self in a world that denies such autonomy to women. Yet other critics see in the ending the confirmation of the novel's discreet but real religious content. A reexamination of some of *La Princesse de Clèves*'s fundamental structures will help us assess more clearly what is at stake in the riddle of Mme de Clèves's "exemples de vertu inimitables."[2]

Lafayette uses a number of narrative strategies to shape our perception of the princess's story. The narrator, sometimes omniscient, sometimes with limited knowledge, sometimes disinterested, sometimes involved, provides readers with a view that at one and the same time mimes the princess's perception of events and takes a small step back, allowing assessment of the princess's choices and actions. Thus, the reader is encouraged to think twice from the very beginning.

The narrator suggests that things are not quite what the official, self-congratulatory rhetoric of the court would suggest. The opening hyperbolic account is punctuated by touches of ironic commentary. Mme de Valentinois dresses "avec tous les ajustements que pouvait avoir Mlle de Marck, sa petite-fille, qui était alors à marier" (35). And Saint-André has known an extraordinary rise, through the King's favor alone: Saint-André "était un des favoris, et sa faveur ne tenait qu'à sa personne; le roi l'avait aimé dès le temps qu'il était dauphin, et depuis, il l'avait fait maréchal de France, dans un âge où l'on n'a pas encore accoutumé de prétendre aux moindres dignités" (39). From its very first pages, *La Princesse de Clèves* carries insidious traces of an ironic subtext that underlies the glittering surface of the court.

In addition, especially in the early parts of the novel, the narrator's judgmental interventions, although limited, serve to back up and justify the princess's behavior and reactions, and to underline the ways in which she differs from those who surround her. In the scene at the jewel merchant's, for example, we read the following description of the young woman's embarrassment as M. de Clèves stares at her: "Il [le prince] s'aperçut que ses regards l'embarrassaient [Mlle de

2. Madame de Lafayette, *La Princesse de Clèves*, ed. Antoine Adam (Paris: Garnier-Flammarion, 1966), 180; hereafter cited parenthetically in the text.

Chartres], contre l'ordinaire des jeunes personnes qui voient toujours avec plaisir l'effet de leur beauté" (42). The princess constitutes the exception to "toujours," and this uniqueness on the moral plane grounds a defense against any accusation of bad faith in her apparently favorable disposition toward M. de Clèves, a reaction dictated by the fact that "Mlle de Chartres avait le coeur très noble et très bien fait" (49), as the narrator tells us.

In describing the heroine's relationship to the Chevalier de Guise, the narrator now intervenes twice to further solidify the favorable evaluation of Mlle de Chartres's character. Her pity for Guise is justified: "il [Guise] avait tant de mérite et tant d'agréments qu'il était difficile de le rendre malheureux sans en avoir quelque pitié" (51). Likewise, the narrator subscribes to Mme de Chartres's admiration of her daughter's sincerity: "Mme de Chartres admirait la sincérité de sa fille, et elle l'admirait avec raison, car jamais personne n'en a eu une si grande et si naturelle" (51).

If the narrator is relatively overt in her approval of Mlle de Chartres's beauty and her reactions to M. de Clèves and other men at the court, she is somewhat more reticent in the description of Nemours's first encounter with the princess. The narrator does provide some subtle justification for the *coup de foudre* through the use of the locution, "il était difficile": "Ce prince était fait d'une sorte qu'il était difficile de n'être pas surprise de le voir quand on ne l'avait jamais vu, surtout ce soir-là, où le soin qu'il avait pris de se parer augmentait encore l'air brillant qui était dans sa personne; mais il était difficile aussi de voir Mme de Clèves pour la première fois sans avoir un grand étonnement" (53). The narrator does not serve simply as an approving voice, however. Because the novel is structured around the gradual coming to consciousness and speech of the princess, the narrator, as a character with opinions, plays a larger role in the earlier parts of the text.

The interventions just discussed are not the only way in which the narrative is shaped so as to induce readers to make a positive evaluation of the princess. In several passages, the narrator intervenes in such a way as to appear almost indistinguishable from one of the characters. The clearest example is provided by reflections on the court. One such passage opens with the statement, "Mme de Chartres, qui avait eu tant d'application pour inspirer la vertu à sa fille, ne discontinua pas de prendre les mêmes soins dans un lieu où ils étaient si nécessaires et où il y avait tant d'exemples si dangereux" (44). The reader is given no indication whether the judgments are those of Mme de Chartres or of the narrator. The subsequent reflections on the court, fused with additional scene-setting material, cannot as such be considered a phase of Mme de Chartres's thought. Through the indetermination of the sentence above, however, the two points of view are merged, and the additional authority of such statements gives even more weight to Mme de Chartres's attitudes. In a subsequent passage, as Rousset points out,[3] Mme de Chartres, through her perspicacity, appears to take over the narrator's function. When her daughter makes no mention of Nemours's feelings for her, "Mme de Chartres ne le voyait que trop, aussi bien que le penchant que sa fille avait pour lui" (61). Here again the shared perspective adds authority to Mme de Chartres's views.

However, this technique also creates the kind of aesthetic distance characteristic of *La Princesse de Clèves*. Initially, the reader is led to accept Mme de Chartres's moral position as valid, in much the same way that her daughter does. On the one hand, this is a means by which readers share the heroine's perception of reality. On the other, readers know, always a little before Mme de Chartres, the degree of Mme de Clèves's attachment to Nemours. This method can already be seen in the initial presentation of Nemours. The narrator's description of the couple's first meeting (52–54) and the placement of the Chevalier de Guise's surmise that they are destined to fall in love (54) succeed in giving the reader a fuller perspective on the situation than that of the characters without ever using direct statement. Mme de Chartres's perception, related after the narrator's comments, the court's reaction to the couple, the introductions, and the passage concerning Guise, arrive for readers with the same *retard fatal* of which Rousset speaks in relation to Mme de Clèves's own reflexions.

Like the various stances of the narrator, direct discourse and early forms of interior monologue are deployed to frame the tale so that the reader both shares Mme de Clèves's perspective and retains a certain

3. Jean Rousset, *Forme et signification: Essais sur les structures littéraires de Corneille à Claudel* (Paris: José Corti, 1962), 30. On this point, also see Barbara R. Woshinsky, *"La Princesse de Clèves": The Tension of Elegance* (The Hague: Mouton, 1973), 105.

distance from it. Direct discourse is used to foreground those elements that are the most striking to the title character. When Mme de Clèves returns to the court after her mother's death, for example, she is visited by the Reine Dauphine. Their conversation is presented in two modes. A brief résumé covers the future queen's expressions of sympathy on the death of Mme de Chartres, and the "plusieurs choses particulières" (80) about the court that she tells Mme de Clèves. However, direct discourse is used when the Reine Dauphine comes to her main piece of gossip: "il est certain que M. de Nemours est passionnément amoureux et que ses amis les plus intimes non seulement ne sont point dans sa confidence, mais qu'ils ne peuvent deviner qui est la personne qu'il aime" (81). The direct discourse conveys the importance that this piece of news has for the princess. This technique is used quite often to mime for the reader the sudden focusing of the princess's attention on matters having to do with Nemours.

The reader is also privy to Mme de Clèves's reflections through the use of a technique that stands on the threshold between résumé and interior monologue in the modern sense. After reading the lost letter, Mme de Clèves's reaction is presented at first in a résumé, into which the narrator intervenes, to clarify what the princess feels: [la princesse] "se trompait elle-même, et ce mal, qu'elle trouvait si insupportable, était la jalousie avec toutes les horreurs dont elle peut être accompagnée" (99). As the passage continues, however, we move closer to interior monologue:

Elle voyait par cette lettre que M. de Nemours avait une galanterie depuis longtemps. Elle trouvait que celle qui avait écrit la lettre avait de l'esprit et du mérite. . . . Elle voyait, par la fin de cette lettre que cette personne se croyait aimée; elle pensait que la discrétion que ce prince lui avait fait paraître, et dont elle avait été si touchée, n'était peut-être que l'effet de la passion qu'il avait pour cette personne à qui il craignait de déplaire. (99–100)

As witnesses to Mme de Clèves's reflections, readers observe the slow unfolding of her understanding of her attachment to Nemours, an attachment of which the reader is already powerfully convinced. As the tale progresses the princess is presented as becoming gradually more conscious and more active. She moves from being the listener, the hearer of the none-too-efficacious exemplary tales, gossip, and surmises of others, to being a speaker in her confession and the renunciation scene.[4] The ultimate effect of Lafayette's narrative strategies is double. On the one hand, the character's final choice is endorsed. On the other hand, the aesthetic distance created by the text's ironies allows the reader to assess the complexity and meaning of Mme de Clèves's final decision to leave not only Nemours but the world of the court.[5]

It is not through narrative strategy alone that Lafayette demonstrates the fundamental validity of Mme de Clèves's final choice. Indeed, the whole world portrayed by the novel conspires to demonstrate that retreat alone permits one to retain some kind of integrity. La Princesse de Clèves offers a thoroughgoing examination of the impact of patriarchy's power on human relationships, whether they be between women and men, among women, or among men.

What gives life at the court its flavor and fascination is the visible proximity to power. The spectacle of kingship, in the particular person of Henri II, holds all in its thrall. The predilections of the king determine those of the courtiers, and chief among these is the king's penchant for mixing affairs of the heart and affairs of state, as witnessed by the dominance exercised by his mistress, Diane de Valentinois. For the nobles, taking their sign from the king, ambition and gallantry are stirred together in an intoxicating brew that all too often proves deadly. And, according to La Princesse de Clèves, the admixture of love and politics is not peculiar only to the time of Henri II, as the interpolated tale of Anne de Boulen illustrates. Alain Niderst reminds us that La Princesse de Clèves is shot through with a conception of history, commonly found in memoirs of the time, that holds that individual passions rather than principles or convictions are the driving force of events.[6] Hence, the factions at court are split along lines of

4. On this point, see Edward C. Knox, *Patterns of Person: Studies in Style and Form from Corneille to Laclos* (Lexington, Ky.: French Forum, 1983), 122, passim; and Suzanne Relyea, "Elle se nomme: La Représentation et la lettre dans *La Princesse de Clèves*," in *Onze études sur l'image de la femme dans la littérature française du dix-septième siècle*, ed. Wolfgang Leiner (Tübingen, Germany: Gunter Narr, 1984), 110.

5. For a more detailed discussion of these strategies, see my *Narrative Strategies in "La Princesse de Clèves"* (Lexington, Ky.: French Forum, 1976), 13–67.

6. Marie-Madeleine de Lafayette, *Romans et nouvelles*, ed. Alain Niderst (Paris: Bordas, 1989), 449n51, 451n78. For a different discussion of disorder, history, and the meaning of *La Princesse de Clèves*, see Laurence A. Gregorio, *Order in the Court: History and Society in "La Princesse de Clèves"* (Saratoga, Calif.: Anma Libri, 1986), passim.

personal jealousy, and, as the story of Anne de Boulen makes clear, great political changes, such as England's rupture with the Catholic church, are rooted in individual passions.

In *La Princesse de Clèves,* this conception of history is placed in the context of the painful lessons that the young Mme de Clèves learns about passion's capricious and unreliable nature. The story of Henri II and Diane, the first explanation of the court's realities that the young woman hears, provides a key to the implications of the conception of history that the novel enacts. In this world where things are often, but not always, not what they seem—"ce qui paraît n'est presque jamais la vérité" (56)—the ordered ceremonial of the court is doubled by a surprising disorder, where women seem to wield power, and men are the toys of their passions. It has been suggested that in *La Princesse de Clèves* Lafayette is showing that real, effective power lies in the hands of women.[7] In the short run this is often true, as demonstrated by Mme de Valentinois's pervasive influence. In the long run, however, power resides in the king, and any power that Diane, the queen, or the Reine Dauphine might exercise is held only by proxy. Although this does not make the women's power less dangerous, or less ruled by passion, as the fate of the Vidame de Chartres illustrates, in the final analysis this secondary power is ephemeral. It can be withdrawn at any point, by an accident, such as the death of Henri II, or by a caprice, such as Henry VIII's sudden murderous jealousy.

While in many ways the positions of women and men at the court are very different, they do share a certain communality in that both men and women are dependent on the king, or the conception of kingship, for their power. The shift in factions in the court at Henri II's death provides a powerful illustration of this fact. Nonetheless, the men retain numerous privileges as partners in the gendered patriarchy, one of the simplest and most devastating for Mme de Clèves being their relative freedom of movement. The privilege of aggression, whether on the battlefield or in the field of love, is reserved for men.[8]

7. In this regard, see the following two articles by Michael G. Paulson: "The Equality of the Two Sexes in *La Princesse de Clèves,*" *Cahiers du dix-septième siècle* 2 (1988): 57–66, and "Gender, Politics and Power in Madame de Lafayette's *La Princesse de Clèves,*" *Papers on French Seventeenth-Century Literature* 15 (1988): 57–66.

8. Margaret J. MacRae emphasizes Diane's status as an outlaw who manipulates the

Mme de Clèves suffers in her passion not only because of her own pain, confusion, and bad conscience, but also because of Nemours's aggressions and repeated invasions of her space. Many critics have commented on the opposition of court and country that is central to *La Princesse de Clèves*; indeed, the geography of the novel is the geography of a woman's struggle for autonomy. Yet wherever she goes, Mme de Clèves's personal territory, be it parlor or pavilion, is encroached upon by Nemours. In the incident of the lost letter, Nemours uses M. de Clèves to invade Mme de Clèves's room, as he also penetrates the gardens at Coulommiers, whether secretly or openly. Even Mme de Clèves's one moment of perfect passion, the evening in the pavilion at Coulommiers, is disrupted with fatal consequences by Nemours.

In *La Princesse de Clèves* power is both orderly and disordered, like the court itself. On the one hand, the social hierarchy is perfectly clear: all power radiates from the king. On the other hand, because decisions are most often motivated by passions, power circulates in a surprising and disorderly fashion only comprehensible if one knows the human motivation behind events, the kind of motivation that Mme de Chartres explains to her daughter in the story of Diane de Poitiers.

The conception of history found in *La Princesse de Clèves* accentuates the capricious and unpredictable, although not inexplicable, unfolding of events. As a consequence, the courtiers are driven by ambition and/or passion and engage in complex game playing. The interpretation of signs, those direct and indirect indices of passion, are thus the keys to understanding one's own position and advancing one's own cause at court. Hence, the constant interference of appearance and reality, the mutual spying and voyeurism, and the multiple strategies of interpretation in which all the characters are engaged. And because passion insistently betrays itself, through speech or silence, through involuntary looks or blushes, everyone is perforce drawn into the game.

It is into this world that Mme de Chartres brings her daughter. For the princess, Mme de Chartres seems an indispensable help in time

---

court's system to her own ends. Her power is only borrowed, however. See Margaret J. MacRae, "Diane de Poitiers and Mme de Clèves: A Study of Women's Roles, the Victim and the Conquerer," *Papers on French Seventeenth-Century Literature* 12 (1985): 559–73.

of trouble, a sorely missed ally, and a disinterested confidant. Yet even Mme de Chartres's behavior is subject to scrutiny, as the narrator suggests when she presents the character. Mme de Chartres's educational principles are subtly endorsed by the narrator, who uses a generalization to suggest that this exceptional technique is a worthy one: "La plupart des mères s'imaginent qu'il suffit de ne parler jamais de galanterie devant les jeunes personnes pour les en éloigner. Mme de Chartres avait une opinion opposée" (41). And it is through the outline of Mme de Chartres's educational principles that the first substantial questions are raised about the glittering and beguiling surface of court life. Nonetheless, Mme de Chartres is not exempt from the court's seduction. She herself is "extrêmement glorieuse" (41), and her choices in potential suitors for her daughter's hand take rank and glory into account, relegating other considerations to a secondary place. Mme de Chartres's famous maxim—"ce qui seul peut faire le bonheur d'une femme . . . est d'aimer son mari et d'en être aimée" (41)—is more troubling than its lapidary form suggests. She brings her daughter into that social order where women serve as the currency of an economy based on rank, wealth, and proximity to power, while at the same time speaking of love and durable happiness. In this context Mme de Chartres must mean something very particular by both of these terms. She speaks of the love that comes from the acceptance of marriage as a relationship that involves considerations larger than those of the individual. Indeed, Mme de Chartres stands in the text as a representative of the tradition that prioritizes the public and social over the individual, and suggests that the duty of the moral woman is to refuse passion. Unfortunately, this maxim and the careful delineation of public and private on which it is based serves as much as a hindrance to the princess's understanding of her situation as it does as an aid. Mme de Clèves does not see the "amitié" (122) that she feels for her husband as the love of which her mother spoke. Instead she persists in reading in her mother's words an injunction suggesting that her only salvation would have been to love her husband as she loves Nemours. This places her in a situation of guilt without remedy. This misunderstanding is compounded by the fact that, in M. de Clèves, the princess marries a man who reverses the importance of public and private as Mme de Chartres would have had them. In pursuing his marriage, M. de Clèves overcomes all social obstacles to pursue an individual passion.

Indeed, that ideal balance of glory, morality, and individual quietude that Mme de Chartres posits is at odds with everything *La Princesse de Clèves* tells us about life in society, both past and present. Seduced by her own vanity, Mme de Chartres asks her daughter to live by a rule that runs counter to all the norms of the society in which she finds herself. The mother seems to solve the contradictions between her view and the reality of the world around her by engaging in a logic that makes women responsible for morality, even in immoral situations. In assessing the relationship between the king and Diane, Mme de Chartres comments:

Il est vrai . . . que ce n'est ni le mérite, ni la fidélité de Mme de Valentinois qui a fait naître la passion du roi, ni qui l'a conservée, et c'est aussi en quoi il n'est pas excusable; car si cette femme avait eu de la jeunesse et de la beauté jointes à sa naissance, qu'elle eût aimé le roi avec une fidélité exacte, qu'elle l'eût aimé par rapport à sa seule personne sans intérêt de grandeur, ni de fortune, et sans se servir de son pouvoir que pour des choses honnêtes ou agréables au roi même, il faut avouer qu'on aurait eu de la peine à s'empêcher de louer ce prince du grand attachement qu'il a pour elle. (55–56)

This statement, which opens Diane's tale, tells the young Mme de Clèves many things. Passion is not based on beauty or virtue. It can be exploited to one's own ends. Moral responsibility is distributed according to gendered rules. If Mme de Valentinois had been a faithful, disinterested mistress, the *king*'s passion could have been excused, and indeed he might even have been admired for his great attachment. There is no suggestion that if she had espoused the alternative conduct that Mme de Chartres outlines, Mme de Valentinois would have been a candidate for praise. At most she might have merited that her behavior be covered in silence, as Mme de Chartres does not reveal the name of the Duc d'Orléans's discreet mistress. It is characteristic of patriarchy both to deprive women of choice and to make them responsible for morality. The absence of choice makes true morality impossible, and one may understand Mme de Clèves's feelings of guilt as arising from this contradiction. Indeed, it is only when she is widowed, that particularly privileged and empowering position for women in seventeenth-century society, that Mme de Clèves makes an authentic choice, and thus purchases her autonomy and moral integrity.[9]

9. In this regard, see Roger Duchêne, "La Veuve au XVIIe siècle," in *Onze études sur*

If her death leaves inimitable examples of virtue, it is not so much because of Mme de Clèves's desperate gesture of confiding in her husband, as because of her ability to see that in the society she knows, there is no possibility of preserving individual integrity. She knows that her mother's maxim is insufficient, as are the multiple and contradictory seductions of passion. *La Princesse de Clèves* consistently underscores the haremlike atmosphere of the court, and suggests that the coherent life can be lived only outside of it. While it is true that all the males at court are subordinated to the king, and thus they are in what might be termed feminized positions, vying for the king's favor as do the women, men nonetheless have privileges that women lack. At the bottom of the hierarchy of power, caught in the contradictory messages of patriarchy, Mme de Clèves puzzles out the riddle of her own life. The narrative structure of the novel and its conception of history endorse Mme de Clèves's withdrawal.

The novel is revolutionary, not in the modern sense, but in the same way that the retreat of certain of the *solitaires* of Port Royal was revolutionary. The view of history that suggests that the ways of nations are determined by the particular passions of its rulers, in combination with an understanding of passion as a dangerous and capricious power, can only suggest that the examined life is not livable in such a society.

Clearly, there are religious overtones to the princess's actions. However, as Jean-Pierre Dens's analysis suggests,[10] piously motivated retreat should be seen as a complex process more likely to occur as motion along a continuum than a sudden and radical rupture with the world. The princess has taken steps along a road that might indeed lead to conversion in the radical rather than the Salesian sense. However, there is nothing to indicate that such a conversion has occurred within the lifetime given her in the novel. Religion is indeed present as a reference and a model in the text. In her struggle for self the princess follows patterns from it. This does not in any way obviate the fact that the primary emphasis of the text is on a struggle for self and for autonomy. Such a struggle might or might not lead to au-

---

l'image de la femme dans la littérature française du dix-septième siècle, ed. Wolfgang Leiner (Tübingen, Germany: Gunter Narr, 1984), 167–68.

10. Jean-Pierre Dens, *"Thanatos* et mondanité dans *La Princesse de Clèves," Papers on French Seventeenth-Century Literature* 15 (1988): 431–39.

thentic conversion. But what the novel foregrounds is this highly individual and lonely quest, a secular coming to *contemptus mundi*.

Nonetheless, Mme de Clèves is presented as eschewing a full break with the world. Such a gesture, like the retreat to Port Royal, brings one again under the scrutiny of society. In this sense, her muted withdrawal is more radical than a spectacular renunciation of all things worldly. The princess refuses to make that final gesture that would have allowed society to write its ending to her tale. Thus the character retains the same privilege of anonymity that DeJean has so ably discerned in the author's stance.[11] Lafayette leaves her character in the enigmatic world of the final lines.

Like so much of the language of cliché in *La Princesse de Clèves*, the princess's "exemples de vertu inimitables" (180) take on particular meaning in the context Lafayette has created for them.[12] The princess's solution, her *vertu*, is not a simple formula, but a complex whole composed of the moments of her struggle: her understanding of her passion, her complicity with it, her confession to her husband, and her final renunciation. Precisely because the novel does not deal in simplified formulae, and indeed works constantly to show the margin of uncertainty that passion introduces into the behavior of even those who most strive for coherence and virtue, at the end Mme de Clèves is not the incarnation of virtue, but one who leaves some examples of it.

Thus, if in these lines we move from the novel to the hackneyed world of the funeral oration, is it not because in this way Lafayette inscribes a meaning for which the world has no discourse? The particular concatenation of unlikely circumstances—the husband in love with his wife, the untimely death of her mother, Nemours's fortuitous presence at the confession, the partial and misleading report of M. de Clèves's spy—does indeed make the princess's story extraordinary. Nonetheless, the dilemma she faces, the extremely limited range of choices that her world offers her, all of them equally unsatisfactory, is not extraordinary at all. Mme de Clèves's retreat is a gesture that cuts

11. Joan DeJean, "Lafayette's Ellipses: The Privileges of Anonymity," chap. 2 of the present volume, 46–47, 62–67.

12. Once again, see Niderst, ed., *Romans et nouvelles*, 458n197. For a discussion of Lafayette's contextualized use of language, see my *Narrative Strategies in "La Princesse de Clèves,"* 71–116.

through the very bases on which courtly society is founded. In this sense, Mme de Clèves's examples of virtue are inimitable. But they are also inimitable because the discourse of partriarchy has no words for its own undoing. More powerful than the confession, this action is one without a maxim. It is this quality that the adjective *inimitables* inscribes. The formula of the funeral oration is subverted, as all formulaic knowledge has been subverted throughout the novel. Lafayette writes what cannot be inscribed, or represented: the story of a woman who has wrested control of her own life from the hands of patriarchy.

PART 2 Sociocritical Readings

4 Aristocratic Ethos and Ideological Codes in *La Princesse de Clèves*

RALPH ALBANESE, JR.

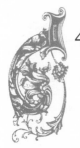

I N HER oft-quoted letter to Leschairaine in 1678, Mme de Lafayette states one of the key objectives of her historical narration: "[la] parfaite imitation du monde de la Cour et de la manière dont on y vit."[1] She fancies herself a memorialist, and she envisages the court as a model setting, underlining the mimetic value of her portrayal of the courtly nobility. The court is perceived as a fixed essence, since very little, in her view, has changed from the Valois to the Bourbon dynasty. Hers is a portrait of the ritualized existence of courtly life *sub specie aeternitatis*. History involves the recounting of an irretrievable past and, as Manfred Kusch has shown, the naming of protagonists confers a particular reality upon them: they appear as disembodied historical figures.[2] The novel's *entrée en matière* is no mere epiphenomenon, since the historical framework constantly informs the narrative structure. The eulogistic, somewhat wistful tone of the opening portraits contributes to this exemplary manifestation of the aristocratic ideal embodied in the court of Henri II. The heroic figures presented in these portraits represent the giants of the sixteenth-century French aristocracy; by their very loftiness, they personify, to varying degrees, forms of human greatness, and each portrait serves

I would like to thank Tom Carr and Jules Brody for their editorial assistance in the preparation of this manuscript.

1. Mme de Lafayette, *Correspondance*, 2 vols., ed. André Beaunier (Paris: Gallimard, 1942), 2:63.

2. Manfred Kusch, "Narrative Technique and Cognitive Modes in *La Princesse de Clèves*," *Symposium* 30 (1976): 314.

to give the measure of each character's capacity for sociability. The social qualities of the courtiers are their title, their genealogy, and their place in the hierarchy: "éclat" and "élévation" are particularly significant attributes for worldly success.

Courtly life is depicted as the epitome of taste, politeness, and wit. Magnificence permeates the series of princely diversions that constitute much of the historical décor: hunting, banquets, music, dance, theater, and, above all, the urbanity of civilized discourse. According to this idealized perspective, existence at court is designed to create a sense of wonder. Hence, the fairy-tale atmosphere enveloping the physical beauty of Nemours and Mme de Clèves at their first meeting. Inasmuch as the highest encomia are reserved for these characters—"un chef-d'oeuvre de la nature" and "une beauté parfaite, puisqu'elle donna de l'admiration dans un lieu où l'on était si accoutumé à voir de belles personnes"[3]—they incarnate the ideal couple, their very presence commanding the attention of all those around them. Magic seems to prevail in this scene, a spectacle in the highest degree, as the dancing couple stands out among the illustrious assemblage of royalty: "Quand ils commencèrent à danser, il s'éleva dans la salle un murmure de louanges" (53–54). Public acknowledgment of their perfection as a couple, the fact that they both love at first sight and remain obsessed with their love, and the princess's inaccessibility are all part and parcel of the *fabula* of the fairy tale.

As the centralized locus of sociability, the court constitutes the totality of experience: all social reality in the novel is reduced to the level of courtly existence. As a self-contained, autonomous social unit, the court represents a hermetically closed world to which only the elite have access. The ceremonial events that punctuate the narrative of *La Princesse de Clèves*—visits, balls, and marriages—underline the perfect insularity of life at court. One calls to mind, in this respect, La Bruyère's pertinent observation: "La cour ne rend pas content; elle empêche qu'on ne le soit ailleurs" ("De la cour," 8)—one is at court or one is literally nowhere; anything outside the parameters of the court is relegated to nothingness. As members of the social elite, courtiers are motivated by a profound desire for prestige; hence their attempt,

3. Mme de Lafayette, *La Princesse de Clèves*, ed. Antoine Adam (Paris: Garnier-Flammarion, 1966), 37, 41; hereafter cited parenthetically in the text.

outwardly at least, to idealize and adore themselves in the mirror of royalty. The tendency to glorify one's social existence is proportionate to one's rank; self-glorification presupposes not only the exertion of power but, more importantly, its transformation into an object of symbolic representation. For members of the court, the highest sense of distinction is not among themselves, but with social groups that do not even enjoy access to narrative representation. By categorically excluding characters from the first and third estates, Mme de Lafayette demonstrates her exclusive preoccupation with the nobility and, more specifically, the courtly nobility. It should be noted, however, that two nonaristocratic characters, the Italian jeweler and the silk dealer, do appear in the novel, but their presence is muted, since they have no right to spoken discourse. It is equally significant that in these two scenes involving, implicitly at least, a financial transaction, the merchants are engaged in the sale of luxury items. Moreover, the acquisition of external attributes of nobility, such as a luxurious home, suffices to allow the jeweler to pass for noble: "Cet homme était venu de Florence avec la reine, et s'était tellement enrichi dans son trafic que sa maison paraissait plutôt celle d'un grand seigneur que d'un marchand" (42). Just as the jeweler is referred to as "cet homme," Mme de Clèves's servants are simply called "gens": designating them as "servants" would draw attention to their immediate functional reality. The world of domesticity (servants, retainers, and so on) is thus absent from *La Princesse de Clèves,* despite the very real need of their services on the part of the upper social ranks in seventeenth-century France.

Noble status is a pure given in *La Princesse de Clèves,* and the image of a self-satisfied, self-enclosed class permitting no questioning of its values from outside its ranks is an integral part of the aristocratic ethos. This value system held that the aristocrat is, by definition, the best, that is, a member of the ethical *aristoi* whose possession and enjoyment of material goods were provided to him by the labor of the productive classes and, therefore, taken for granted. If nobles were indeed "privilégiés," it was literally because they benefited from private laws—*leges privatae*—designed to protect them. Strict avoidance of behavioral patterns characteristic of a commoner was considered a significant honorific duty based on the principle of *non-dérogeance.* Thus, for example, caste prejudice against the practice of a lucrative trade, which could entail the loss of rank, reflected the parasitic existence of the nobility. When the silk merchant says of Nemours, disguised as an artist, "il n'a guère la mine d'être réduit à gagner sa vie" (166), he implies that it is unseemly for an aristocrat to have to "earn" his livelihood, since such an obligation, presented here in pejorative terms, only befalls members of the third estate. Nothing was further from the ideal of heroic transcendence than lowly material concerns. Mme de Clèves's considerable wealth and ownership of land sheds light on the fact that her sentimental life is, in essence, a pure luxury: she is simply not obligated to work. A final example along these lines is the sumptuous feast offered by the Maréchal de Saint-André. In preparing this supper fit only for a king, the latter indulges in a "dépense éclatante qui va jusqu'à la profusion" (61), or what Jean-Marie Apostolidès has aptly called "un spectacle de l'abondance."[4] What is particularly evident in this scene is the principle of nonproductive expenditure. The phenomenon of prestige consumption is a key feature of the ideology of noblesse oblige, according to which the need to display rank takes the form of a powerful compulsion: luxury constitutes a necessity, and expenditures are dictated by rank and social obligation. Within the workings of such an economics of waste, ostentation reigns as the aesthetics of culinary preparation and display prevail over the physiology of food, whose biological function is now transcended; in short, gratuity takes precedence over utility.

Peter Brooks has identified *La Princesse de Clèves* as a novel of "worldliness" celebrating patterns of aristocratic sociability at court.[5] Although the narrator takes pains to maintain an atmosphere of magnificence at court, there is a definite movement from external harmony and brilliance to internal agitation and despair. The Pascalian dialectic of external *grandeur* and internal *misère,* expressed in terms of a contradiction between superficial éclat and moral imperfection, serves to illuminate the workings of the aristocratic ethos in the novel. From the outset, the reader develops a profound distrust of surface reality, since what is perceived is almost always subject to ambiguity: "Si vous jugez sur les apparences en ce lieu-ci, répondit Mme de

4. Jean-Marie Apostolidès, "Le Spectacle de l'abondance," *L'Esprit créateur* 21 (1981): 26–34.

5. Peter Brooks, *The Novel of Worldliness* (Princeton: Princeton University Press, 1968).

Chartres, vous serez souvent trompée: ce qui paraît n'est presque jamais la vérité" (56). By his example, the king sets the tone of moral laxity characteristic of the court, since he institutionalizes permissiveness: "Ce prince était galant, bien fait et amoureux; quoique sa passion pour Diane de Poitiers, duchesse de Valentinois, eût commencé il y avait plus de vingt ans, elle n'en était pas moins violente, et il n'en donnait pas des témoignages moins éclatants" (35). Henri II's behavior openly mocks the sanctity of marriage. It is significant, accordingly, that there are no happy couples in the novel. The king is indeed the ultimate guarantor of political order, but this order is undermined by erotic desire. Politics at court can be measured in terms of constantly shifting sexual alliances.[6]

The court is, in short, a deleterious presence, just as much a locus of vulnerability as one of sociability: its ordered or controlled agitation—"une sorte d'agitation sans désordre" (45)—encompasses the intrigues inherent in the courting ritual. Dissemblance was thus an integral part of the maintenance of appearances, since life at court entailed a constant observation of the actions of others as well as one's own. Hence, the emergence of the courtly ideal of self-observation, intimately linked to that of self-mastery, notably in the areas of body and verbal language. On several occasions, the princess's behavior fails to conform to the model proposed by La Bruyère: "Un homme qui sait la cour est maître de son geste, de ses yeux et de son visage; il est profond, impénétrable, il dissimule les mauvais offices, sourit à ses ennemis, contraint son humeur, déguise ses passions, dément son coeur, parle, agit contre ses sentiments" ("De la cour," 2). The relevancy of the queen's admonitions to the Vidame de Chartres becomes, then, immediately apparent: "On vous observe, on sait les lieux où vous voyez votre maîtresse, on a dessein de vous y surprendre" (104). The perpetual watchfulness of society assumes the dimensions of a spy system at court. Given the radical subordination of the private self to the imperatives of public scrutiny, one witnesses the systematic crushing of intimacy, the virtual impossibility of private relationships. As a result of the collective eyes and ears of the court, public

6. As Erica Harth has shown, this accounts for the "anomaly" of M. de Clèves's constancy toward his wife and the unprecedented nature of her confession to him, since it too violates the norms of plausibility; see her *Ideology and Culture in Seventeenth-Century France* (Ithaca: Cornell University Press, 1983), 217.

discourse is necessarily oblique. The highly stylized and controlled language of civility—of which Nemours is an exemplary practitioner—presupposes the suppression of individual discourse. The king, of course, serves to regulate the terms of social intercourse at court and, to this extent, it is impossible to separate the "personal" character of his actions from their "public" or political significance. His power resides in his being both an object of visual representation and an agent of vision at court; in this capacity, he excels in practicing a kind of "ocular imperialism." Thus, the profound irony of the fatal wound to his eye, a source of strength and vulnerability at the same time.

The constraining influence of the court can best be measured by the fact that all courtiers, regardless of rank, are subjects of the king. Ceremonies serve to exalt royal greatness and elaborate patterns of social ritual exert a powerful pressure on the courtier, since *bienséance* requires his presence at courtly activities at all times. M. de Clèves, for example, sees service to the king as the heart of his duties: his need to reside at court is primordial, and he follows the rule of decorum, which holds that public appearances must at all costs be maintained, contact between spouses made, and so on. This public obligation to remain on permanent display is a cornerstone of the courtier's existence. Representation of the self precludes the possibility of solitude. The courtier's highly problematic status stems from his intensive infighting with others to win royal favor: his raison d'être depends upon his ability to reside (i.e., succeed) at court. The code of *bienséance* exerts a regulatory function for such a self-conscious existence by offering the theoretical underpinnings for the politics of dissimulation: it creates a formal distance between individuals since it tends to depersonalize one's behavior; politeness serves as a buffer preventing the intrusion of the real world upon the self. Since the courtly ethic is grounded in *libido dominandi* and *libido sentiendi,* the various amatory strategies used by the characters of *La Princesse de Clèves* lead to a radical devalorization of the ideal of love. Whereas this ideal implies a true sense of commitment and a gift of self, the essence of gallantry and coquetry is a desire to remain supremely uninvolved by withholding the self.[7] If the fundamental idleness of the courtiers

7. On this point, see Robert McBride, "*La Princesse de Clèves*: A Tale of Two Ethics," *Studi francesi* 87 (1985): 470.

helps to account for the collective amorality, artificiality, and empti-
ness of individual lives, an irreducible link exists between the enslavement of courtly existence and the enslavement of passion. This
notion of undifferentiated sameness subverts an aristocratic code governed by the profound desire to be "distinguished," that is, to be
perceived as radically different from others.[8] Thus, although characters are presented as "incomparable"—the adjective used to describe
both Nemours and the Vidame de Chartres—they are, in fact, essentially interchangeable. This paradox is amply illustrated by the
confusion caused by the "lost letter," since Nemours's sexual behavior
has been strikingly similar to that of the Vidame de Chartres.

The ambiguous nature of language and human behavior, the dis-
turbing uncertainty deriving from the interchangeability of signs,
finds its ultimate expression in the characterization of the novel's titu-
lar heroine. *La Princesse de Clèves* portrays, in essence, the evolution of
an inexperienced young woman to one who has attained an exceptional
degree of self-awareness. Her entrance into courtly society can be
viewed as a virtual coming into being, a kind of birth, whereas her
departure from this society would come to signify her death. This all-
too-soon withdrawal from the world, which Jean Rousset rightly calls
the "brève histoire d'une extinction,"[9] is perfectly consistent with her
somewhat unexpected appearance at court. Presented from the outset
as an ingénue, Mlle de Chartres is guided by the principles of a rigorous moral education administered by her mother *away* from court.
Mme de Chartres teaches her daughter the value of utter self-reliance
and self-restraint. By condemning the moral bankruptcy of the court,
she initiates the discourse on values; in particular, she teaches her
daughter to guard against the vulnerability of love ("une extrême défiance de soi-même" [p. 41]). To the extent that she presents herself
as a standard-bearer of virtue, a quality conspicuously absent from
court, Mme de Chartres represents an ideological model. She exerts a
pedagogical role in relating various courtly intrigues (e.g., the rela-

8. According to Susan Tiefenbrun, Henri II's court is marked by a "paradigm of
uniqueness." . . . "[it is a] . . . world where everyone and everything is uniformly exceptional" ("The Art of Repetition in *La Princesse de Clèves,*" *Modern Language Review* 68
[1973]: 46).

9. Jean Rousset, *Forme et signification: Essais sur les structures littéraires de Corneille à
Claudel* (Paris: José Corti, 1962), 84; hereafter cited parenthetically in the text.

tionship between Diane de Poitiers and Henri II). She instills in her daughter high expectations, prompting her to aspire to physical and moral perfection. Although such a lofty ideal of self-worth is predicated upon a "mystique of uniqueness,"[10] Mme de Chartres's admonitions are part of an ideology of decorum, a concept of virtue based on social appearances that the princess will eventually transcend. In her effort to find a suitable match for her daughter, the mother is motivated, clearly, by the ideal of *gloire,* thus underlining the exclusively political nature of aristocratic marriages in sixteenth-century France. A reflection of royal marriages brokered by heads of state, the union of M. de Clèves and Mlle de Chartres represents the fruit of long negotiations between families. If the princess is heir to exceptional material and social comfort, it is because her marriage presumably involves a significant property settlement and, as a noblewoman, Mme de Chartres oversees the management of the family fortune.

Aristocratic pride is at the root of the princess's elevated idea of self, inculcating in her a provisional sense of her superiority to others ("éclat" and "élévation"); her high birth, beauty, and wealth confer upon her a status of exceptionality unknown to all other females at court. Virtue constitutes her most precious personal quality and, if exemplariness is a principal aristocratic trait, the princess is absolutely peerless in this regard. As we have noted, she arrives at court as a neophyte in matters of love and passion: gallantry is a term she only knows conceptually. The abrupt awakening of passion in her marks an evolution from the theoretical to the real, from external "peinture" to internal torment. Passion will represent for Mme de Clèves an absolute spontaneity previously unknown to her. Its effect on her will be disruptive, destructive, and permanently destabilizing, for it calls into question the calm and security of the idealized vision of the court. Love unleashes the discovery of hidden elements of her psyche: secretly fascinated by this prototype of masculine beauty and charm, she tends to idealize Nemours, projecting onto him exceptional qualities. The heroine's inability to deal with her passion in public accounts for her need for reflective solitude and her constant need to flee the court.[11]

10. This term comes from William O. Goode, "A Mother's Goals in *La Princesse de Clèves*: Worldly and Spiritual Distinction," *Neophilologus* 56 (1972): 402.

11. Jean Rousset defines Mme de Lafayette's narrative technique as the art of coun-

Nemours's public theft of her portrait distresses the princess since she now must contend with her own vulnerability. By consenting to this figural, formal appropriation of her being, she tacitly accepts a symbolic loss of self and, accordingly, must act in a manner that will contribute to her self-representation. The "lost letter" has a devastating effect on the heroine since she experiences the ravages of jealousy as a result of this episode. The force of this self-destructive passion is such that she spends a sleepless night. She ultimately realizes that total and exclusive possession of one's lover is an illusion. More importantly, perhaps, in accepting Nemours's love and concomitant feelings of jealousy, the princess would have to recognize the existence of rivals and thus be reduced to a more common level of humanity.

La Princesse de Clèves portrays the perils of a married woman at court. The four digressive episodes amply illustrate the lack of happiness among couples in the novel. Whereas other members of the court accept the principle of compromise, Mme de Clèves distinguishes herself by her essentially uncompromising posture. The heroic idealization of her character stems in large measure from the fact that she eschews the ethics of accommodation. By respecting the principle of conjugal fidelity and honoring her marital vows, she gives expression to a cult of sincerity reaching heroic proportions. She feels revulsion and a sense of moral superiority vis-à-vis Mme de Tournon and Mme de Valentinois, to say nothing of the pervasiveness of adultery at court. Her *aveu* is truly an unprecedented action forming the basis of her individual identity: it is a supreme example of behavior characteristic of those few individuals worthy of membership in an ethical elite. [12]

Thanks to Nemours's indiscretion, the princess's confession becomes a mere object of court gossip. By retelling her story, Nemours

---

terpoint, that is, a movement from society to the inner conscience, thus highlighting the fundamental contradiction between public and private selves (*Form et signification,* 21). On time and passion in the novel, see Georges Poulet, "Madame de Lafayette," in *Etudes sur le temps humain* (Paris: Plon, 1950), 122–32.

12. Such anomalous behavior defies the comprehension and logic of those around her, as well as the catalogued judgment of seventeenth-century maxims; see Gérard Genette, "Vraisemblance et motivation," in *Figures II* (Paris: Seuil, 1969), 75. By defying imitation, this extraordinary measure also violates the notion of plausibility shared by seventeenth-century readers. On this point, see Dalia Judovitz, "The Aesthetics of Implausibility in *La Princesse de Clèves,*" *Modern Language Notes* 90 (1984): 1054.

undermines its status as an exceptional, private exchange between husband and wife: his impropriety, a manifestation of male vainglory, suggests that he would be less than faithful as a husband. The princess's profound disillusionment stems from the fact that Nemours's vanity prevents her from perceiving herself as "different." Furthermore, rather than difference—"cet homme que j'ai cru si différent du reste des hommes" (138)—she discovers in his character an ultimate sameness. By not yielding to Nemours's power of seduction, she steadfastly refuses to "fall"—"tomber comme les autres femmes" (68)—an action tantamount to prostituting herself, to lowering herself to the level of a common woman.[13] Although she constantly flees the danger of his presence at court, Mme de Clèves ultimately comes to terms with the duke. During her sole interview with him, she exhibits sincerity, self-mastery, and free will in rejecting his marriage proposal. This rejection implies, first, her escape from the immutable representation of self in her portrait. Mme de Clèves discovers the fragility of passion, its essentially ephemeral nature. She also comes to realize the nefarious consequences of passion, inimical to the preservation of self; one may very well attribute the death of her husband to its fatal power. By refusing to marry Nemours, the princess rejects the inauthenticity that such a relationship would represent and, paradoxically, preserves her ideal of everlasting love. In short, she seeks permanence and order in a volatile universe. Given the ultimate sterility of the erotic impulse, she seeks, in the final analysis, the comfort and repose of *ataraxia,* a perfect serenity of mind and body.

By settling on her country estate, Mme de Clèves breaks with the traditional spatial pattern of the novel: movement to and from the court (locus of facticity and the comedy of virtue) to Coulommiers (locus of sincerity and authenticity). Her final movement is from self-effacement to self-exile. Her rejection of "tout commerce avec le monde" is a rejection of the notion of exchange, of aristocratic sociability, at least in its degraded form, at court. Her inability to internalize the social norms of the court justifies flight from her legitimate

13. Mme de Chartres's admonition ("tomber comme les autres femmes") is curiously reminiscent of the silk merchant's observation regarding the unknown "artist" ("réduit à gagner sa vie"): both expressions designate a commonness of experience, that is, a "fall" to a level of fundamental sameness, whereas the act of rising above one's peers requires truly exceptional behavior.

social group; in this respect, her virtue constitutes an eminent form
of cognitive dissonance. Whereas the heroine's experience of falling
in love is involuntary, one would be hard-pressed not to notice the
selective nature of her withdrawal from love and, by extension, from
courtly society. This heroic attempt to preserve her independence at
all costs represents the greatest assertion of her freedom and a liberation from the power of social imperatives. The end of the novel suggests that the princess transcends the limits of the material world—
"les choses de cette vie" (179)—and appears to arrive at an almost
metaphysical *prise de conscience,* at a Pascalian awareness of her own
nothingness. Her attainment of *anagnorisis* implies a progression from
passion to knowledge.[14] If *La Princesse de Clèves* highlights the narration of an aristocratic conscience—through introspection—the
novel ends, in fact, with the heroine's withdrawal from the world,
that is, from the universe of representation. Yet the significance of
this gesture should be understood as a valorization of a newfound
"ethic of self" diametrically opposed to the courtly "ethic of worldliness."[15] Such a radical affirmation of self implies a resolutely personal
sense of duty: this act of self-transcendence is also a supreme manifestation of her moral autonomy. The heroine vows to adhere to a standard of behavior that would not have warranted the disapproval of her
mother, who advised her to adopt "des partis trop rudes et trop difficiles" (68). Having provided her daughter with an example of stoic
detachment from life, Mme de Chartres continues to exert a powerful
influence on the latter's superego, serving as a perpetual *mémoire
d'outre-tombe.* Like her confession, Mme de Clèves's withdrawal from
society is a profoundly extramimetic gesture by which she rejects established modes of representation and strives to obtain autonomous,
self-motivated representation. Whereas Nemours's passion fades away
in time, she places herself on a spatiotemporal plane beyond the continuum of History. Her philanthropic commitment to the "occupations saintes" of the convent is a sign of aristocratic *largesse* and a
worthy substitute for the gallant preoccupations of the court.[16] To the

14. Jules Brody envisages Mme de Clèves as a tragic heroine: "her conduct . . . describes a triumphant inner journey from illusion to illumination" ("*La Princesse de Clèves*
and the Myth of Courtly Love," *University of Toronto Quarterly* 38 [1969]: 133).

15. On this point, see Peter Brooks, *The Novel of Worldliness,* passim.

16. As the ultimate manifestation of her inner worthiness and exemplary rank, the

extent that the eventuality of dishonor is, for the heroine, a source of motivation, *La Princesse de Clèves* would appear, then, to exalt the triumph of private selfhood among the courtly nobility.

The self-reflexive dimension of the novel, illustrated primarily by the heroine's retrospective mode of self-analysis, allows us to grasp the workings of an aristocratic conscience. By way of conclusion, I will now examine some of the sociocultural and historical implications inherent in the life-style of the courtly elite and its underlying ethos. First of all, as an heroic novel, *La Princesse de Clèves* offers the dominant class a format in which to highlight its value system, an aesthetic sublimation designed to embellish members of the elite, perceived to incarnate all manner of perfections. It depicts the Valois court of Renaissance France, the last flowering of aristocratic narcissism, the final moment of tranquillity before the Wars of Religion. The novel offers seventeenth-century readers a feeling of solidarity with the great ancestry of the nobility. According to the heroic conception, the aristocratic self bases its identity on a highly idealized vision of reality, on an enduring sense of magnanimity, and on an ethics and aesthetics of formal perfection. The valorization of self-mastery as a means of mastering others and the exaltation of sincerity and honor also contribute to the superhuman dimension of the privileged few, giving *La Princesse de Clèves* an unmistakable sense of grandeur. This portrait of the nobility at the height of its power and glory is made, however, through the retrospective view of an aristocratic conscience: "historical distance" is nothing more than a nostalgic projection into Renaissance France, when the nobility was more secure in its position. Given the decline of the socioeconomic status of the French nobility from the middle of the sixteenth century on, leading to the concomitant erosion of its values, the novel represents, as we shall see, an oblique commentary on the political disenfranchisement of this class.

---

heroine's final *refus* illustrates the validity of Kristen Neushel's analysis of the nobiliary ethos in sixteenth-century France. According to this historical perspective, the representation of the nobleman's self in society was designed to elicit support for his behavior, to have his deeds perceived as honorable; the principal objective in the "exchange of honor" characteristic of relationships among nobles is the creation and strengthening of one's personal identity: "The center of any nobleman's world had to be himself, and all of his relationships functioned to sustain and to nurture his identity" (*Word of Honor: Interpreting Noble Culture in Sixteenth-Century France* [Ithaca: Cornell University Press, 1989], 97).

According to Davis Bitton, the French nobility underwent a protracted "crisis of identity or adjustment" from 1560 to 1640.[17] Its social preeminence in decline, it needed to present a convincing justification for its privileges and reformulate a coherent self-image. In fact, the public perception was that the nobility was becoming more and more dysfunctional and even obsolescent.[18] Nostalgia for a "golden age" of nobility in early Renaissance France became a topos of sixteenth and early seventeenth-century juridical writing on this class. Idealized as a paragon of the highest virtues, that is, devotion to king and country, the nobleman was portrayed as a public servant par excellence. Guillaume d'Oncieu classifies the primacy of public interest over private interest as "the first law of nobility."[19]

The transformation of a warrior nobility into a courtly aristocracy, that is, from an independent to a relatively subdued class, constitutes a fundamental sociopolitical reality of seventeenth-century France, indeed one of the principal consequences of the consolidation of the state. There occurred a transfer in the roles of military leadership from nobles to nonnobles (i.e., royal bureaucrats or *intendants*), and criteria for advancement were no longer based on the military prowess of a nobleman. The economic dependency of the nobility on the king accounted for its subservience to courtly rituals. The fact that Louis XIV routinely absorbed the debts of his courtiers is an indication of how courtly society helped preserve the nobility and at the same time control it. "Civilizing" the courtly nobility was also a means of policing, domesticating, and disarming an otherwise turbulent class, and the obligatory nature of the nobleman's presence at court assured the king of his loyalty. Norbert Elias's study of the sociogenesis of the European courtly system—"[la] dernière grande formation non bourgeoise de

17. Davis Bitton, *The French Nobility in Crisis, 1560–1640* (Stanford: Stanford University Press, 1969), vii.

18. On the basis of his analysis of a considerable body of judicial treatises and pamphlets from this period addressing the subject, with many of them defending the noble life-style, Bitton has identified the emergence of a need to redefine rigorous distinctions between noble and nonnoble and thus avoid the problematic issue of "status confusion"; hence, the elaboration of numerous prohibitions against *dérogeance* (*French Nobility in Crisis*, 65, 69, 93–94).

19. Guillaume d'Oncieu, *La Précédence de la noblesse sus un différent en cas de précédence* (Lyon, France: J. B. Buisson, 1593), 43–46, cited by Bitton, *French Nobility in Crisis*, 73.

l'Occident"[20]—sheds light on this fundamental type of social formation in early modern France: the court formulated models that contributed to the molding of social conduct, to the civilizing of behavior.
To express rank, for example, was an absolute necessity. Thus—and
this is clearly the case in the fictive universe of *La Princesse de Clèves*—
nobles needed to display the trappings of wealth; their obligation to
lead a public life, within "le monde," was unquestioned and constituted for them a cornerstone of their social identity. According to Max
Weber, luxury represented, for the courtly nobility, an essential mode
of self-assertion, an integral part of the strategy of "conspicuous consumption." At a time when aristocratic values were increasingly subverted by bourgeois materialism, the courtly nobility—"cette élite
monopoliste pré-industrielle" (Elias, 307)—devoted itself to the cultivation of leisure. Leisure was indeed the hallmark of the privileged
class, an unquestionable sign of social superiority. Libertinage, or the
constant pursuit of pleasure, was a principal outlet for a courtly nobility operating within an ethics of leisure and luxury. Gallantry had
a particularly alienating effect on this class, heightening its domes-
tication and forever estranging it from its military function. Passion
entailed, as we have seen, the disruption of aristocratic harmony, a
"fall from grace" of the exalted figures at court. Jean Rousset has
argued convincingly that love was an agent causing one to lose one's
"substance," one's identity (24); as an expression of the anarchic self,
love wreaked havoc on the aristocratic conscience.

The fundamental model derived from courtly society was the perfect aristocrat. In *La Princesse de Clèves,* almost all of the characters
are "well born" and beautiful. In this respect, Max Weber's notion
of "charismatic" rule can be applied to the fascination exerted by certain aristocrats; hence, their "specifically extraordinary character."[21]
The novel portrays the relationship between a ruler and an elite central
group: the notion of *gloire* constitutes a prestige fetish allowing the
king to justify his existence, and Mme de Clèves and Nemours are
clearly bearers of charisma; the latter serves as a primus inter pares at
court, a perfect embodiment of courtly values and a powerful model

20. Norbert Elias, *La Société de cour* (Paris: Calmann-Lévy, 1969), 15; hereafter cited
parenthetically in the text.

21. Max Weber, *Economie et société* (Paris: Plon, 1971), 253.

for other courtiers, who become, more or less, "des Nemours ratés."
The king, however, represents the only figure of immutability at
court, and this is due to the institutional permanence of kingship,
depicted in the transfer of power from Henri II to François II: "Le roi
est mort, vive le roi!" The nobility, on the other hand, is vulnerable
to the essential mutability of passion; its precarious position is a result
not only of its utter dependence on royal favor but also of the extreme
uncertainty of its affairs of the heart: given the various degradations
and sense of decline wrought by the latter, love can indeed function
as a metaphor for History in *La Princesse de Clèves*. Thus, the courtly
nobility is reduced to an entirely decorative, ceremonial function:
spectacular display serves as a compensation for an inner void. Jean
Rousset postulates the triumph of the imaginary world, contending
that History is, in this novel, nothing more than a fallacious décor
(21). The mythorepresentative value of Mme de Lafayette's narrative
resides in her projection into an irretrievably heroic past; paintings
such as the *Siège de Metz* constitute iconic representations of a bygone
era. History inevitably destroys past perfections and contributes to
the creation of a wistful longing for an inaccessible ideal. In offering
unapologetic nostalgia for aristocratic splendor, Mme de Lafayette
sounds the death knell of the nobility. For French aristocrats of 1678,
her novel signals the degradation of noble values or, more precisely,
the radical "difficulty of being" an aristocrat. The internal contradictions experienced by a would-be heroic aristocracy are portrayed in the
character of the protagonist, whose flight from reality mirrors the
status of her class: aristocratic *gloire* gives way to a silent renunciation
of the world. Her withdrawal from society represents a negative and
implicitly subversive value;[22] her quest for an unadulterated form of
love is an unmistakable sign of her marginality. The powerlessness of
the court to assimilate her into its value system underlines her non-
conformist, atypical behavior, her adherence to anachronistic values.

22. Mme de Clèves's introspective, solipsistic character betrays the problematic status
of the aristocratic persona, reduced to self-contemplation, a prisoner of its own image,
experiencing "le constat de ruine de la personnalité humaine réduite à elle-même" (Claude
Vigée, *"La Princesse de Clèves* et la tradition du refus," *Critique* 159–60 [1960]: 725).
The cultivation of emotional privacy also calls into question the heroine's political loyalty,
and her final departure from society implies latent political opposition to the monarchical
order.

The princess's deviancy from normal patterns of behavior offers, in fact, a striking illustration of anomie theory:[23] she personifies the extreme "individuation" of those types who have difficulty adapting to the imperatives of courtly society; her case suggests a breakdown in the socialization process, and the issue of her residence at court is, as we have noted, an existential one. She is in direct violation of the code of *honnêteté,* which facilitated the integration of the nobility at court in the 1660s by valorizing its group identity; the code thus sought to restrain individuals from developing too strong a sense of self by preventing them from adopting forms of behavior that were aesthetically incorrect. Mme de Clèves's moral intransigence is, in 1678, part of an outmoded heroic ideal, and her final withdrawal from court foreshadows the progressive disenchantment of certain nobles at Louis XIV's court (e.g., Fénelon, Saint-Simon).

In the final analysis, by her *retraite* and the ontological status of her death, the heroine typifies the future extinction of her class; she offers, in the process, a muted protest against its historical degradation. Her action also contributes to the preservation of the dignity of her class, since it implies a paradoxical escape from History. At the end of the novel, the princess's existential choice is made not against love but rather against the radical impossibility of leading a life in harmony with the traditional aristocratic ethos (virtue, honor, exemplarity, *maîtrise de soi,* and so on). She comes to represent, quite simply, a profound inability to be. Nourished by an impending sense of decline, her world-view presupposes an awareness of the irremediable loss of a prestigious past, and latent feelings of betrayal and remorse that were those of an aristocratic conscience previously galvanized by heroic action. She incarnates, in an imaginary mode, the destruction of the feudal aristocracy after the Fronde, now obliged to take refuge in a mythic representation of self. Marie-Odile Sweetser is justified in denouncing the historical contradiction inherent in the critique of the princess's character, that is, her refusal to assume the role of the ro-

---

23. See my article, "Théâtre et anomie: Le Cas du *Misanthrope,*" *Cahiers internationaux de sociologie* 64 (1978): 113–26. Although Alceste's marginality vis-à-vis the values of courtly society is expressed in a comic mode, it nonetheless sheds light on the sociological notions of anomie and deviancy, and on the dysfunctioning of norms and regulatory mechanisms.

mantic heroine.[24] Instead of a feminist declaration of independence, it is more to the point to view in her refusal a profoundly class-oriented decision; she seeks to preserve intact a traditional class identity; she steadfastly refuses to betray the ancestral ideals by which the aristocracy defined itself. She is, ultimately, beyond mimesis, a living and dying model of "vertu inimitable."

24. Marie-Odile Sweetser, *"La Princesse de Clèves* et son unité," *PMLA* 87 (1972): 489.

5 The Economy of Love in *La Princesse de Clèves*

PHILIPPE DESAN

ESPITE appearances, Mme de Lafayette wrote a social novel. I do not intend to determine whether this was indeed her intention or to demonstrate that she was conscious of the ideological tensions present during the latter half of the seventeenth century; rather, setting issues of authorial intention and circumstantial determinism aside, I will explore the ways in which *La Princesse de Clèves* provides us with an opportunity to examine the economy of human relations in the seventeenth century. Numerous passages in the novel refer directly to human relations as a commercial activity, and I will argue that within its scope women represent a veritable *commerce*. Indeed, this economic aspect of love appears essential to any interpretation of the novel. Its theories are developed largely in the first part of the work, where the reader encounters a complex network of sentimental and political exchanges occurring in the *marketplace* represented by the court of Henri II, a site where sentiments and politics inevitably commingle.

The purpose of such marketplace exchange is to place a value upon individuals who themselves are transformed into objects within an economy of human relations. John Lyons has argued that what is traded in this novel are "marks" of passions, or, as he puts it, "it is the mark which constitutes the mediation between the public and the private, the object of gaze and the money of exchange. All the characters, including the heroine, find themselves confronted with the dilemma of all economic systems: if one gives too many marks of passion these marks lose value, but if one does not give any mark they do not circulate and therefore have no value."[1] The idea of the circulation of passions will help us interpret this novel and analyze the exchange process as it is determined by the forces of the market itself.

Critics customarily ignore the first part of the novel, claiming that the description of Henri II's court contributes nothing to the movement of the plot and even detracts from the psychological development one expects from a "modern" novel. For when we read *La Princesse de Clèves* today, we usually consider it the first modern novel. Having grown so accustomed to psychological drama, our reading of this text has become somewhat restricted. I would like to show that *La Princesse de Clèves* is also a social novel, a novel that narrates the confrontation of two conflicting ideologies. When we read the novel this way the description of the court is essential to the novel's representation of the normative limits placed on human behavior. In other words, the court is both social setting and ideological setting.

The seventeenth century is profoundly marked by a contradiction between two moral systems, that of the nobility, which remains in existence only as an idealization, and a more pragmatic moral system, an emanation of the rising bourgeoisie also prevalent at the court. As Laurence Gregorio has noted, "It is an era in which society finds itself grappling with the growing influence of the bourgeoisie, and with corruption and political disunity within the nobility."[2] Mme de Clèves's problematic situation in the novel results from the irresolvable ideological contradiction between these two systems.

Instead of discussing these competing ideologies in depth, I will merely outline their general contours. The declining ideology of the nobility still defends the purity of emotions, espouses courtly love and moral honesty, and seeks to perpetuate virtuous relations; but these nobiliary values are being degraded or transformed into a new ideology, one that functions on the basis of profit, utility, and necessity. The court serves as a privileged site for the meeting of these incompatible ideologies. Within this rigid economic framework, in which feelings and power freely circulate, the woman serves as a form of currency. She is a medium of exchange that allows men to accrue value

1. John D. Lyons, "L'Économie des marques dans *La Princesse de Clèves*," *Neuphilologische Mitteilungen* 81 (1980): 326.

2. Laurence A. Gregorio, *Order in the Court: History and Society in "La Princesse de Clèves"* (Saratoga, Calif.: Anma Libri, 1986), 29.

by participating in economic transactions. As the novel's protagonists come to discover, however, in keeping with the workings of a bourgeois economy founded on principles of exchange and the marketplace, it is the exchange itself (the means) rather than the use to which it is put (the ends) that confers value on the desired object. Precisely because she is caught between these two ideologies—the one that she ideally claims as her own, the other to which she must submit—the Princesse de Clèves experiences an inner crisis. This crisis, rendered visible to the reader by way of the passions, is in fact ideological. Mme de Clèves seems to be the only character fully conscious of the double system of values paradoxically surrounding her.

The balls and the court festivals function as markets where individuals gain and lose value. Courtiers agree to participate in these gatherings in hopes of deriving a profit. During the course of these assemblies, the woman facilitates circulation; it is she who will ultimately determine the value of the "objects" placed on the market, "objects" understood here as reputation, value, friendship, passion, and so forth. It is the woman's function to determine the rising value or the bankruptcy of each of these objects, all merchandise at hand having to undergo her inspection. However, the woman's position is problematic because she, too, is an object bearing a particular value, and as such she must expose herself to the covetous glances of others. In the bourgeois economy of love, the marketplace plays an essential role for it is the only place where exchange values are determined. Human emotions lose their use value and constantly need to be *shown* in order for them to acquire meaning. What good is it to be loved if that love is not openly declared? This is perhaps the most crucial issue raised in *La Princesse de Clèves*.

Since the woman's value is determined by the practices of the bourgeois marketplace, she cannot avoid the court. Unless she places herself on the market, she will have no exchange value. But when she does place herself on the market, she necessarily throws herself into an ideological battle of feelings, a battle of perception and representation. Whereas in a courtly economy the *value* of love lies in the well-kept secret, in a bourgeois economy it is the potential for amorous exchange (and the avowal of this potential) that determines its price. For an exchange to occur, however, it is equally necessary that there be competition, thus requiring that one display one's wares publicly in the marketplace. Sentimental value is calculated in the bargaining process. Love in *La Princesse de Clèves* must always be exhibited; it must be *spoken* to a third party. Placing love on the market propels the narrative forward—the letter, M. de Nemours's avowal to the vidame, and so on—the required avowal transgresses the sacred code of courtly passion, thus precipitating the heroine into a modern economy of the passions. Jean-Marie Delacomptée notes that "undeclared love joins lovers together into an ideal couple that declared love draws apart; the avowal renders love impossible. Such is courtly passion."[3]

The ball is the perfect place for the display of one's goods, since all those who will contribute to the valuation of the desired object will gather there; the ball becomes a site of political intrigue and carnal schemes. Attending a ball, like all public assemblies, involves certain risks, for one must engage oneself with all of the paradoxes of the market. M. de Nemours, for example, has a perfect grasp of the laws regulating value in the marketplace, yet he discovers the problematic nature of the coveted object once the exchange is taking place. In the case of the ball offered by the Maréchal de Saint-André, we are informed through the Prince de Condé of the many contradictions inherent in the marketing of the object that one hopes to carry away from the marketplace: "Je crois qu'il [M. de Nemours] a quelque maîtresse qui lui donne de l'inquiétude quand elle est au bal, tant il trouve que c'est chose fâcheuse, pour un amant, que d'y voir la personne qu'il aime" (62).[4] The lover's contradictory position is explained by two possible attitudes later described to us.

Mme la Dauphine is astounded by the fact that a lover would not wish to see his mistress at the ball. While easily imagining that a husband might feel this way, she cannot imagine that a lover would. And yet the feelings expressed by M. de Nemours possess their own bourgeois logic: "lorsqu'elles sont au bal, elles veulent plaire à tous ceux qui les regardent; . . . quand elles sont contentes de leur beauté, elles en ont une joie dont leur amant ne fait pas la plus grande partie" (62). Indeed, value is determined only in relation to a series of offers based upon a quantitative principle of emotions: if only one person

3. Jean-Michel Delacomptée, *"La Princesse de Clèves": La Mère et le courtisan* (Paris: Presses Universitaires de France, 1990), 6.

4. All quotations from *La Princesse de Clèves* are taken from the text edited by Antoine Adam (Paris: Garnier-Flammarion, 1966); hereafter cited parenthetically in the text.

demonstrates interest in a given object, the price of that object will never increase; it is competition (the laws of supply and demand) that determines the object's value.

In the market economy of sentiment played at the court, an object's use is determined only after its confrontation with other objects having the same potential use. The intrinsic superiority of one object over another can be ascertained only in accordance with its continued demand. Thus, the Princesse de Clèves's value is not determined by any personal quality (her beauty, for example), but rather by the number of prospective buyers (M. de Clèves, M. de Nemours, the Chevalier de Guise) vying for the object she has become. Value here is purely quantitative, necessitating that the lover places his coveted object on the market, despite his consciousness of the dangers inherent in the process. In order for his object to acquire an increased exchange value, he must subject himself to the risk of losing the desired object. The risk involved is an integral component in the economy of bourgeois emotions. M. de Nemours's inner contradiction, while distressing to him, is nonetheless essential to the optimal functioning of market processes: it exemplifies the contradiction inherent in the law of supply and demand. The terms of exchange fluctuate continually and are fixed only by means of the bargaining process; they are no longer solely dependent on the feelings one individual experiences toward another.

Whereas within a nobiliary mentality feelings are judged in terms of their use value, with no concern for the market, the mercantilist mentality, increasingly gaining the upper hand even among the court, no longer considers the use value of the desired object a reliable indicator of its worth. This is true because the protagonists no longer view the use to which feelings are put as ends in themselves. Like any other object, love must submit to market forces in order to be assigned a value. It is precisely this play of market forces that enables man to draw pleasure once the value of the object that he desires to possess is determined. Morality too varies in accordance with repeated exchanges, and has lost its status as the referential axiom that once served to organize human behavior. An extensive network of interdependencies now regulates the economy of the passions. For this reason, M. de Nemours's attraction for the Princesse de Clèves is more than a personal idiosyncrasy; it reveals the normative behavior of a subject held captive by the bourgeois notion of love.

M. de Nemours's fear in approaching this interaction is in fact two-fold, for there is a second conceivable attitude vis-à-vis the public display (the ball) of the desired object: "quand on n'est point aimé, on souffre encore davantage de voir sa maîtresse dans une assemblée; . . . plus elle est admirée du public, plus on se trouve malheureux de n'en être point aimé; . . . l'on craint toujours que sa beauté ne fasse naître quelque amour plus heureux que le sien" (62). Although hard to accept, this state of mind is, once again, inevitable. This latter possibility provides yet another occasion for the "trader" to gain acceptance, for making him accept the idea of the ball as a marketplace perpetuates the "exchangeable" quality of Mme de Clèves. Although perhaps not yet loved, M. de Nemours nevertheless still has every chance of acquiring the love that he is "working" on. What he is capable of giving for the object is judged insufficient at this point, but it is merely a question of time and strategy—of his negotiations, one might say—for him to achieve his goal. The ball provides a momentary opportunity for carrying out a new transaction; it facilitates the exchange.

As we know, Mme de Clèves decides not to go to the ball offered by Saint-André: "il fallait donc qu'elle fît la malade pour avoir un prétexte de n'y pas aller" (63). By doing this, she hopes to spare M. de Nemours the sufferings I have just discussed. But she is mistaken in thinking she is sparing him, for she does not understand the rules of the marketplace and the commerce of women that prevails at the court. When she refuses to display herself on the market, declines to appear at Saint-André's ball, she denies herself all possibility of being valued as an object for others. As a result, her use value alone comes under consideration. But what good is use value when the entire economy of human relations is founded on the complex nature of the exchange and the value that derives from it? Mme de Clèves is naïve to the extent that she does not recognize that she alone thinks this way with regard to the market. Even her own mother "combattit quelque temps l'opinion de sa fille" (63) in an attempt to convince her to attend the ball. To keep oneself off the market is to earmark oneself for a single buyer, but it is also to devalue one's "merchandise" and therefore displease whoever hopes to acquire this particular article. In a bourgeois society, use itself is dependent on exchange: one can always create a use for what appears to be useless—collections are a pertinent example—but an object that possesses only functionality and is never introduced to the market becomes worthless in society's view.

M. de Nemours maneuvers within an economy whose rules he unconsciously accepts. Mme de Chartres is not mistaken when she sees in M. de Nemours a man who "deals" in women: "Elle se mit un jour à parler de lui; elle lui dit du bien et y mêla beaucoup de louanges empoisonnées sur la sagesse qu'il avait d'être incapable de devenir amoureux et sur ce qu'il ne se faisait qu'un plaisir et non pas un attachement sérieux du commerce des femmes" (65). The "pleasure of commerce" is quickly transformed into an end in itself: pleasure resides in the exchange (the process of conquest) rather than in the enjoyment (possession) of the object that one seeks to possess. The "serious attachment" Mme de Chartres speaks of refers directly to an economy whose goal is the acquisition of "needs" based on their use value. But this era is long gone. It is clear to her that the market transactions occurring at the court have become ends in themselves for M. de Nemours. Mme de Chartres's words leave an indelible mark on the Princesse de Clèves, for at the end of the novel she will pronounce the same words to M. de Nemours, seeming at last to comprehend the rules of the market economy: love (value) resides in the quest for the desired object and not in the object itself.

While one derives pleasure from the exchange process itself, one may also destructively desire to possess the object fully, even for an instant. Thus, M. de Nemours's conscious goal is to possess Mme de Clèves, but he is blind to the bourgeois and reifying nature of his desire. The fulfilled desire for complete possession transforms the mistress into a wife, consequently destroying the value she has accrued in the conquest. The possession and enjoyment of the object inevitably entail the object's degradation, resulting in its progressive depreciation in value in the opinion of the other "merchants." In order for an object to have value, it must circulate *freely* on the market; at the very least the others involved in potential transactions must *perceive* the object as being free. The free circulation of objects and bodies is an implicit requirement in the development of a bourgeois economy of the passions. Mme de Clèves's only hope for preserving her love intact is to withdraw the desired object—herself—from the market and keep it out of reach of male commercial transactions. Such a situation is at once impossible and suicidal, yet it is completely consistent with a nobiliary logic in which the qualitative reigns. This nobiliary logic resolutely opposes the quantitative bourgeois economy of the passions. Once Mme de Clèves discovers the famous "reason of the passions" so central to this novel, she finds herself confronted with an unresolvable problem.

The reader becomes aware on several occasions that Mme de Chartres recognizes at once the danger present at court, and the futility of trying to escape. The Princesse de Clèves's entire value resides in the desire she provokes in others during the course of her encounters on this complex market where bodies and feelings are exchanged. Her withdrawal from the court remains a ready solution, but such an action would imply the simultaneous acceptance of her existence as one man's use value. This, as we shall see, places her in a precarious position, because that one man may lose interest in her. Although she tears him apart with jealousy, she continues to reassure him regarding his own sentimental commerces. In order to justify her actions, Mme de Clèves would need to find within the court an *Identical Other,* a male who adheres to the same moral code she does. Such a quest remains an ideal that the practice of everyday reality gradually tarnishes. Yet, she remains "pure" of bourgeois ideology, even refusing to belong to her husband. Her love is inaccessible, for it occupies a position outside of the market and all exchange. Even in her marriage to M. de Clèves, the princess never succumbed to an economy of love that positions conjugal love as a solution to the perpetual circulation of bodies. Let us keep in mind that for her husband she continues to be a desirable object that he insistently seeks to return to the market in order to win all over again. Thus, with each of her withdrawals from the court, M. de Clèves asks that she return. The husband's contradictory behavior—according to all logic, he should want to withhold his possession, putting an end to others' covetousness—can be explained by an unconscious slippage between two value systems: the affirmation of use value inherent in marriage and the desire to play the lover's role of competing against other potential lovers/buyers in the marketplace symbolized by the court.

M. de Clèves quickly comes to overestimate his wife, precisely because she withholds from him the type of love that only a mistress is capable of giving. But by persisting in being a *potential* mistress for her husband, Mme de Clèves is able to preserve the entire value attributed to her prior to her marriage: she never allowed herself to become use value because her body was never objectified in marriage. M. de Clèves continues to hope for the love that only mistresses—those women constantly on the market—know how to give: "Vous m'estimez plus que je ne vaux" (69), Mme de Clèves exclaims, objecting to her husband. While she is conscious of the high price placed on her by her husband, the Chevalier de Guise, and M. de Nemours, the Princesse de Clèves does not control this value; it lies beyond her influence. She has become an object whose value fluctuates in accordance with its process of exchange. Like a pawn thrown into the market, her feelings no longer belong entirely to her; they always fall under the sway of the *price* placed upon her by those who traffic in passions at the court.

The portrait incident reveals another characteristic of the economy of love in *La Princesse de Clèves*. When individuals themselves become unobtainable, one may acquire a substitute object that allows one to feel a similar sense of possession. The portrait becomes such a substitute for M. de Nemours: Mme de Clèves's portrait replaces Mme de Clèves herself. This is why M. de Nemours considers the theft of the portrait his first victory; it allows him to anticipate materially his ultimate goal. Thus we learn that "Il y avait longtemps que M. de Nemours souhaitait d'avoir le portrait de Mme de Clèves. Lorsqu'il vit celui qui était à M. de Clèves, il ne put résister à l'envie de le dérober à un mari qu'il croyait tendrement aimé" (92).

The theft of the locket becomes significant only if it implies a diversion of the object of desire away from the husband. Let us look for a moment at the implications of this theft. The locket is a reified representation of M. de Nemours's love for the Princesse de Clèves, symbolizing his desire to take *immediate* possession of the highly coveted object—outside the normal channels of exchange where he has not yet met with success. But the theft likewise becomes significant only if it is discovered by Mme de Clèves who, by her silence (and whatever reason put forward by the narrator), is thus willing to see her husband dispossessed of her. Let us bear in mind that the portrait has exactly the same value for the two male protagonists, for M. de Clèves is still trying to win his wife's affection. The "battle" of the portrait makes reference to a *political economy* of love.

The discovery of the theft will serve to unveil M. de Nemours's true desires and, as a result, will reinforce Mme de Clèves's dependency on a market beyond her control. Once she recognizes the principle that governs the exchange, she must also place her feelings toward M. de Nemours inside this system. This is what she would like to avoid at all costs: "La raison voulait qu'elle demandât son portrait; mais, en le demandant publiquement, c'était apprendre à tout le monde les sentiments que ce prince avait pour elle, et, en lui demandant en particulier, c'était quasi l'engager à lui parler de sa passion" (92). But there is no way out of such a situation: exposing M. de Nemours is an acknowledgment that she exists as an object of desire for another (and therefore for *all* others); disclosing her passion is tantamount to defining herself as an integral component in the market of love, an object capable of being possessed. Either admission would erase her carefully maintained difference from other women, other circulating objects in the court's economy of love.

It is with this sudden *prise de conscience* that the Princesse de Clèves recognizes and feels her alienation. She henceforth perceives that her sense of herself and the objectified view that the novel's other protagonists have of her are quite different. Her love, in this case, would be no more than the reflection of others' love, as it would be perceived simply as a response to a market operation—an investment of passion on the part of her suitors. It is impossible for her to accept the conditions of the exchange and others' vested interest in her if she hopes to preserve the quality and future (although never realizable) use of her own passion. Within the primitive and symbolic economy of love in which she functions, her love is a *gift* that lies outside the market's system of exchange. But the gift of passion, in an era when intrigue, conspiracy, and machination predominate, is already anachronistic, as the reader can tell from the description of the daily life of the court of Henri II in the first part of the novel.

Critics concur that the incident of the letter represents a decisive turning point in the psychological evolution of the Princesse de Clèves. Reading the letter confirms her suspicions, at least those that her mother had imparted to her: "Combien se repentit-elle de ne s'être pas opiniâtrée à se séparer du commerce du monde" (100). Separation from the world remains one viable solution; the reader senses its approach and, as we know, it will close the novel. However, Mme de Clèves at first withholds this solution and resists abandoning the court. Instead, she attempts to impose her own values on the court, to redefine the rules of exchange according to her own criteria. Her effort notwithstanding, such an attempt can only fail. She has established a dialogue of the deaf between herself and the other protagonists in which words are spoken but nothing can be heard.

Mme de Clèves is not like other women and she knows it; but her self-awareness does not suffice. She must also communicate this message to others. In doing so, she derails all the regulative mechanisms of the court's system of exchange of the passions. Mme la Dauphine clearly perceives this "destructive" aspect of the Princesse de Clèves: "il n'y a que vous de femme au monde qui fasse confidence à son mari de toutes les choses qu'elle sait" (116). For speech no longer necessarily has to accompany an act; a new era in human relations is becoming visible on the social and political horizon. One no longer asks an individual to explain his or her actions, or at least some actions possess their own logic and elude traditional morals. On several occasions Mme de Clèves experiences the need to divulge her feelings while knowing fully that such an avowal can only evoke *reactions* from the other protagonists. For the other characters in the novel, the avowal is not an end in itself, but rather the motive for actions that must inevitably follow such a declaration; for Mme de Clèves, the avowal itself represents the means of reestablishing a moral balance. It is for this reason that her avowal is unique and qualitative; no action, no exchange, could alter its value.

If the avowal scene is problematic, it is because the avowal is in fact only half an avowal. Above all, it is not of the kind one would make to one's husband: "je vais vous faire un aveu que l'on n'a jamais fait à son mari" (122), Mme de Clèves confides. But herein lies a system of morals at work on two irreconcilable levels: the level of conscience and the level of actions. Feelings are never dependent upon the reactions they produce, and vice versa: "si j'ai des sentiments qui vous déplaisent, du moins je ne vous déplairai jamais par mes actions" (122), admits Mme de Clèves. But it is also with this mistaken conception of idealized love that the Princesse de Clèves exposes her difference from the society in which she moves. Everyone else believes that thought can have no bearing or produce an outcome if it is not followed by action; this is precisely the lesson we learned from Corneille's tragedies. The Machiavellian ethic in which a man is judged by his actions has replaced a Ciceronian (perhaps Jansenist) ethic in which the origin of deviant and therefore detestable behavior can be recognized in thought. According to this outmoded ethic, the princess has sinned, for she is indeed guilty of her thoughts. Yet the Princesse de Clèves cannot fathom that this sin, this moral offense, is irrelevant for the novel's other characters, who judge everything on the basis of actions alone. Freedom of conscience does not come into play in an economy where exchange is the only thing that matters. Desiring exchange will not guarantee the success of the transaction; therefore, desire in itself has no value. It, like matters of conscience, occupies a position outside the modern economy.

Jealousy too becomes problematic only if it is *verifiable* in actions. M. de Clèves therefore must verify his wife's actions incessantly. Similarly, from the moment he knows that the Princesse de Clèves loves him, M. de Nemours anticipates the moment when her love will be concretized by an action. Jealousy is merely a sign of potential action, a feeling concealed beneath its imminent translation into practice. Since love becomes visible only when the lovers are present, the proximity of bodies rather than the proximity of souls favors the unveiling of the passions. And yet M. de Nemours's repeated attempts to approach Mme de Clèves physically get him nowhere. He makes no tangible progress toward love, since the object he seeks cannot be grasped. Mme de Clèves *is* on the market, but she refuses every offer, a response incomprehensible to the other protagonists. After all, what kind of individual accepts the market's existence but refuses to trade in it? Mme de Clèves's total withdrawal from the commerce of the court would be more understandable to her way of thinking, but since she agrees to take part in this commerce, men also expect her to accept its rules, signing herself over to the buyer who gives the greatest proof of his love and in this way pays a fair price for her passion.

To become jealous is to fall back temporarily into the lover's role. M. de Clèves's declaration is symptomatic in this regard: "Je m'étais consolé en quelque sorte de ne l'avoir pas touché par la pensée qu'il était incapable de l'être. Cependant un autre fait ce que je n'ai pu faire. J'ai tout ensemble la jalousie d'un mari et celle d'un amant; mais il est impossible d'avoir celle d'un mari après un procédé comme le vôtre" (123). The avowal that Mme de Clèves makes to her husband transforms him into a lover, for, owing to her declaration, the princess rediscovers a love that she never let go of and that, finally, never severed its ties with the market. Her husband understands that he no longer has even the advantage of marriage, namely the spouse's silence. Mme de Clèves's manner of dealing with the situation goes against society's rules to the extent that she declares that she is desired by someone who already possesses her, thereby effacing her husband by placing him on the same level as any other lover. An avowal of this sort can only provoke M. de Clèves's despair: "Vous me rendez malheureux par la plus grande marque de fidélité que jamais une femme ait donnée à son mari" (123). Such moral devotion has no value for M. de Clèves, for he cannot imagine the relation between his wife's words and her future actions. Mme de Clèves offers him a last chance to believe in the perfect harmony existing between her speech and her actions, trying to find in what she already has this Identical Other who would agree to participate in an economy of the gift rather than in a market economy: "Fiez-vous à mes paroles; c'est par un assez grand prix que j'achète la confiance que je vous demande" (124). Even if as a husband M. de Clèves were to accept and respect his wife's word and avowal, as a lover his jealousy is redoubled. The avowal will have served no purpose, and as the narrator tells us, "la singularité d'un pareil aveu, dont elle ne trouvait point d'exemple, lui en faisait voir tout le péril" (125).

Since truth is considered no more than the reflection of possible actions, not divulging the name of the man one loves will be taken as proof of a reprehensible action. When all is said and done, it is the half or incomplete avowal that leads to the death of M. de Clèves. The latter could have endured his wife's silent unfaithfulness, but for her to speak without taking action is incomprehensible to him. Mme de Clèves could have become another's mistress, but she still would have remained his spouse. Each object bears two values: a use value found in marriage and an exchange value accrued at the court, outside of marriage. However, the exchange value always destroys (or determines) the use value. For M. de Clèves, the rules of marriage—not declaring one's love for another as long as no action has unbound one's marital ties—disappear before the avowal of one's passions. Mme de Clèves's virtue is destructive because it represents an incomprehensible exception to the rules: "Pourquoi m'éclairer sur la passion que vous aviez pour M. de Nemours, si votre vertu n'avait pas plus d'étendue pour y résister? Je vous aimais jusqu'à être bien aise d'être trompé, je l'avoue à ma honte; j'ai regretté ce faux repos dont vous m'avez tiré. Que ne me laissiez-vous dans cet aveuglement tranquille dont jouissent tant de maris? J'eusse, peut-être, ignoré toute ma vie que vous aimiez M. de Nemours" (162).

Mme de Clèves's avowal also poses a problem for M. de Nemours. What baffles him is that action will not follow this avowal; he cannot see the avowal as an end in itself. In Mme de Clèves's mind the avowal truly is such an end, although she knows that others expect some action to follow this type of declaration. Because of this expectation, M. de Clèves does not fall sick after her avowal, but only after he has sent a spy to see if her avowal has been transformed into an act. For all but Mme de Clèves, any declaration of love has two distinguishable moments: speech and action. However, this artificial distance between the avowal and the act is untenable in the nobiliary mentality within which Mme de Clèves wishes to conduct herself. For her, the avowal *is* an act: speech alone suffices to show one's passion. M. de Nemours cannot imagine the concealment of love except as a temporary measure, never as a finality. He poses the problem in the following fashion: "Si je n'étais point aimé, je songerais à plaire; mais je plais, on m'aime, et on me le cache" (157). This analysis symbolizes the great dissimilarity in logic between these two different forms of behavior, which rely on two opposing ideologies. Nemours believes that when the mind turns toward the object it desires, it decides then and there to acquire it; the avowal is therefore necessary at that moment as the object calls for a contract, a fixed price required for the exchange to take place. But the contract is merely a preliminary sign of a real operation concretized in the performance of an act. In his confused state, Nemours no longer knows how to act. Since he knows that he pleases Mme de Clèves, he cannot imagine what is preventing her from taking action. His confusion is expressed clearly when he says, "Je sais mon bonheur; laissez-m'en jouir" (157). M. de Nemours finds himself locked into a situation that he considers absurd.

The Princesse de Clèves knows that she holds singular views: "il n'y a pas dans le monde une autre aventure pareille à la mienne; il n'y a point une autre femme capable de la même chose" (136). Her recognition of her own singularity gives rise to the feeling of having been abandoned by her counterparts. She begins to feel alienated when she realizes that the moral code preventing her from acting goes against the current of the moral code that will henceforth prevail. Her alienation and resultant isolation, however, only serve to reinforce her value in the eyes of society: now it is because of her difference or rarity that she becomes a coveted object. For rarity produces value within the bourgeois economy. Having discovered this, use becomes entirely devoid of significance; it is purely the difficulty of procuring the desired object that counts from this point on. Mme de Clèves's detachment and inner retreat do not affect the objective value that she represents for others: "Quelque triste que fût Mme de Clèves, elle ne laissa pas de paraître aux yeux de tout le monde, et surtout aux yeux de M. de Nemours, d'une beauté incomparable" (141). The protagonists would be more than happy to abandon all of the prerogatives that by right belong to the husband were it possible, if only for a moment, to play the lover's role. For M. de Nemours, the avowal of Mme de Clèves's passion grows to the point of obsession, as it announces an action to come and indicates a first step toward a practice of love.

M. de Clèves finally comes to the realization that he must distance his wife from the commerce of the court. Her half-avowal literally changed him, and he henceforth doubts his wife's word: "quelque bonne opinion qu'il eût de la vertu de sa femme, il voyait bien que la prudence ne voulait pas qu'il l'exposât plus longtemps à la vue d'un homme qu'elle aimait" (148). Experience prevails against opinion and M. de Clèves is incapable of conceiving his wife's situation. For him, action is all, and truth can be determined only in relation to one's physical behavior. This is why the reproach made by M. de Clèves to his wife turns on the notion of a full avowal: "vous n'avez pu me dire la vérité tout entière, vous m'en avez caché la plus grande partie; vous vous êtes repentie même du peu que vous m'avez avoué et vous n'avez pas eu la force de continuer" (151). Love and passion must be reduced to a name; love absolutely must be objectified.

M. de Clèves cannot imagine why his wife does not take action once she has made her avowal. Since he cannot comprehend the meaning of her declaration, he feels inferior when faced with his wife's unshaken moral ideals: "Je ne me trouve plus digne de vous; vous ne me paraissez plus digne de moi, je vous adore, je vous hais, je vous offense, je vous demande pardon; je vous admire, j'ai honte de vous admirer. Enfin il n'y a plus en moi ni calme, ni raison" (151). Mme de Clèves rises up against the reason of the passions, thereby questioning modern society's moral order.[5] She appeals to a different logic, not dependent on cause-and-effect reasoning. For her, immobility becomes a way of life that runs counter to the court's intrigues, the perfect answer to the perpetual movement created by the circulation of feelings on the market of the court.

What purpose does a passion serve if it cannot be put into practice? What reason is there for a love that will produce no outcome? A vaguely decipherable Cartesian architecture lies just beneath the surface of the text, depriving Mme de Clèves of all chances of playing any role whatsoever in this society founded upon individualism and the accomplishment of one's foreseen goals. The Princesse de Clèves has become imprisoned in the world of means; it is a world that can formulate moral norms only on the basis of political and commercial practices. Conventional morality is transmitted through politics and subject to an economic logic oriented toward exchange with an ever-present profit motive. Of what use is a market if not for facilitating the exchange of objects? When the court no longer houses a set of higher moral values but replicates the commercial operations of the public square, the nobility falls subject to a bourgeois handling of its passions and of love in particular.

What purpose would the court serve if all persons put themselves on display—as if placed on display in a merchant's shop window—without allowing for the possibility of an exchange, a conquest? A world where one returns home with the same feelings one brought to the market would be absurd—it would be the world of the courtly novel. Exchange in *La Princesse de Clèves* is not symbolic: it is very real. Mme de Clèves is the last remaining believer in the possibility of symbolic exchange rooted in silence and inward withdrawal. Her idealized concept of exchange is founded on the quality of the moment of human interaction rather than on the quantitative valuation of the object placed on the market. For her the moment of human interaction promises nothing, no long-term development. Because she realizes that her concept of exchange is incomprehensible to others, she rec-

5. According to Serge Doubrovsky, Madame de Lafayette supposedly thus indirectly repudiated any inheritance from Cartesianism by means of the Princesse de Clèves ("*La Princesse de Clèves*: Une Interprétation existentielle," *La Table ronde* 138 [1959]: 39–51).

ognizes the impossibility of bringing such an exchange into action and can only withdraw from the world.

The reader anticipates the princess's inevitable *withdrawal of her body*. In the end, she acknowledges that her mother had been speaking the truth: any attempt to reconcile these two opposing modes of social and economic organization is doomed to failure. Mme de Clèves would have preferred to ignore the world's overly concrete reality; but once she understands that she is alone in believing in the viability of symbolic interactions, no other choice remains for her but to withdraw her body from the commerce of men. She decides to isolate herself and therefore never "live" the love she had idealized.

The Princesse de Clèves thus decides to replace the man she loves with various substitutes: a portrait of M. de Nemours at the siege of Metz and a cane from India that formerly belonged to him. She replicates M. de Nemours's practice of object substitution, but this time the substitute objects are not intended to be temporary replacements: they *are* desire and are enough to satisfy her passion. Love has become religion, with the icons cherished just as dearly as the man they are meant to represent. These substitute objects allow Mme de Clèves to envision a form of exchange that ultimately leads nowhere: "elle s'assit et se mit à regarder ce portrait avec une attention et une rêverie que la passion seule peut donner" (155). From this point on, passion is inseparable from introspection; it is an inner, almost religious experience culminating in a perfect communion of souls. Mme de Clèves no longer makes avowals; she withdraws into silence and immobility, for she realizes that her desire to speak about her love was a mistake.

When M. de Nemours observes Mme de Clèves in the silence and immobility that her retreat to Coulommiers came to symbolize, he reflects upon the events that led him there: "Il se mit à repasser toutes les actions de Mme de Clèves depuis qu'il en était amoureux; quelle rigueur honnête et modeste elle avait toujours eue pour lui, quoiqu'elle l'aimât" (157). Honesty has become an obsolete notion, replaced within bourgeois ideology by the notion of utility. To be considered reasonable, each act must now possess some sort of utility. The type of thought deemed honest takes pleasure in the meanders of virtue and of the isolated subject rather than useful and goal-oriented commerce with the world. The reader no longer sees any workable solution to the reconciliation of these two worlds, which the novel now represents as geographically distant. Mme de Clèves's retreat necessarily presages the end of the novel: the positions are externally fixed; there is no longer a solution that can move the plot forward.

Before dying, M. de Clèves pronounces these last words that retrospectively constitute a premonition: "vous connaîtrez la différence d'être aimée, comme je vous aimais, à l'être par des gens qui, en vous témoignant de l'amour, ne cherchent que l'honneur de vous séduire" (162). This analysis, however, without being wrong, applies equally to M. de Clèves. By admitting this economic reality, he evicts his wife from the market and gives her little choice but to withdraw: no one else shall have what he himself was unable to acquire. Henceforth Mme de Clèves suffers from a certain sense of guilt: "Elle repassait incessamment tout ce qu'elle lui devait, et elle se faisait un crime de n'avoir pas eu de la passion pour lui, comme si c'eût été chose qui eût été en son pouvoir" (165). She perhaps understands that by attempting to make her husband accept her moral code, she precipitated his death. Let us remember that it was precisely the "absurdity" of the avowal scene that sparked a veritable outcry on the part of critics when *La Princesse de Clèves* first appeared. One must admit that this avowal is indeed absurd in a bourgeois economy of the passions.

The final avowal Mme de Clèves makes to M. de Nemours comes too late, but for the first time it allows her to act: her sole action is her withdrawal. If the half-avowal made to her husband kept her on the market, the full avowal made to M. de Nemours is social suicide, precipitating Mme de Clèves outside the commerce of men. M. de Nemours does not recognize the full import of this declaration of the passions. He rejoices before this avowal and throws himself at the princess's feet. He does not realize that what he has just gained by her speech will be forever lost to him by its realization, that is, no action will ever follow from the avowal, since the avowal is already her ultimate action. Silence alone offers the theoretical possibility of a passage between speech and action. By avowing her passion and thereby taking the first step in the direction of a bourgeois morality, Mme de Clèves also eliminates all possibility of actually living her passion. She alone grasps the illusory nature of her avowal: "Je ne vous apprends, lui répondit-elle en souriant, que ce que vous ne saviez déjà que trop" (171). M. de Nemours's reply attests to the new mercantilist mentality reigning at the court: "Ah! madame, répliqua-t-il, quelle différence de le savoir par un effet du hasard ou de l'apprendre par vous-même, et de voir que vous voulez bien que je le sache!" (171). That sentimental display has become more important than the feelings themselves reassures M. de Nemours of his chances of obtaining the object he has long desired, because he believes that with this avowal the bargaining process has been initiated.

M. de Nemours deludes himself by thinking that the obstacles Mme de Clèves's raises do not truly exist, nor the rules of decorum to which she makes reference: "Il n'y a point d'obstacle, madame, reprit M. de Nemours. Vous seule vous opposez à mon bonheur; vous seule vous imposez une loi que la vertu et la raison ne vous sauraient imposer" (175). Once again he is correct within the logic of his contemporary world, but Mme de Clèves does not share this world; her rules belong to another era. Her dilemma is pitiful but not truly tragic, as the tragic is usually defined, because it is engendered solely by the prejudices dating from another era that she has preserved within her. By refusing to accept the new social rules, Mme de Clèves thus attempts to safeguard the waning ideology of a thoroughly outmoded moral code. M. de Nemours is so deeply persuaded that such an attitude is ultimately untenable and must be the temporary effect of despair caused by a sense of guilt that he cannot imagine her maintaining this attitude for very long: "il demeura d'accord avec M. le vidame qu'il était impossible que Mme de Clèves demeurât dans les résolutions où elle était" (176).

The novel's central crisis stems, perhaps, from its attempt to propose a modern definition of all types of human associations, marriage in particular. Modern man—this eternal trader who cannot rest—once he has acquired possession of love, immediately places this object back on the market in order to launch himself into the search for a new conquest. He defines his being in relation to this endless activity. In a certain manner, marriage proscribes the free circulation of goods. Mme de Clèves fully perceives the finality of all commercial exchanges: "Je sais que vous êtes libre, que je le suis, et que les choses sont d'une sorte que le public n'aurait peut-être pas sujet de vous blâmer, ni moi non plus, quand nous nous engagerions ensemble pour jamais. Mais les hommes conservent-ils de la passion dans ces engagements éternels?" (173). Indeed, passion is merely a feeling that is born and matures through a series of transactions and exchanges.

Were M. de Clèves the only man alive to preserve love through marriage, as Mme de Clèves believes, the endurance of his passion could be attributed only to her willingness to remain for him a future mistress.

This moment of consciousness brings the novel to an end as the heroine comes to realize that love dwells in those obstacles that separate speech and action: "je crois même que les obstacles ont fait votre constance" (173), she declares to M. de Nemours before she leaves him for the last time. Modern man is quite responsive to a logic of repetition and quantity: "Vous avez déjà eu plusieurs passions, vous en auriez encore; je ne ferais plus votre bonheur: je vous verrais pour une autre comme vous auriez été pour moi. J'en aurais une douleur mortelle et je ne serais pas même assurée de n'avoir point le malheur de la jalousie" (174). If Mme de Clèves abandons all hope of marrying M. de Nemours, it is to a certain extent so that she may save her own life and all that life represents—the last bastion of a courtly and nobiliary ideal rapidly dissolving into the everyday fabric of a bourgeois conception of feelings and passions.

The novel reveals a paradox in the bourgeois mode of thinking: when love functions according to an economic logic that requires individuals to compete in the marketplace, the objects they desire will be found valuable only if they are coveted by others. Marriage strips the object of its essential function, which is to circulate, and thereby simultaneously strips it of its true value, its exchange value. Marriage thus sets off a depreciation of the passions, passions that will only regain their "true" value through the parallel relationship of mistress and lover. In order to recover his essence, which is based on his ability to excel at commercial conquest, man must continually return to the market, where there are always new objects to be discovered, always new sources of temptation. The Princesse de Clèves is aware that this economic ordering of the world is linked to a concept of modernity. Her conscious decision to withdraw from this world provides the last historic example of a nobiliary morality founded upon the eternally kept promise and the silence of the passions.

The Princesse de Clèves's unrealizable dream is to live with her feelings and to preserve them intact. Her renunciation of the world allows her to reinforce her own moral values and to claim them as her destiny. Because her strict adherence to this moral code aims to leave behind "des exemples de vertu inimitables" (180), the novel can be considered a success. The last words of the novel bear a fateful resonance, for the withdrawal of the Princesse de Clèves exemplifies the waning of passion and morality from a bygone epoch, one that appeared to contemporary critics as a highly unlikely variant in a new society seeking to draw itself closer to a more pragmatic, earthbound reality.

PART 3 Ethical and
Religious Readings

6 Trapped between Romance and Novel

A Defense of the Princesse de Clèves

STEVEN RENDALL

A DEFENSE of the Princesse de Clèves implies that she has committed some offense. I propose to bypass the various complaints registered by readers over the past three hundred years in order to focus attention on the principal indictment formulated in the novel itself—and on the heroine's response to it.

In his final conversation with the princess,[1] the Prince de Clèves charges her with two related offenses: adultery and causing his death. She denies the first allegation, but makes no immediate response to the second. The reader knows, of course, that although the princess may harbor adulterous desires, she has not committed adultery. The justice of the prince's second accusation is more difficult to determine. The narrator, while not explicitly endorsing the prince's allegation, offers no alternative explanation for his death. Indeed, everything in the text suggests that he does in fact die as a result of his belief that his wife has committed adultery. The question posed by the novel is whether, or to what extent, we can be held morally responsible for the consequences of other people's *perceptions* of our behavior.

The novel does not answer this question. Instead, as Helen Kaps has pointed out, it maintains a delicate balance between the indul-

1. Mme de Lafayette, *La Princesse de Clèves,* ed. Antoine Adam (Paris: Garnier-Flammarion, 1966), 135–38; henceforth cited parenthetically in the text.

gent, courtly moral perspective of the narrator (seconded by characters like the dauphine, the vidame, and Nemours) and the heroine's more severe, uncompromising view.[2] The princess clearly regards herself as morally responsible for her husband's death. The narrator tells us that when she began to reflect on her bereavement,

> et qu'elle vit quel mari elle avait perdu, qu'elle considéra qu'elle était la cause de sa mort, et que c'était par la passion qu'elle avoit pour un autre qu'elle en était la cause, l'horreur qu'elle eut pour elle-même et pour M. de Nemours ne se peut représenter. . . . La douleur de cette princesse passait les bornes de la raison. Ce mari mourant, et mourant à cause d'elle, ne lui sortait point de l'esprit. Elle repassait incessamment tout ce qu'elle lui devait, et elle se faisait un crime de n'avoir pas eu de la passion pour lui, comme si c'eût été une chose qui eût été en son pouvoir. (164–65)

We should notice here how the narrator implicitly endorses the princess's conviction that she is the cause of her husband's death (the verb "considéra" presupposes the truth of the propositions it introduces) but undercuts her view of its moral significance by describing her scruples as excessive ("la douleur de cette princesse passait les bornes de la raison"). The narrator tends to regard the mutual attraction that draws the princess and Nemours together as both natural and inevitable and, in the concluding sentence of the passage just quoted, uses the imperfect subjunctive to suggest that the princess is wrong to blame herself for not reciprocating the prince's passion. The implication is that one is not accountable for what one cannot control— but, as we shall see, this is an implication that the princess does not accept.

This same passage might also be taken to indicate that in the princess's opinion, it was the fact that she loved Nemours, and did not love her husband, that led to the latter's demise. The narrator tells us, however, that the prince's fatal illness does not start when his wife reveals to him, in the famous "confession scene" (122–23), that she is in love with another man, but instead begins when he receives a report that seems to indicate that she has committed adultery (160). I believe it would be a mistake to see this as evidence for the view

---

2. Helen Karen Kaps, *Moral Perspective in "La Princesse de Clèves"* (Eugene: University of Oregon Press, 1968), 52; henceforth cited parenthetically in the text.

that the heroine has a masochistic inclination to blame herself for everything.

The complexity—and the rigor—of her analysis can best be seen in her final conversation with Nemours, where she accuses *him* of being the cause of her husband's death:

> Il n'est que trop véritable que vous êtes cause de la mort de M. de Clèves; les soupçons que lui a donnés votre conduite inconsidérée lui ont coûté la vie, comme si vous la lui aviez ôtée de vos propres mains. Voyez ce que je devrais faire, si vous en étiez venus ensemble à ces extrémités, et que le même malheur en fût arrivé. Je sais bien que ce n'est pas la même chose à l'égard du monde; mais au mien il n'y a aucune différence, puisque je sais que c'est par vous qu'il est mort et que c'est à cause de moi. (172)

The princess's concluding words are an assertion that both she and Nemours are guilty, but in different ways. As the context shows, the princess is claiming that Nemours's behavior was the *cause* of the prince's death—though both he and the prince acted as they did *because* of their love for her. That is the point of her discreet allusion to a hypothetical duel between the prince and Nemours: had they fought over her, and had her husband been killed, her moral duty would prevent her from marrying the victor. She recognizes that while courtly society would not regard the two situations as analogous, she herself does, because she knows that her husband's death resulted from his belief that he had lost his battle with Nemours.

Thus in the princess's view, her "inclination" for Nemours caused him to act as he did, and this in turn caused the prince's death. I want to make three observations concerning the princess's argument: (1) It presupposes that one is morally responsible for acts that others perform on one's account. (2) In drawing an analogy between her situation and that of a woman whose husband and lover engage in a fatal duel over her, she ignores what others might regard as a significant difference—namely, that there is no reason to believe that Nemours deliberately provoked the prince or sought to kill him. (3) The causal chain connecting the princess with her husband's death depends upon its intermediate link, the inference that the prince draws from Nemours's conduct. Each of these points is crucial to an understanding and assessment of the princess's view.

The first two points both suggest that moral responsibility does not necessarily depend upon intention. While it is clear enough that the princess is not wholly displeased by Nemours's attentions to her, and that Nemours welcomes the opportunity offered him by the prince's demise, the text provides no grounds for concluding that the princess intentionally leads Nemours on, or that he intends to cause her husband's death. The third point mentioned above raises another and even more interesting issue, one I want to explore in some detail. The text makes it clear that the chain of responsibility linking the princess with her husband's death is anchored in his *perception* of what she has done. As we shall see, his interpretation of the evidence is based on the category of plausibility or *vraisemblance,* and it is the very implausibility of the truth that frustrates the princess's efforts to persuade him that she has not committed adultery.

Seventeenth-century debate about the novel's verisimilitude focused on the famous scene in which the princess confesses to her husband that she loves another man. Is it plausible that such a wife would make such a confession? Is it wise or right for her to do so? What is often not noticed is that the princess herself asks these same questions. When she tells her husband, "je vais vous faire un aveu que l'on n'a jamais fait à son mari" (122), she recognizes that what she is doing is not "normal," and suggests that it is even unprecedented. Valincour and others maintained that this latter claim is false because Mme de Villedieu had described a similar confession in her novel *Les Désordres de l'amour,* which had been published a few years before Lafayette's book. This criticism not only curiously conflates fiction and reality, but fails to recognize how the princess's remark functions within the fiction. What is unique is, by definition, *invraisemblable,*[3] and in saying that her confession is unprecedented, she marks it as the first in a series of implausible occurrences that powerfully determine the subsequent development of the action, and, ultimately, her own fate.

The *invraisemblance* of the confession is repeatedly stressed in the

---

3. As several scholars have shown, in seventeenth-century French reflections on literature an event or situation is considered *vraisemblable* to the extent that it can be regarded as an example of a general rule. See Gérard Genette, *Figures II* (Paris: Seuil, 1969), 71–79; and John Lyons, *Exemplum: The Rhetoric of Example in Early Modern France and Italy* (Princeton: Princeton University Press, 1989); Lyons will hereafter be cited parenthetically in the text.

following pages. Reflecting on her act, the princess "en fut si épou-
vantée qu'à peine put-elle s'imaginer que ce fut une vérité. . . . La
singularité d'un pareil aveu, dont elle ne trouvait point d'exemple, lui
en faisait voir tout le péril" (125). On finding the princess so cool to
him, Nemours also doubts the confession's reality: "Il ne savait quasi
si ce qu'il avait entendu n'était point un songe, tant il y trouvait peu
de vraisemblance" (128). And when the dauphine later tells the princess a story about a wife who confesses to her husband that she loves
another, the princess replies, "Cette histoire ne me paraît guère vraisemblable, Madame" (132). After listening to Nemours, the dauphine
herself says she is nearly convinced the princess is right in saying that
"cette aventure ne peut être véritable" (134).

The princess's reply continues to address the issue of *vraisemblance*,
but shifts its focus from the ontological question—did it happen?—
to an epistemological one—how can it be known? The story can
hardly be true, she says, for if it were, how could it have been revealed?
"Il n'y a pas d'apparence [i.e., it is *invraisemblable*] qu'une femme,
capable d'une chose si extraordinaire, eût la faiblesse de la raconter;
apparemment son mari ne l'aurait pas racontée non plus, ou ce serait
un mari bien indigne du procédé que l'on aurait eu avec lui" (134).
Nemours immediately seizes the opportunity to reinforce the princess's suspicion by suggesting an explanation: the husband might have
told someone else in an ignoble attempt to satisfy the desire to discover
his rival's identity. In this way Nemours confirms the binary logic
implicit in the princess's question: the only *plausible* explanation is
that either the husband or the wife told a third party what occurred.

This logic dominates the ensuing discussion between the princess
and her husband. When the prince denies her accusation that his jealous curiosity has led him to betray their secret, the princess responds:
"il n'y a pas dans le monde une autre aventure pareille à la mienne;
il n'y a point une autre femme capable de la même chose. Le hasard
ne peut l'avoir fait inventer; on ne l'a jamais imaginée et cette pensée
n'est jamais tombée dans un autre esprit que le mien" (136). She
argues that precisely *because* her confession is unique and unprecedented, the story cannot plausibly be about another couple—or even
a fiction coincidentally invented by someone else. Therefore, since she
assumes that only she and the prince could know what happened in

the garden at Coulommiers, it must necessarily follow that he confided in a friend, who in turn told Nemours, who told the vidame, who told the dauphine.

The prince accepts the premise that only the two of them could know, and argues on the same ground of plausibility that "Il est plus vraisemblable que ce soit par vous que par moi que ce secret soit échappé. Vous n'avez pu soutenir toute seule l'embarras où vous vous êtes trouvée et vous avez cherché le soulagement de vous plaindre avec quelque confidente qui vous a trahie" (136). The princess's judgment is based on the maxim suggested to her by Nemours ("la jalousie . . . et la curiosité d'en savoir peut-être davantage que l'on ne lui en a dit, peuvent faire bien des imprudences à un mari," [p. 135]); the prince's is implicitly based on another generalization about human conduct, which might be formulated as "women are unable to bear misfortune silently."

The prince's analysis of the situation is logically symmetrical with his wife's, and equally rigorous: "il était assuré de n'avoir rien redit; c'était une chose sue; ainsi il fallait que ce fût par l'un des deux . . ." (137). The princess, we are told, "pensait à peu près les mêmes choses, elle trouvait également impossible que son mari eût parlé et qu'il n'eût pas parlé." But Nemours's comment seems to apply so well to her husband's case that "elle ne pouvait croire que ce fût une chose que le hasard eût fait dire; et cette vraisemblance la déterminait à croire que M. de Clèves avait abusé de la confiance qu'elle avait en lui" (137).

As these passages make clear, the category of the plausible or *vraisemblable* plays a central role in the prince's and the princess's attempts to explain what has happened. In order to grasp the key to the enigma they would have to consider the possibility they repeatedly reject— that is, the possibility that against all likelihood, someone else has overheard their conversation. The prince and the princess are trying to tell a story governed by the norms of *vraisemblance,* but the material with which they have to deal more properly belongs to the genre of romance, in which the action frequently turns on arbitrary coincidences, and improbable events occur without any explanation other than sheer chance.

The text does not attempt to motivate Nemours's witnessing of the confession; on the contrary, it suggests that his presence is almost wholly aleatory. While hunting near his sister's estate, he gets lost in the forest. On inquiring as to his whereabouts, he learns that he is near Coulommiers; then, "sans faire aucune réflexion et sans savoir quel était son dessein, il alla à toute bride du côté qu'on le lui montrait" (120). When he arrives at the prince's property, "il se laissa conduire au hasard par des routes faites avec soin, qu'il jugea bien qui conduisaient vers le château" (120). Instead of leading him to the castle, the paths lead him—by chance—to the *pavillon* on the castle's grounds at the exact moment when the prince and princess get there. Nothing in this account diminishes the implausibility of Nemours's overhearing the confession, and that is the point. It is precisely because it is implausible that neither the prince nor the princess can conceive of it as a solution to their dilemma or incorporate it into the explanatory narrative they are struggling to construct.

While the princess's confession is a great blow to the prince, he can still interpret it as an index of her sincerity and fidelity. But their inability to arrive at a plausible explanation of the enigma that does not imply that one of them has betrayed their secret arouses a new sense of mistrust between them, and constitutes a serious aggravation of their malaise. Moreover, it leads the prince to seek to resolve his doubts by employing a man to spy on Nemours, and this action in turn results in still another crucial misperception of events interpreted in accord with notions of *vraisemblance.*

When the spy makes his report, he cautions against drawing hasty conclusions: "Je n'ai rien à vous apprendre," he tells the prince, "sur quoi on puisse faire de jugement assuré. Il est vrai que M. de Nemours a entré deux nuits de suite dans le jardin de la forêt, et qu'il a été le jour d'après à Coulommiers avec Mme de Mercoeur" (160). But the prince ignores the spy's implicit distinction between observed facts (*le vrai*) and what can plausibly but not certainly be inferred from them. He moves directly to the only conclusion he regards as *vraisemblable,* that the princess has been unfaithful to him, and sends the spy away without asking for further clarification.

The prince is so shaken by what he takes to be clear proof of his wife's infidelity that he falls ill with the fever that eventually kills him. The text suggests that the proximate cause of his death is his perception, based on a plausible but false extrapolation from the available evidence, that the princess has betrayed him. In his final conversation with her, he accuses her of making a hypocritical show of grief: "Vous versez bien des pleurs, madame, lui dit-il, pour une mort que vous causez . . . je meurs du cruel déplaisir que vous m'avez donné" (161). He goes on to say, with considerable bitterness, that once he is dead, she will be at liberty to "rendre M. de Nemours heureux, sans qu'il vous en coûte des crimes" (162)—that is, she will no longer have to commit the crime of adultery. He suggests that her infidelity has made a mockery of her confession: "Fallait-il qu'une action aussi extraordinaire que celle que vous aviez faite de me parler à Coulommiers eût si peu de suite?" (161–62). When she proclaims her innocence, saying "je n'ai jamais fait d'action dont je n'eusse souhaité que vous eussiez été le témoin," he replies scornfully, "Eussiez-vous souhaité . . . que je l'eusse été des nuits que vous avez passées avec M. de Nemours?" (162–63).

Finding the circumstantial evidence strongly against her, the princess cries, "Ecoutez-moi, pour l'amour de vous-même: il est impossible qu'avec tant de vérité, je ne vous persuade de mon innocence" (163). She gives her version of what happened in the garden, and urges the prince to ask her servants if he wants to confirm her story. But although the narrator assures us that "la vérité se persuade si aisément lors même qu'elle n'est pas vraisemblable," the princess succeeds only in *almost* convincing her husband that she has not been unfaithful to him. "Je ne sais, lui dit-il, si je me dois laisser [aller] à vous croire" (163). In any event, her explanation comes too late, for the prince dies a few days later.[4] It is not his wife's confession that she loves another man that has broken his spirit, but rather the "discovery" that she has not kept her promise of fidelity. Unlike the stereotypical jealous

4. The comments on these scenes by Lafayette's contemporary Valincour show how the notion of *vraisemblance* can be used to conceal its own functioning. He finds it *invraisemblable* that the prince is so easily convinced of his wife's infidelity: "Sur la seule mine de son Gentilhomme, il croit sa femme coupable, il se condamne à mourir"—a formulation that obscures the extent to which the prince's inference is itself based on *vraisemblance*. And, according to Valincour, the prince is immediately convinced of his wife's innocence when she defends herself ("dès que sa femme ouvre la bouche pour luy dire qu'elle n'a rien fait contre son devoir, il condamne ses premiers sentiments, et se repent de l'avoir accusée"), a shift he finds implausible ("c'est changer trop légèrement sur une matière si importante"). Valincour's reading of this scene seems clearly to underestimate the resistance offered by the *vraisemblable* to the establishment of the truth. See the excerpts from Valincour's book quoted in Emile Magne's edition of *La Princesse de Clèves* (Geneva: Droz, 1950), 229.

husband of novella and comedy, whose moral flaw seals his fate, the prince is the victim of an epistemological error.

The text implies, then, that the princess can correctly accuse Nemours of causing her husband's death, even if he has not done so intentionally but only by acting in such a way as to provide apparent grounds for the prince's belief that she has been unfaithful. But whereas the narrator regards all this as insufficient grounds for holding her morally responsible for his death, the princess does not. In her eyes, to accept Nemours's proposal would be to compound her own guilt by marrying the man who caused her husband's death.

Helen Kaps suggests that the princess's view is in accord with Catholic church law, which specifically forbad a woman to marry her husband's assassin. In a treatise on "les empeschemens du mariage," Lafayette's contemporary Jean Gerbais explains that when "un Epoux, par exemple, conspire à la mort de son Epouse, de concert avec une autre créature afin de pouvoir l'épouser; si cet Epoux et cette créature exécutent leur pernicieux projet, ils ne peuvent plus déslors se marier ensemble; et s'ils se marient, leur Mariage est nul" (Kaps, 21, note 5). But the princess's judgment of her own case goes considerably beyond the circumstances envisaged in this example, since no one plots the prince's death—though Nemours certainly welcomes it. The princess eschews the excuses offered by the notion of "intention," and according to the distinction between "fact" and "interpretation"— that is, the key concepts of classical and modern casuistry—her analysis of her ethical situation is both lucid and coherent. Her acceptance of the prince's judgment that she has caused his death, and her consequent refusal to marry Nemours, are not based on mere masochism or blind obedience to socially imposed norms. Rather, they are based, at least in her own eyes, on the conviction that she is morally responsible for acts performed on her account, and also, in the absence of a transcendental viewpoint—that of an omniscient God, for instance— that would make it possible to sort out the *vrai* from the *vraisemblable,* for what she is perceived to do as well as for what she "actually" does.

Acknowledging that the prince had reason to believe that she had betrayed him, that her alleged infidelity was *vraisemblable* though not *vrai,* the princess insists on taking responsibility for the consequences of her husband's *interpretation* of her conduct—even if it is a *mis*interpretation. Moreover, she is consistent in holding Nemours to the same standard, insofar as she regards him as morally responsible for her husband's death, even though she has no reason to believe that he acted with malicious intent, and knows that the inference the prince drew from his behavior was false.

However, the princess offers *two* kinds of reasons for her refusal to marry Nemours after her husband's death: her moral duty and her peace of mind (*le devoir* and *le repos* [pp. 174, 175, 177, 178, etc.]). In her interview with Nemours, she explains at length why, even though in the eyes of society there is no remaining obstacle to their marriage, it would bring her nothing but unhappiness. Nemours would inevitably fall in love with someone else, she says, and she would find herself in the position of her late husband—hopelessly in love with someone who did not love her.[5]

In arriving at this judgment, the princess relies, like her husband, on the category of *vraisemblance*. When her jealousy is aroused by her mistaken belief that Mme de Thémines's letter is addressed to Nemours, she recognizes for the first time "combien il était peu vraisemblable qu'un homme comme M. de Nemours, qui avait toujours fait paraître tant de légèreté parmi les femmes, fût capable d'un attachement sincère et durable" (119). That is, she considers Nemours as an example of a class of men of a certain type, and assumes that such men generally act in the same way—just as her husband assumes that a man like Nemours does not spend two nights alone with a beautiful woman without making love to her. In the same way, when Nemours proposes marriage, the princess asks, "Mais les hommes conservent-ils de la passion dans ces engagements éternels?" (173). The implicit answer to this rhetorical question is clearly "No, generally they do not."[6] She suggests that her husband may have been the only ex-

5. Serge Doubrovsky, "*La Princesse de Clèves:* Une Interprétation existentielle," *La Table ronde* 138 (1959): 36–51. But in recognizing the importance of the princess's concern for her "repos," we should not ignore the text's insistence that "devoir" is an equally significant factor in her decision. "Ce que je crois devoir à la mémoire de M. de Clèves serait faible s'il n'était soutenu par l'intérêt de mon repos," the princess says, "et les raisons de mon repos ont besoin d'être soutenues par celles de mon devoir" (175).

6. Lyons points out that the case of Henri II's passion for Diane de Poitiers, evoked in the novel's opening paragraph, suggests the possibility that "a man can have a lasting passion" (227). But it is not clear that this case is relevant to the princess's question, since she is talking about *marriage,* and suggests that even her husband's enduring love might have flagged if she had returned it.

ception to this rule, and to think Nemours might be another is tantamount to hoping for a personal miracle: "Dois-je espérer un miracle en ma faveur . . . ? (173).

A miracle—that is, an extraordinary event produced by divine agency and contradicting "natural laws" or conventional expectations—is by definition *invraisemblable*. The rejection of "miracles" is characteristic of both bourgeois rationalism—notably represented in the late seventeenth century by Bernard le Bovier de Fontenelle, who attacked miracles and enthusiastically defended *La Princesse de Clèves*— and the nascent realist novel, which rose along with the middle class. The canon of verisimilitude that governs the realist novel tends to exclude not only supernatural interventions in the action but also the quasi-miraculous coincidences that are the staple of earlier romances such as Mme de Lafayette's *Zayde,* and which are parodied in Voltaire's *Candide.*

La Princesse de Clèves straddles the border between romance and the (realist) novel. As I have already suggested, when the prince and the princess strive to understand how the latter's "confession" could have become known, they are trying to find a plausible explanation for an event that has none within the framework of the novel. Similarly, when the prince interprets his spy's report as indicating that his wife has been unfaithful to him, he is reading it in accord with the conventions of the realist novel—above all those of *vraisemblance* and plausible "motivation." The princess reads Nemours's conduct in the same way, projecting a "realistic" future she refuses.

As John Lyons has recently pointed out, the narrator repeatedly draws attention to facts that are true but unlikely—for instance, Henri II's long-lasting passion for Diane de Poitiers and his death in a freak jousting accident (225–26, 228–29). Yet the narrative constantly depends on appeals to verisimilitude—that is, to received ideas about the world, and particularly about human psychology. It does so, for instance, when it explains why Nemours tells the vidame about the confession—"il tomba dans une imprudence assez ordinaire, qui est de parler en termes généraux de ses sentiments particuliers et de conter ses propres aventures sous des noms empruntés" (126)—or explains why the vidame violates his promise of confidentiality—"L'envie de s'éclaircir, ou plutôt la disposition naturelle que l'on a de conter tout ce que l'on sait à ce que l'on aime, fit qu'il redit à Mme de Martigues l'action extraordinaire de cette personne, qui avait avoué à son mari la passion qu'elle avait pour un autre" (131). Such examples could be multiplied almost indefinitely.

The narrator does not acknowledge the role played by such appeals to *vraisemblance* in her narrative, however, so that their functioning, highlighted in her analysis of the characters' thought and discourse, remains occulted in her own. This is not surprising, and indeed might be said to be generally characteristic of the classical "psychological" narrative of which *La Princesse de Clèves* is often considered the first major example. In Lafayette's novel, however, the implicit critique of judgments based on verisimilitude undermines the authority of the narrator's appeals to them and thus opens, or widens, an ironic gap between implied author and narrator. While the text questions the reliability of such judgments, it proposes no alternative to them; at most, as Mme de Chartres suggests (55–56), they can be refined through a critical awareness that things are not as simple as they seem.

By including romance plot elements within a text governed by the norm of verisimilitude characteristic of the realist novel, Mme de Lafayette shows what this norm excludes, and at what price. The price is paid by her heroine, who is left trapped in a no-man's-land between two genres.

7 The Princess and Her Spiritual Guide

On the Influence of Preaching on Fiction

WOLFGANG LEINER

ONE would search Mme de Lafayette's novel in vain for the spiritual guide figuring in the title of this chapter; there is no explicit reference substantiating the existence of such a guide in the princess's universe. At no time does the author employ this word, and with the same discretion she avoids all mention of religious practice. Neither during the time of the princess's marriage, nor during the pending moments of death of those individuals particularly close to her—and we are told that her mother and her husband took two or more days to die[1]—does the author supply us with the least bit of information about how the dying prepared themselves for death (68). One sent for the doctors, but of the priests there is no mention. The church with its rites, sacraments, and ceremonies, with its priests and dignitaries,[2] was not present. Is not this universe deliberately situated away from Christian values and institutions? The question is justified, for dying with a "constance

---

1. "Elle vécut encore deux jours, pendant lesquels elle ne voulut plus revoir sa fille, qui était la seule chose à quoi elle se sentait attachée" (Madame de Lafayette, *La Princesse de Clèves,* ed. Antoine Adam [Paris: Garnier-Flammarion, 1966], 68; all of my citations come from this edition and are hereafter cited parenthetically in the text). "Il voulut continuer; mais une faiblesse lui ôta la parole. Madame de Clèves fit venir les médecins; ils le trouvèrent presque sans vie. Il languit néanmoins encore quelques jours et mourut enfin avec une constance admirable" (164).

2. Except for one mention of the pope.

admirable"[3] is not an exclusively Christian virtue. The vaguely described convents (164, 180) in our text do little to ease our doubts about the religious atmosphere. God makes only one discreet appearance,[4] and he is named a mere three times. This lack is noteworthy when one considers the frequency with which other words occur: passion (111 times), woman (104 times), beauty (50 times), love (49 times), mistress (42 times), and gallantry (22 times).[5] The court, so often evoked and named ninety-three times, whose magnificence (8 times) is an object of fascination for the author and her characters, is not at all the celestial court, as perceived by Saint-Genest,[6] but rather the court of France at the time of Henri II.

To all appearances we find ourselves in the presence of a work occupied to a greater extent with worldly realities than with the problems of moral and Christian conduct. We have before us one of those novels that, according to Bourdaloue, demonstrates that there is "rien de plus propre à corrompre un coeur."[7] There is reason to believe, however, that this appearance is deceiving and that, upon closer inspection, the novelistic discourse and the teachings of Christianity in *La Princesse de Clèves* are not at all antagonistic and exclusive realities. There are in fact indications in the novel that would justify the title of this chapter. Is not Mme de Clèves's behavior itself determined by those directing principles inspired by a moral system manifested in the words of the well-known preachers of Louis XIV's epoch? Behind Mme de Chartres, as behind the Princesse de Clèves and the Duc de Nemours, who are the most imaginary of fictional characters—"le monde ne produit pas des gens de cette espèce," said Pierre Bayle[8]— stands the profile of Mme de Lafayette's shadow. She is the one who sets them into motion, and it is her ideas and ethics, her vision of the characters, that determine the outcome of her novelistic creation. It

3. We are told that Monsieur de Clèves "mourut enfin avec une constance admirable" (164).

4. "Plût à Dieu que vous me . . . puissiez persuader" (163).

5. See Jean de Bazin, *Index du vocabulaire de "La Princesse de Clèves"* (Paris: Nizet, 1967). This index was the source of much of my information.

6. Jean de Rotrou, *Le Véritable Saint-Genest* (Geneva: Droz, 1973).

7. Louis Bourdaloue, *Oeuvres complètes.* 4 vols. (Paris: Louis Vivès, 1890), 2:124; hereafter cited parenthetically in the text.

8. Pierre Bayle, *Nouvelles Lettres critiques sur l'histoire du Calvinisme* (Janvier, 1685).

would be astonishing not to see the ideologies of the period reflected in the protagonists' conduct, and indeed surprising if the moral options available to Mme de Lafayette's contemporaries did not, in any way, make a mark on a work that purposefully strives to avoid the impression of being fictional.

Other readers have emphasized, long before me, the interdependence of this fictional work and the society of the time. Harry Ashton pointed out in 1922 that it was natural for the Christian religion as an essential element of this society—which was simultaneously both a model and an audience for the novel—to function as the basis for the ideology underlying the work.[9]

Mme de Chartres's behavior, her life, and her death lead one to the conclusion that she was a sincere Christian. The happiness that she hopes to attain "en sortant de ce monde"[10] evidences her piety and indicates that she confronted death with the belief that she will achieve this blessed state promised to those who live in the fear of God. Assuredly, as I have already said, references to a Christian God and the Christian religion and its doctrines are almost nonexistent. The novel's last sentence provides us with a good example of the vague religious allusions pervading the text: "[Mme de Clèves] passait une partie de l'année dans cette maison religieuse et l'autre chez elle; mais dans une retraite et dans les occupations plus saintes que celles des couvents les plus austères; et sa vie, qui fut assez courte, laissa des exemples de vertu inimitables" (180). This vagueness should not be viewed, however, as a confirmation of indifference with regard to religion. On the contrary, it is more likely her respect for belief and religion that prevents the author from speaking more specifically.[11]

9. Harry Ashton, *Madame de La Fayette: Sa vie et ses oeuvres* (Cambridge: Cambridge University Press, 1922).

10. "Si quelque chose était capable de troubler le bonheur que j'espère en sortant de ce monde" (68).

11. Helen Karen Kaps concisely summarizes this problem: "The absence of overt references to a Christian God or to Christian doctrine indicates not so much that Mme de Lafayette has dispensed with the sanctions of formal religion to bolster the moral principles in *The Princesse de Clèves* as they do her compliance with a code of propriety which excluded from fiction matters unsuitable by their extreme dignity as well as those unsuitable by their lack of it" (*Moral Perspective in "La Princesse de Clèves"* [Eugene: University of Oregon Press, 1968], 25; hereafter cited parenthetically in the text.

Yet if one agrees with Helen Karen Kaps that the novel is inspired by the values of Christianity, and that the princess's refusal to remarry after the death of her husband is above all motivated by her concerns about Christian virtues and not by the fear of life and love (26), one must then also admit that such a conclusion arises less from the few allusions that an attentive reading reveals than from a comparison made between that which is given in the novel and the elements of reality outside the text.[12]

I would like to throw new light on this situation by drawing a parallel between certain passages of Mme de Lafayette's novel and the texts of Bourdaloue and Bossuet. Clearly, this process will not involve establishing an exhaustive list of borrowings that the novelist took from these two men of the church. Certain passages taken from the works of the preachers were actually published some time after the appearance of the novel. In approaching these texts with such a contradictory order of appearance, I propose to demonstrate that the church's morality, as it was officially presented by the most well-known preachers, is echoed even in a novel where the church is essentially absent. In this frivolous world of the court, where magnificence and gallantry rule with gilded tongues, the church still brings forth its voice through intermediaries, through spiritual guides such as Bourdaloue. A statement from Mme de Sévigné establishes proof of Bourdaloue's authority: "tout ce qui est au monde" is present at his sermons.[13] It is also Mme de Sévigné who brings to the attention of her daughter the admiration that Mme de Lafayette has for this famous preacher.[14]

12. Identical objectives are formulated by Ilse Stempel in "Desillusionierung und Kritik: Madame de Lafayette und die Entzauberung des höfischen Helden," in *Die französische Autorin vom Mittelalter bis zur Gegenwart,* ed. Renate Baader/Dietmar Fricke (Wiesbaden, Germany: Athenaion, 1979), 98, in an argument against the interpretation proposed by R. Francillon in his book, *L'Oeuvre romanesque de Madame de La Fayette* (Paris: José Corti, 1973).

13. Letter to Madame de Grignan, March 13, 1671. Marie de Rabutin-Chantel Sévigné, *Correspondance,* 3 vols., ed. Roger Duchêne (Paris: Gallimard, 1972), 1:185.

14. In reference to Bourdaloue, Madame de Sévigné said that he blasted out his words like a bull crashing through a china shop. The letter to Madame de Grignan, cited in the preceding footnote, includes this famous exclamation: "Ah! Bourdaloue, quelles divines vérités nous avez-vous dites aujourd'hui sur la mort! Mme de Lafayette y était pour la première fois de sa vie, elle était transportée d'admiration."

One attempting to illustrate the impact of Christian morality on this court milieu, so frequently exposed to the most diverse temptations, would without doubt find Mme de Chartres the most convincing example. Her exemplariness makes her an exceptional character who, graced by her just morals, exerts a significant influence upon those persons living in her entourage.[15] Mlle de Chartres is, above all, influenced by her personality. The moral education of her daughter and the regulation of her conduct seem to be the essential tasks assigned to Mme de Chartres. All her conversations with the novel's protagonist confirm this hypothesis. Her system of values is based on two key concepts: virtue and duty. These two ideals anchored together deep in the princess's conscience serve as a protective shield for the young woman against the temptations of the court and the dangers that threaten married women. The mother's pressing appeals to her daughter not to lose sight of the ideal of virtue and not to forget her duties are like echoes reverberating with the exhortations of the Christian morality preached by the Jesuits. In accordance with the principles presented by Bourdaloue in the "Sermon sur l'état du mariage" (2:16–27), Mme de Chartres considers this union a sacrament, therefore an indissoluble union. It is the sacramental nature of marriage that requires a married woman to have an "extrême défiance de soi-même et un grand soin de s'attacher à ce qui seul peut faire le bonheur d'une femme, qui est d'aimer son mari et d'en être aimée" (41). Just before her death, in their last conversation, Mme de Chartres feels obligated to exhort the princess: "Songez ce que vous devez à votre mari, songez ce que vous devez à vous-même" (68). She encourages her daughter to be firm and courageous, never to fear taking harsh and difficult measures, and never to let herself be obligated by "d'autres raisons que celles de la vertu et [du] devoir" (68). Her aim had always been to give her daughter "de la vertu et à la rendre aimable" (41). When Mlle de Chartres made her initial entrance into the court, the mother "qui avait eu tant d'application pour inspirer la vertu à sa fille ne discontinua pas de prendre les mêmes soins dans un lieu où ils étaient si nécessaires et où il y avait tant d'exemples si dangereux" (44).

15. I am here referring to Georges Forestier's study, "Madame de Chartres, personnage-clé de *La Princesse de Clèves,*" *Les Lettres romanes* 34 (1980): 67–76.

One would almost have to apologize for wanting to demonstrate, with citations from sermons, how many specific novelistic characters of Mme de Lafayette are inspired in their principles of conduct and in their perception of the world by the moral precepts dictated by the well-known preachers of the time. It is necessary, however, to emphasize the parallelism between Mme de Lafayette's novel and the sermons, as this analogy gives the work a precise sense that cannot be perceived by one who ignores this relatedness. The connections that exist between the "Sermon sur l'état du mariage" and *La Princesse de Clèves* are evident. Here it is sufficient to emphasize that the preacher and the novelist are in obvious agreement in that they do not consider marriage a mere social affair, without moral obligations (Bourdaloue, 2:19), but rather the result of a passion that explains and legitimizes the love at the core of the union. The opinion that love outside of marriage could be nothing other than a sin is shared by Bourdaloue, the novelist, and her characters: "Elle vit alors que les sentiments qu'elle avait pour [le Duc de Nemours] étaient ceux que M. de Clèves lui avait tant demandés, elle trouva combien il était honteux de les avoir pour un autre que pour un mari qui les méritait" (65).

Bourdaloue regards these "amitiés criminelles"—a term that will also be used by Mme de Lafayette (91)—as relationships tarnished by sin (4:447). One thus understands why Bourdaloue, in his sermon "Sur les tentations," compels his readers "de ne pas aller au-delà du devoir, de ne pas compter parmi les devoirs tel ou tel attachement dont la seule passion est le noeud" (1:230). It would therefore be important, as he states in his sermon, "Sur la pensée de la mort," "de trouver un moyen qui nous délivrât de ces incertitudes affligeantes, et de ces craintes si opposées à la paix intérieure de nos âmes" (1:172).

Bossuet argues along the same lines: a human being could not function "sans règle et sans conduite, au gré de ses aveugles désirs."[16] We note the importance that he accords, in his *Oraisons funèbres,* to the attention that individuals in the past devoted to their duties. Of Henriette d'Angleterre he says, "les inclinations . . . ne l'attachaient pas moins fortement à tous ses autres devoirs. . . . Combien a-t-elle été maîtresse (de son coeur!), avec quelle tranquillité a-t-elle satisfait à tous ses devoirs" (125, 146).

16. Bossuet, "Oraison funèbre de Henriette d'Angleterre," in *Oraisons funèbres,* ed. P. Jacquinet (Paris: 1844), 104–5; hereafter cited parenthetically in the text.

Mastery of oneself is the necessary ingredient for honor and dignity. This lesson comes from the Prince de Clèves, who proves himself a worthy successor to Mme de Chartres: "Ayez du pouvoir sur vous-même pour l'amour de vous-même et s'il est possible pour l'amour de moi" (129–30). Is this not an echo of the encouragement given by Mme de Chartres to the princess? "Ne craignez point de prendre des partis trop rudes et trop difficiles, quelque affreux qu'ils vous paraissent d'abord: ils seront plus doux dans les suites que les malheurs d'une galanterie" (68). Mme de Chartres encourages her daughter to take the narrow road—the only road, according to Bossuet in his "Oraison funèbre de Henriette de France"—that could lead to virtue: "Accourez, dit Saint-Grégoire, puissances du siècle: voyez dans quel sentier la vertu chemine: doublement à l'étroit, et par elle-même, et par l'effort de ceux qui la persécutent: secourez-la, tendez-lui la main: puisque vous la voyez déjà fatiguée du combat qu'elle soutient au dedans contre tant de tentations qui accablent la nature humaine, mettez-la du moins à couvert des insultes du dehors" (27ff.).

Duty and virtue: novelist and preacher alike maintain that these are the essential values for those who would escape painful but hopeless remorse on Judgment Day. The novelist and the preacher concur as well that virtue and a sense of duty are indispensable for life at court as well as life in the household. Is this by chance? Or is this congruity more likely explained by the novelist's intention to make references to the Christian ideology?

The presentation of the court in France that opens the novel immediately brings to our attention the importance that this court will have in the story of the Princesse de Clèves. From the first sentence we recognize which values dominate in this world: magnificence and gallantry. In a milieu where men use every available tool to attract attention to themselves, in a world where gallantry and its false or real passions determine social relationships, one can imagine the degree of artificiality, the hypocritical behavior of the individuals, their inclination to deceive and to let themselves be deceived. It is a theater in which each person wears a mask that is exchangeable according to the necessity of the moment. It is a dangerous universe where temptations are numerous. The inconstancy of the individual is the only constant; everything in this universe is done for the sake of appearance: "Dans ce commerce d'amitiés mondaines, et par conséquent impures, combien de fausses apparences? Combien de dissimulations? Combien de tromperies, de ruses, surtout quand l'ambition ou l'intérêt engage l'une [la personne qu'on aime] à jouer tel personnage."

This warning from Bourdaloue's sermon, "Sur l'éloignement et la fuite du monde" (2:311), plays an important role in many of Mme de Chartres's conversations with her daughter. We are told that Mme de Chartres judged that such precautions were necessary to protect the princess against the temptations of the court: "où il y avait tant d'exemples si dangereux . . . dans un lieu dont l'ambition et la galanterie étaient l'âme . . . [où] personne n'était tranquille, ni indifférent, [où l']on songeait à s'élever, à plaire, à servir ou à nuire" (44–45). Like Bourdaloue, she denounces false appearances, double-crossings, and deception: "ce qui paraît n'est presque jamais la vérité" (56). Mme de Lafayette's novel is a work that chips away illusion's facade.

The story of Mme de Tournon brings the princess to the realization that the very person whom she believed incapable of love and deception was actually thoroughly well-versed in the game of gallantry and double crosses (80). As one who listened to Bourdaloue, such a discovery should not have been a surprise. One reads in the sermon "De la charité chrétienne et des amitiés humaines":

On sait assez quel est l'esprit de la cour; et parce que les intérêts y sont beaucoup plus grands que partout ailleurs, les passions y sont aussi beaucoup plus vives et plus ardentes. Qu'est-ce, en effet, que la cour? Le siège de la politique, mais d'une politique la plus intéressée. On n'y est occupé que de sa fortune, et l'on n'y a d'autre vue ni d'autre soin que de s'avancer, de s'élever, de se maintenir au dépens de qui que ce soit. Telle est l'âme qui anime tout, tel est le mobile qui remue tout, tel est le principal agent qui met tout en oeuvre. (4:435)

The court's reputation described in this sermon is confirmed in Mme de Chartres's conversations with her daughter and, as well, in the series of episodes that justify certain precautions: the court is the place of temptation, a place of contagion, a place of perversion, a place of corruption: the metaphorical court of the world. "Si vous jugez sur les apparences en ce lieu-ci, vous serez souvent trompée" (56). Jean Mesnard sees in this maxim a summary of the court's true nature.[17]

17. Jean Mesnard, ed., *La Princesse de Clèves,* by Mme de Lafayette (Paris: Lettres Françaises, Imprimerie Nationale, 1980), 35; hereafter cited parenthetically in the text.

"Le monde est contagieux, et nous sommes faibles," claims Bourda-loue in a statement that echoes that of Mme de Chartres: "Il faut absolument fuir le commerce du monde, et y renoncer pour jamais dès que nous voyons qu'il nous pervertit et que nous sentons les pre-mières atteintes de sa corruption" ("Sur l'éloignement et la fuite du monde," 2:311). The conduct suggested here by the Jesuit Father resembles exactly what Mme de Chartres recommends to her daughter. After having taken her to a refuge away from that place of perdition that is the court, she counsels her, "ayez de la force et du courage, ma fille, retirez-vous de la cour" (68). The temptation to which the princess is exposed resembles an epidemic prevalent throughout the court. As Bourdaloue proclaims:

Oui, chrétiens, la cour est un séjour de tentations, et de tentations dont on ne peut presque se préserver, et de tentations où les plus forts succombent; mais pour qui l'est-elle? Pour ceux qui n'y sont pas appelés de Dieu, pour ceux qui s'y poussent par ambition, pour ceux qui y entrent par la voie de l'intrigue . . . pour ceux qui y demeurent contre leur devoir. . . . Mais quel est souvent le principe du mal? Le voici: c'est qu'à la cour, où le devoir vous arrête, vous allez bien au-delà du devoir. Car . . . comptez-vous parmi vos devoirs tel ou tel at-tachement dont la seule passion est le noeud, et qu'il faudrait rompre tant d'as-siduité auprès d'un objet vers qui l'inclination vous porte, et dont il faudrait vous séparer? ("Sur les tentations," 1:230ff.)

Mme de Chartres's fear "de voir [sa fille] tomber comme les autres" (68) should not surprise us since we are told that, according to the rule, all women succumb to temptation. Mme de Chartres's Christian orientation of conduct clearly explains her apprehension at seeing her daughter distance herself, like the others, from Christian morality. Marriage, for her, is apparently still a sacrament. Certainly, the nov-elist reflected on this fact when she ended the last conversation be-tween mother and daughter by noting that Mme de Chartres would gladly accept death should her daughter ever succumb like other women (68). We are now at a turning point in the novel. Here the dilemma expressed in Mme de Lafayette's novelistic discourse becomes evident: a married woman, living in a world where gallantry dictates the laws, is confronted with the problem of conjugal fidelity. The last words of Mme de Chartres thus indicate the two options offered to the princess: live like others *or* distinguish yourself, follow the wide path of gallantry and pleasures *or* take it upon yourself to follow the narrow path of Christian virtue. While orienting her conduct according to her mother's maxims, the princess will distinguish herself, assert herself, and identify herself as different from other women. She will conduct herself in accordance with her mother's and her spiritual guides' expectations rather than with those of the court. She will resist temptation, that is, the obsessive temptation that haunts her in the form of the Duc de Nemours. His name appears 323 times in the text, whereas the names of Mme de Chartres and the Princesse de Clèves together appear only 284 times. The disproportionate frequency with which the two male protagonists' names occur reflects the seriousness of the menace that hovers over the married princess: the Prince de Clèves is named 116 times, whereas the tempter is named 323 times. Is it the maternal figure's authority, or is it the princess's adhesion to principles of Christian morality that explains her conduct? The question is of little importance. What is of real significance is that the ethic preached by the church is the one that triumphs—and the novelist is the artisan of this triumph. In whatever manner one views the author's clever orchestration and use of narrative elements, one can clearly see the conformity between religious teachings and novelistic discourse.

By emphasizing two precise elements in the structure, I would like to focus once more on the hidden correspondence between the two orders of discourse that are of interest here. The first structuring element that merits attention is that of the *retraite*; and here I am thinking of the word itself as much as its meaning. After the death of Mme de Chartres, the princess is led to the countryside by her husband, as he seeks to distance her from a place that merely augments her sorrow. In this retreat, she learns of Mme de Tournon's death. M. de Clèves helplessly watches his wife suffering anew from this report and, attempting to lessen her pain, he admonishes her not to mourn the deceased woman as a "femme pleine de sagesse et digne de votre estime" (69). Mme de Clèves is completely astonished to hear such a statement from him, particularly because the prince had held, in past times, much esteem for Mme de Tournon. "Il est vrai, répondit-il, mais les femmes sont incompréhensibles et, quand je les vois toutes, je me trouve si heureux de vous avoir que je ne saurais assez admirer mon bonheur" (69). One notes that once again the princess is set up in contrast with all other women. As readers we are more aware of the flow of things than the prince and so can both sense the ironic tone that the author wanted to give to the prince's statements and grasp the melancholy that lies behind the princess's response: "Vous m'estimez plus que je ne vaux, répliqua Mme de Clèves en soupirant, il n'est pas encore temps de me trouver digne de vous" (69).

No, it is not yet time because she has yet to undergo and overcome the ordeal successfully. However, if the solemn moment that the princess has passed with her mother has the sense that we attribute to it, if it is possible, as I believe, to see in Mme de Clèves that *Kontrastfigur* proposed as an example to all women who fall into temptation, then she is not unworthy of the prince's confidence, despite the fact that he dies before her Christian virtue is put to its final test. I stress the analogy between Mme de Tournon's and the princess's situation in order to emphasize that the former's story brings us face to face with a widowhood prefiguring that of the latter. Yet these are indubitably two widowhoods of opposite natures. To understand this apparent contradiction, let us first hear Bossuet's voice:

La princesse palatine est dans l'état le plus dangereux de sa vie. Que le monde voit peu de ces veuves dont parle Saint Paul, qui "vraiment veuves et désolées," s'ensevelissent, pour ainsi dire, elles-mêmes dans le tombeau de leur époux; y enterrent tout amour humain avec ces cendres chéries; et, délaissées sur la terre, "mettent leur espérance en Dieu, et passent les nuits et les jours dans la prière!" Voilà l'état d'une veuve chrétienne, selon les préceptes de Saint Paul: état oublié parmi nous, où la viduité est regardée, non plus comme un état de désolation, car ces mots ne sont plus connus, mais comme un état désirable, où affranchi de tout joug, on n'a plus qu'à se contenter soi-même, sans songer à cette terrible sentence de Saint Paul: "La veuve qui passe sa vie dans les plaisirs"; remarquez qu'il ne dit pas, la veuve qui passe sa vie dans les crimes; il dit: "La veuve qui la passe dans les plaisirs, elle est morte toute vive"; parce qu'oubliant le deuil éternel et le caractère de sa désolation, qui fait le soutien comme la gloire de son état, elle s'abandonne aux joies du monde. Combien donc devrait-on pleurer comme mortes, ces veuves jeunes et riantes, que le monde trouve si heureuses! (279–80)

Compared with the episode related in this extract from the "Oraison funèbre de Anne de Gonzague de Clèves," Mme de Tournon's retreat reveals itself to be less in accordance with the high exigence of the church. She leaves her retreat in order to remarry and to begin her life anew. Her sudden death prevents the realization of this plan while, at the same time, it reveals her hypocrisy and double crosses. This episode is closely bound to the story of the Princesse de Clèves herself. The account of Mme de Tournon's behavior influences her both in an immediate sense and in terms of her future decisions. Upon hearing about the other woman's escapades, the princess recognizes the dangers that lie in wait for her outside her refuge—even she must struggle to avoid these tantalizing temptations. In the future, the princess will not forget this lesson of how *not* to conduct herself. Whereas Mme de Tournon, in love with Sancerre and "résolue à l'épouser . . . commença même à quitter cette retraite où elle vivait et à se remettre dans le monde" (75) and, once repossessed by the world, plays a double game in leading Sancerre to believe that she loved him while explaining to Estouteville "que c'était lui qui était cause qu'elle quittait cette grande retraite" (80), Mme de Clèves transforms the retreat, where "la bienséance l'obligeait à vivre" (178) after the death of her husband, into a retreat whose significance cannot be ignored by M. de Nemours, "une retraite plus sainte que celle des couvents les plus austères" (180).

The word *retraite* appears three times in these final pages of *La Princesse de Clèves* and, curiously enough, these three "retreats" are like an echo of the three mentions of this word in the pages consecrated to Mme de Tournon's story. In no other part of the novel does this word reappear. It would be difficult to believe that chance alone explains the author's use of the word *retraite* in a work so intelligently, so ingeniously, so mysteriously structured. I believe even less that the mention of "austere retreat" opening the account of Mme de Tournon's widowhood and closing the account of Mme de Clèves's religious life could be an effect of chance. The position of one single epithet indicates that we are in the presence of two experiences diametrically opposed, or, even more, of two identical experiences revolving in opposite directions: whereas Mme de Tournon leaves her austere retreat to reenter the world, Mme de Clèves enters her retreat with the first steps onto the narrow road leading to virtue, thus conforming, as Bossuet worded it, to the high expectations of the church and the apostles: "Voilà l'état d'une veuve chrétienne selon les préceptes de Saint Paul: état oublié parmi [les autres]."

Casting a final quick glance on the theme of death that, like a silent counterpoint, accompanies the evocation of the courtly world full of splendor, gallantry, and glitter, we are once more able to verify to what extent this novel illustrates the essential ideas of the church's teachings. The shadow of death stands silently but ever present in our novel and numerous characters fall under its darkness: Mme de Chartres, Mme de Tournon, the king, the Prince de Clèves. Death punctuates the story's development; yet, like Mme de Chartres's personality and the interspersed stories of others' lives, it is an element that orients the princess inexorably toward the point of escape at the novel's end: the austere retreat. One should not be in the least bit astonished that the spectacle of death is so dominantly present in a literary text from a century fascinated by life's end and the "hereafter." Mme de Lafayette's novel reflects certain religious preoccupations that characterize the entire "post-Tridentine" literature. I am not seeking to annex *La Princesse de Clèves* to the domain of the baroque, yet, upon closer examination, it becomes evident that the moral lesson suggested by these numerous evocations of death is not fundamentally different from that given in the *Stances de la mort*. On an aesthetic level, however, the difference is considerable. The spectacle of death is integrated into the literary work and produced, so to speak, for the characters in the novel, primarily for Mme de Clèves and not for the reader, as it is in certain texts at the end of the sixteenth and the beginning of the seventeenth century. It is only through identification with our protagonist that one grasps—on the rebound so to speak—the significance of these death scenes. Death has the function of disillusioning the princess who is dazzled by the magnificence of the spectacle surrounding her, and of both reminding her of the fragility of her condition and orienting her and perhaps the reader's attention toward the permanent. Is it necessary to emphasize that these frequent recollections of death's reality aim toward essentially the same dramatic effect in the sermons as in our novel? "On peut juger quel trouble et quelle affliction apporta un accident si funeste dans une journée destinée à la joie" (124). The novelist's commentary about Henri II's death corresponds to Bourdaloue's commentary inspired by thoughts about death: "Je sais que cette réflexion se présente à vous malgré vous; je sais qu'elle vient jusques au milieu de vos plaisirs, parmi les divertissements et les joies du monde, dans les moments les plus heureux en apparence, vous saisir vous troubler; et qu'au fond de l'âme elle vous fait bien payer avec usure cette fausse tranquillité qui ne consiste que dans des dehors trompeurs" (1:175).

What purpose do these numerous deaths serve? They serve to reveal the instability of things, to emphasize the futility of life and passions, and to shatter the charm exercised upon human beings by power, splendor, and passion, so that they will open their souls to God while turning away from this world of deception. According to Bourdaloue, death is:

à notre égard la preuve palpable et sensible du néant de toutes les choses humaines, pour lesquelles nous nous passionnons. C'est elle qui nous le fait connaître, tout le reste nous impose; la mort seule est le miroir fidèle qui nous montre sans déguisement l'instabilité, la fragilité, la caducité des biens de cette vie; qui nous désabuse de toutes nos erreurs, qui détruit en nous tous les enchantements de l'amour du monde, et qui, des ténèbres même du tombeau, nous fait une source de lumières, dont nos esprits et nos sens sont également pénétrés. ("Sur la pensée da la mort," 1:169)

The Princesse de Clèves serves without doubt as a model of Christian virtue. Inspired by the example and moral lessons presented by her mother and moved by the feeling of the futility of passions and human concerns, she detaches herself from the world in order to dedicate herself to devout occupations: "Les passions et les engagements du monde lui parurent tels qu'ils paraissent aux personnes qui ont les vues plus grandes et plus éloignées" (179). The image of Mme de Clèves evoked here by the novelist echoes a Bossuet text published in 1659 relating the experience of a real postulant: "Bien qu'elle sache qu'aux yeux des mondains un monastère c'est une prison, ni [les] grilles, ni [la] clôture ne l'étonnent: elle veut bien renfermer son corps afin que son esprit soit libre à son Dieu, et elle croit que comme le monde est un[e] prison en sortir c'est la liberté."[18]

"Je n'ai nulle inquiétude de votre conduite," said the prince to his wife, "vous avez plus de force et plus de vertu que vous ne pensez" (127). The end of the novel confirms his belief. Thanks to the prince's virtue, and, without a doubt, to the grace of God, the princess will remain faithful to her duties: toward her husband, toward religion, toward herself. If it is necessary to give a meaning to this retreat—

18. Bossuet, "Pour la vêture d'une postulante Bernardine" (1659).

the point of escape toward which the main lines in the novel converge—I would then propose to see it neither as an expression of weakness on the part of Mme de Clèves, nor as evidence of fear originating from a threat of being seduced by the "Don Juan" Duc de Nemours. I also would not see the retreat as a sign attesting to the importance that the protagonist—invented by the novelist and resembling another "religieuse"[19]—gives to Love rather than to the Duc de Nemours. I would be inclined, rather, to interpret this refusal of the world as a logical step resulting from the princess's moral education, her experience with the court, with men, with life, as a necessary step originating ultimately in a Christian concept of life. Would it be foolhardy to imagine that Mme de Lafayette created her princess as a fictional figure embodying the idea of a Christian woman as it was presented by the most illustrious preachers of her time?

Jean Mesnard notes, "L'univers du roman, pour les uns, implique l'absence de Dieu; pour les autres, il s'achève dans la transcendance" (9). My analysis demonstrates that both of the readings pointed out by Jean Mesnard are possible; yet even more my interpretation of the princess attempts to show that only the second could be fully in accordance with the spirit of the work. God is, in effect, absent from the novel's universe—yet only on the condition that one contents oneself with a reading excluding the hidden presence of God in the privacy of the heart. God is absent for the reader who neglects or refuses to take into consideration Christian morality which, in the seventeenth century, gives form to thought in the same way that Marxist ideology is present in thought today.

Reading *La Princesse de Clèves* with such a perspective leads to an essentially psychological interpretation, substantiated by the search for tranquility at the end of the novel. Those who are not, however, tempted to view Mme de Lafayette's novel as a psychological study, but rather as a novel ending in transcendence, will see in the very importance that the princess accords to the search for tranquility, not an argument against their interpretation, but a confirmation of their thesis that *La Princesse de Clèves* brings us face to face with a work of fiction offering women in a society full of temptations the example of

19. One thinks here about Mariane of Guilleragues's *Lettres portugaises* (1669) for whom love and not the lover is of the utmost importance.

154 / Wolfgang Leiner

a Christian woman, of a spouse living according to the principles of
the church's morality. According to Bourdaloue, "En effet, c'est dans
la retraite et la séparation du monde qu'on trouve ce repos où l'on
apprend à connaître Dieu" (1:175). Rather than placing before the
eyes of the reader an example of a controversial woman who, through
her retreat, criticizes a social order unfavorable to women,[20] Mme de
Lafayette offers us, in her central heroine, a literary portrait of the
illustrious sinner and penitent who so intensely haunted the imagination of her entire century.[21]

It has been said that there is nothing more appropiate for withering
piety and for corrupting a heart than these tainted books. Experience
clearly demonstrates this fact, and the confessions of those who have
read such books are tangible proofs. Bourdaloue asks, "A quoi tendent
ces histoires romanesques? A inspirer l'amour" (2:124). This judgment by Bourdaloue, which corresponds to the numerous condem-
nations of romantic novels pronounced in the course of the century,
allows one last emphasis on a specific conformity between the discourse of the preacher and that of the novelist. Mme de Lafayette's
story is not a morally tainted book as defined by Bourdaloue. Instead
of withering piety, Mme de Lafayette's novel fortifies it; instead of
corrupting a heart, *La Princesse de Clèves* elevates it. And if this book
tends to inspire love, it is a love based on the word of God and the
commandments of Christian morality. Obviously Mme de Lafayette's
book should not be classified as a "tainted book." On the contrary,
one could perfectly well conjecture—and the entirely fictitious nature
of Mme de Chartres's character encourages us to see things in this
perspective—that the novelist had in mind, with regard to her readers, the same goal that Mme de Chartres had in mind with regard to
her daughter.

My intention has in no way been to make Mme de Lafayette the
spokeswoman of Bossuet and Bourdaloue, that is, an author who
would seek only to transpose the moral teachings of the church onto
the realm of the novel. I wanted to demonstrate, rather, that it is

20. Stempel, "Die französische Autorin," 98.

21. See my study, "Métamorphoses magdaléniennes," in Gisèle Mathieu, ed., *La
Métamorphose dans la poésie baroque française et anglaise: Actes du Colloque International de
Valenciennes, 1979*, Etudes littéraires françaises 7 (Tübingen, Germany: Gunter Narr,
1980), 43–56.

perfectly possible to establish a precise correspondence between the novelistic discourse of Mme de Lafayette and the discourse of the sermons from these two preachers, who were contemporary to, and well respected by, Mme de Lafayette. Establishing this correspondence appeared to me of extreme interest, as it has not been recognized up until now. Readers and critics of *La Princesse de Clèves* have been able to establish all sorts of congruities with other discourses: with that of Corneille and that of Racine, for example, and with the discourse of the moralists. By limiting itself to literary discourses, literary criticism accomplished that which it set out to do: situate this work in its literary milieu in order to determine, from the very place it occupies there in the network of tendencies and influences, its sense and meaning. This meaning will never be definitive, for every new approach suffices, by enlarging the work's possible spectrum of meaning, to change its sense. Following the footsteps of the sociologists, I wanted to see if there were any connections that could be made with extraliterary discourses.

Jacques Hennequin recently explained that the pulpit exercised the same influence on the seventeenth century that television exercises today. It is therefore not at all astonishing that these sermons left their traces on everything during this period, a proof in itself that a writer in the class of Mme de Lafayette could not—perhaps did not want to—extricate herself from the influence of the preachers. By attracting attention to this connection, to this crossing of discourses, I did not intend to effect a reduction, but rather to propose a new sense that could not but enrich the multisemantic field of Mme de Lafayette's novel.

8 *La Princesse de Clèves* and *L'Introduction à la vie dévote*

PATRICK HENRY

T LEAST since Molière the word *dévot* has had a bad press.[1] When François de Sales published *L'Introduction à la vie dévote* in 1609, however, the word signified more generally one who had taken a vow and lived in a cloister. The great originality of this work lies in the fact that, even if not the first devotional manual for laypeople, it was the first effective and successful one.[2] Its author, perhaps above all interested in the direction of souls, firmly believed that laypeople could become conscious of their religious grandeur and lead holy lives in society. The devout life, formerly restricted to monks and cloistered nuns, would now be a realizable goal for soldiers, statesmen, housewives, the married as well as the celibate.

L'Introduction à la vie dévote[3] is marked by a deep love of God and

This chapter is dedicated to Philip A. Wadsworth, a model teacher, scholar, and friend. I would also like to record my gratitude to Mary Anne O'Neil whose insights were invaluable in the writing of this study and to Ralph Albanese for reading the manuscript and offering helpful suggestions.

1. The *Robert* lists its etymology, "1190; lat. ecclés. *devotus* 'dévoué à Dieu,'" and its pejorative sense "bigot" and synonyms "cafard, cagot, pharisien, tartufe" (Paul Robert, *Le Petit Robert* [Paris: SNL, 1967], 474.

2. Elfreida T. Dubois, "Saint Francis de Sales and Jeremy Taylor: *Introduction à la vie dévote* and *Holy Living*. A Comparison," *History of European Ideas* 2 (1981): 49, 61n.

3. No mention will be made of *Le Traité de l'amour de Dieu,* a later and more advanced work for those further along the road that leads to unity with God. In the preface to that work Saint François explains, "Ce traité donc est fait pour aider l'âme déjà dévote à ce qu'elle se puisse avancer en son dessein" (Saint François de Sales, *Oeuvres* [Paris: Gallimard,

confidence in him, a desire for detachment from the things of this world, and a robust optimism. Perfect union with God is the never attainable but always approachable aim of the devout life; courage, constancy, and struggle are required. Saint François encourages us to get up when we fall and persist in our efforts to remain virtuous. Temptations await us at every turn and, in order to combat them, we must develop the habit of virtue which can only be built upon a knowledge of our weaknesses, the avoidance of occasions of sin, and the striving for union with God. Saint François exhibits a deep hatred for sin but tolerance, patience, sympathy, and love for sinners, who always have the freedom to determine their destiny. If his students persist in the devout life, they will learn to be in the world but not of it, to die to the world, so to speak, as they live in it.

Although one would assume that Mme de Lafayette was familiar with the work of Saint François de Sales—a relative of Mme de Sévigné and a saint canonized in 1665, six or seven years before she began work on *La Princesse de Clèves*—I can find no mention of him in her work or correspondence. In addition, I have been unable to discover even an allusion to him in the numerous books and articles dealing with *La Princesse de Clèves*.[4] I believe, nonetheless, that a reading of this novel in light of *L'Introduction à la vie dévote* will help elucidate its religious nature, which comes most ostensibly to the surface in the final three paragraphs of the text. The princess's final decision not to marry Nemours and to spend "une partie de l'année dans [une] maison religieuse et l'autre chez elle"[5] is not surprising. "Ends are ends," writes Frank Kermode, "only when they are not negative but frankly transfigure the events in which they were immanent."[6]

1969], 342. This same edition will be used for references to *L'Introduction à la vie dévote*, hereafter cited parenthetically in the text).

4. The sole exception is a footnote in an excellent article that discusses *La Princesse de Clèves* at length. It simply refers the reader to *L'Introduction à la vie dévote* where Saint François de Sales mentions that the desert was originally where saintly hermits meditated and atoned. See Domna Stanton, "The Ideal of 'Repos' in Seventeenth-Century French Literature," *L'Esprit créateur* 15 (1975): 88.

5. Madame de Lafayette, *La Princesse de Clèves,* ed. Antoine Adam (Paris: Garnier-Flammarion, 1966), 180; hereafter cited parenthetically in the text.

6. Frank Kermode, *The Sense of an Ending: Studies in the Theory of Fiction* (Oxford: Oxford University Press, 1968), 175.

As in *L'Introduction à la vie dévote,* the goal of the education that Mme de Chartres gives her daughter is happiness through the practice of virtue. In atypical behavior for the seventeenth century,[7] she withdrew from the court for several years to devote herself to that task. She tried not only to cultivate her daughter's mind and beauty but above all to "lui donner de la vertu et . . . la lui rendre aimable" (41). This insistence on rendering virtue lovable is also reminiscent of Saint François, who writes: "Les vertus ont cela d'admirable qu'elles délectent l'âme d'une douceur et suavité non pareille après qu'on les a exercées, où les vices la laissent infiniment recrue et malmenée" (308).

What is once again suggestive of Saint François de Sales—and, according to the narrator, highly irregular for the times—is that, unlike most mothers who think they can best protect young people by never speaking of love in their presence (41), Madame de Chartres predicates her education upon a lucid portrayal and appraisal of human weaknesses. She therefore speaks freely of dissimulation and of the false nature of appearances—"ce qui paraît n'est presque jamais la vérité" (56)—of both the charms and dangers of love, of the infidelity of men, and the unhappiness that love affairs bring to married women. Virtue can only be maintained, she tells her daughter, "par une extrême défiance de soi-même" (41) and fidelity to one's husband.

The virtuous life is the happy life and for a married woman happiness and virtue are found in loving her husband and being loved by him (41). This, of course, is the teaching of Saint François, as is the choice of marriage partner being left to the parents.[8] In this latter respect, Stirling Haig remarks, "Unfortunately, Mme de Chartres has no modern scruples about giving her daughter in marriage to a man for whom she only professes 'less repugnance than for another.'"[9] Marianne Hirsch is closer to the mark when she notes that "the marital 'amour' Mme de Chartres has in mind could naturally grow out of

7. Roger Francillon, *L'Oeuvre romanesque de Madame de La Fayette* (Paris: José Corti, 1973), 142; hereafter cited parenthetically in the text.

8. Saint François imposes "complete and unquestioned obedience on children toward their parents, including the choice of marriage partners" (Dubois, 56, 62n). On the general theme of obedience, see *L'Introduction à la vie dévote,* 161–63.

9. Stirling Haig, *Madame de Lafayette* (New York: Twayne, 1970), 114; hereafter cited parenthetically in the text.

the Princess's feelings of 'respect and gratitude.'"[10] The virtuous life has the additional reward of "tranquillité" (41), which is opposed throughout the novel, as it is in *L'Introduction à la vie dévote*, to the tumult and agitation of the passions.

In two negative readings of the novel, Martin Turnell and Claude Vigée maintain that virtue for Mme de Chartres "means little more than 'keeping up appearances.'"[11] This judgment, however, does not withstand a close reading of the novel. While it is true that she values her daughter's reputation, she nonetheless collapses the classical distinction between *fama* and *virtus,* seeing the former growing out of the latter. Even when she lies about her daughter's behavior, it is not solely or even essentially to keep up appearances, but rather to protect her from danger. In addition, her deathbed Salesian advice, to flee, would, as we shall see, in no way serve to "keep up appearances."

The educational views of Mme de Chartres are clearly in the Catholic tradition, as is her view of marriage. Alain Niderst writes that Mme de Chartres does not teach her daughter that "la vertu est récompensée par Dieu."[12] While it is true that we never hear her say this, we never hear her say the contrary; and not only is "virtue recompensed by God" in the Catholic tradition but, from the text itself, we can much more easily surmise that this is understood than that it is not. Mme de Chartres, "dont le bien, la vertu et le mérite étaient extraordinaires" (41) and who accepts her death "avec un courage digne de sa vertu et de sa piété" (67), speaks on her deathbed of "le bonheur qu' [elle] espère en sortant de ce monde" (68). Certainly we should see some rapport between that "vertu," that "piété," and that "bonheur." Once more, she spends her last two days alone "à se préparer à la mort" (68). As I hope to show repeatedly, religion is not so much absent from the text as it is understated and muted.

One of the essential components of the devout life is the necessity and role of the spiritual director. *L'Introduction à la vie dévote* is addressed to Philothée, the narratee who has the good fortune of having

10. Marianne Hirsch, "A Mother's Discourse: Incorporation and Repetition in *La Princesse de Clèves,*" *Yale French Studies* 62 (1981): 75.

11. Martin Turnell, *The Novel in France* (New York: Vintage, 1958), 39; Claude Vigée, "*La Princesse de Clèves* et la tradition du refus," *Critique* 159–60 (1960): 728.

12. Alain Niderst, *"La Princesse de Clèves" de Madame de Lafayette* (Paris: Nizet, 1977), 117.

the narrator as her spiritual director. "Voulez-vous à bon escient vous acheminer à la dévotion?" he asks rhetorically. "Cherchez quelque homme de bien qui vous guide et conduise; c'est ici l'avertissement des avertissements" (38). The chosen director must be "plein de charité, de science et de prudence: si l'une de ces trois parties lui manque, il y a du danger" (40). Humble souls on the road to devotion will immediately consult their spiritual directors in moments of anxiety so that their troubled hearts will combat the influence of anxiety and maintain the strength necessary to practice virtue and resist temptation (272). "Le grand remède contre toutes tentations grandes ou petites, c'est de déployer son coeur et de communiquer les suggestions, ressentiments et affections que nous avons à notre directeur" (266).

Mme de Chartres is much more than a pedagogue or a mother. After raising and educating her daughter, she functions as her spiritual director, urging her to confide in her and promising her guidance: "Elle la pria, non pas comme sa mère, mais comme son amie, de lui faire confidence de toutes les galanteries qu'on lui dirait, et elle lui promit de lui aider à se conduire dans des choses où l'on était souvent embarrassée quand on était jeune" (45). The princess heeds her advice and after dancing with Nemours at the ball, for example, returns home and "quoiqu'il fût fort tard, elle alla dans la chambre de sa mère pour lui en rendre compte" (54).

Initially far more perceptive and mature than her daughter, Mme de Chartres is able to ascertain her daughter's sentiments before she herself is aware of them. Sensing the danger inherent in her daughter's situation, she takes steps to keep her out of trouble and initiates conversations about Nemours in order to counsel her indirectly. When she falls ill, however, and lies on her deathbed, there is no longer time for circumspection—"je ne suis plus en état de me servir de votre sincérité pour vous *conduire*" (67; my italics), she tells her daughter. Her final spiritual direction is to warn the princess that she stands "sur le bord du précipice" and that "il faut de grands efforts et de grandes violences pour [la] retenir" (68). She advises her to think of what she owes herself and her husband and to flee the court.

After her mother's death, the princess feels particularly "malheureuse d'être abandonnée à elle-même" (68), that is to say, without the assistance of a spiritual director at a time when she is "si peu maîtresse de ses sentiments" (68). She states a definite need for her mother "pour se défendre contre M. de Nemours" (68). Now, aware of both her own weaknesses and the very real danger that Nemours presents, she turns to her husband who replaces her mother in the role of spiritual director. His tenderness toward her at the time of her mother's death makes her more conscious of her duty and she, in turn, shows more friendship and tenderness toward him than she had previously displayed. In this respect, later in the novel, a remark of Mme la Dauphine highlights the unusual closeness of their relationship: "il n'y a que vous de femme au monde qui fasse confidence à son mari de toutes les choses qu'elle sait" (116). His role is still one of direction and protection: "elle ne voulait point qu'il la quittât, et il lui semblait qu'à force de s'attacher à lui, il la défendrait contre M. de Nemours" (69).

One of the great ironies of the novel is that the deepest moment of confidence between them, *l'aveu*, triggers a series of events that ultimately are responsible for the death of M. de Clèves. Despite the extraordinary nature of *l'aveu*, or precisely because of it, it is well prepared in the text. The reader recalls that on her deathbed Mme de Chartres tells her daughter not to fear to undertake "des partis trop rudes et trop difficiles, quelques affreux qu'ils vous paraissent d'abord" (68) and that M. de Clèves tells his wife during his narration of the story of Sancerre, Estouteville, and Mme de Tournon, "Je crois que si ma maîtresse, et même ma femme, m'avouait que quelqu'un lui plût, j'en serais affligé sans en être aigri. Je quitterais le personnage d'amant ou de mari, pour la conseiller et pour la plaindre" (76). In addition, the husband's new role of spiritual director would suggest this possibility and, in fact, the princess had thought of doing so earlier but discarded the idea (93).

Like all confessions, *l'aveu* is a plea for help. This secular one resembles the sacrament of penance in that it is made on one's knees and, as Francillon has pointed out (167), the "sin" is confessed but the partner's name is not revealed. And, of course, it is made to the person who, at that time in the novel, serves as the confessor's spiritual director. "Conduisez-moi," she begs at the time of *l'aveu*, "ayez pitié de moi et aimez-moi encore, si vous pouvez" (122). Later too she still asks him for direction: "réglez ma conduite, faites que je ne voie personne" (127), and he offers it in words that echo her mother's deathbed advice: "Je vois le péril où vous êtes; ayez du pouvoir sur vous pour l'amour de vous-même et, s'il est possible, pour l'amour de moi" (129–30).

Despite its courageous, even heroic nature, *l'aveu* results in a disaster. "Vous avez attendu de moi," M. de Clèves tells his wife, "des choses aussi impossibles que celles que j'attendais de vous. Comment pouviez-vous espérer que je conservasse de la raison" (151). From the Salesian point of view, M. de Clèves lacks the prudence required of all spiritual directors. He is the one who wants to "keep up appearances" and, as a result, he will not let his wife flee to the country either before or after *l'aveu*.

One of the more modern aspects of *La Princesse de Clèves*, one that links it to *le nouveau roman*, is that it is at times self-reflexive and its characters discuss questions theoretically that are germane to the plot in which they are involved. Hence the question of *l'aveu* is discussed in the novel itself. From our perspective the question discussed might well have been: "Can a husband serve as the spiritual director of his wife, when he is madly in love with her and she is in love with another man?" When one considers that the novel also foreshadows another modern novel, namely Proust's *A la recherche du temps perdue*, in its portrayal of the torments and ravages of jealousy, the answer can only be a resounding "No."

In addition to the princess's Christian education and her recourse to spiritual direction, the novel also contains other specifically Salesian practices for warding off temptation. The key for Saint François de Sales, and again this is founded upon human weakness, is to avoid rather than confront temptation. In the chapter entitled "Avis pour conserver la chasteté," he writes that "ce mal [la lubricité] agit insensiblement, et par des petits commencements fait progrès à des grands accidents" (167), adding that "il est toujours plus aisé à fuir qu'à guérir" (167).

When Saint François speaks about flight, he means, when possible, a real "changement de lieu" (190), for he believes in the wisdom of abandoning a place of temptation for extended periods of time—"Le changement de lieu sert extrêmement pour apaiser les ardeurs et inquiétudes, soit de la douleur soit de l'amour" (190). Absence makes the heart grow fonder in the Salesian scheme of things, but fonder only of God if the sinner flees Egypt without the hesitations of Lot's wife fleeing Sodom. Otherwise absence makes the heart grow faster on an aborted journey—"Ah, vous avez donc de la farine d'Egypte, vous n'aurez donc point de la manne du ciel" (284).

We will recall, of course, that the advice to flee the court is precisely the advice that Mme de Chartres offers from her deathbed. Nothing could be more Salesian than this counsel given to the princess by her first "spiritual director": "Retirez-vous de la cour, obligez votre mari de vous emmener" (68). Nothing is more obvious in the novel, despite the princess's weaknesses and love for Nemours, than her desire and attempts, as it were, to get out of Egypt. She sees the court as the locus of tumult and agitation and aspires to the solitude, safety, and "repos" of the country. Exposed to temptation at the court and ultimately aware that flight alone will enable her to resist that temptation, she repeatedly tries to persuade her husband to allow her to spend more time at Coulommiers (86, 119, 148).

M. de Clèves, however, resists his wife's attempts to flee both before and after *l'aveu*. Because of *his* desire to "keep up appearances" and his observance of *les bienséances,* he consistently talks her back into society—"Il est temps que vous voyiez le monde" (80); "le repos . . . n'est guère propre pour une personne de votre âge" (121). Just before *l'aveu,* she begs her husband to let her stay in the country (121) but he will not permit her to do so without a satisfactory explanation. It can be argued, therefore, that *l'aveu* takes place only because M. de Clèves will not consent to her retreat. This would disculpate the princess from the charge of having sacrificed her husband's "repos" in order to ensure her own. It is doubly ironic that the only time he permits her to leave for Coulommiers, a series of events takes place that leads him to believe that she has committed adultery. As a result of this belief, he falls ill and dies.

Inasmuch as M. de Clèves will not let the "changement de lieu" become a reality, the princess is forced to live at court. Here too, when possible, flight is still important. It is always better to flee temptation, Saint François would argue, than to confront it, even if flight simply means leaving the room until the seducer himself departs. The princess has already made up her mind to "éviter la présence de ce prince" and not to enter "dans les lieux où il la pouvait voir" (85). In addition, she has resolved to leave her husband's room whenever Nemours is present. But once again M. de Clèves objects—"il ne voulait pas absolument qu'elle changeât de conduite" (86). Nemours deciphers these signs perfectly: "Ce prince vit bien qu'elle le fuyait et en fut sensiblement touché" (86). In other words, the more she does to avoid temptation, the more the tempter knows she is susceptible to temptation.

The princess never initiates a meeting with Nemours and has recourse to Salesian and more generally Jesuit principles to prevent his success in arranging a rendezvous with her. In his chapter entitled "Quelques autres avis touchant le parler," Saint François writes: "Bien que quelquefois on puisse discrètement et prudemment déguiser et couvrir la vérité par quelque artifice de parole, si ne faut-il pas pratiquer cela sinon en chose d'importance, quand la gloire et service de Dieu le requièrent manifestement" (218). This "directing the intention" which sets up a lawful object (the avoidance of temptation) as the purpose of a dubious action (lying) is a recurring strategy of Mme de Clèves—"[elle] prit le parti de feindre d'être malade" (143); "Elle envoya une de ses femmes à M. de Nemours . . . pour lui dire qu'elle venait de se trouver mal" (149). In addition, she invents a stratagem at Coulommiers "pour éviter que M. de Nemours ne demeurât seul avec elle" (159). As a result, she can, in good conscience, tell her husband on his deathbed, "Je n'ai jamais passé ni de nuits ni de moments avec M. de Nemours. Il ne m'a jamais vue en particulier" (163).

The princess is not, however, always able to flee or to control the situation in such a way as to avoid the presence of Nemours. Oddly enough, it is often due to her husband's demands that societal obligations be met (128) that she is confronted by him (113). Consequently, she is reduced to waging several difficult battles and, in order to win them, employs other Salesian methods of avoiding temptation and sin. "N'écoutez nulle sorte de propositions, sous quel prétexte que ce soit," advises Saint François, because "le coeur et les oreilles s'entretiennent l'un à l'autre, et comme il est impossible d'empêcher un torrent qui a pris sa descente par le pendant d'une montagne, aussi est-il difficile d'empêcher que l'amour qui est tombé en l'oreille ne fasse soudain sa chute dans le coeur" (189). Mme de Clèves complies: "[elle] ne fit pas semblant d'entendre M. de Nemours" (135); "Elle demeurait donc sans répondre" (85). She succeeds so well in silencing his advances that he himself makes an allusion to her about his strategy of indirection: "Il y a des personnes à qui on n'ose donner d'autres marques de la passion qu'on a pour elles que par les choses qui ne les regardent point" (84). She is once again justified in telling her dying husband, "Je ne l'ai jamais souffert, ni écouté" (163).

"Mais qui ne peut s'éloigner que doit-il faire?" asks Saint François. "Il faut absolument retrancher toute conversation particulière, tout entretien secret, toute douceur des yeux, tout souris, et généralement toutes sortes de communications et amorces qui peuvent nourrir ce feu" (190), he affirms. In this respect, the princess acts as if she were consciously and conscientiously following the precepts of Saint François. No longer able to deceive herself into hoping she was not in love with Nemours, "elle songea seulement à ne lui en donner jamais aucune marque" (85). When in his presence, "elle évitait . . . [ses] yeux" (128) or "le quitta sans le regarder" (135). But the more she tries to "éviter ses regards" (88) and to "lui parler moins qu'à un autre" (88), the more he realizes that she is not indifferent to him. It is not only interesting that so many passages of *La Princesse de Clèves* recall the "sous-conversations" in the novels of Nathalie Sarraute but that so many passages of *L'Introduction à la vie dévote* do also.

In short, from the moment she sees Nemours for the first time until the death of her husband, the life of the princess is one long struggle to avoid temptation. Constantly troubled by "une passion violente et inquiète" (52), full of "impatience et . . . trouble" (97), suffering a "douleur insupportable" (97) and "la jalousie avec toutes les horreurs dont elle peut être accompagnée" (99), experiencing despair, torture and misery, she attempts to flee one man while another will not allow her to do so. Her situation has been aptly described as "la situation de bête traquée" (Francillon, 163). Throughout her agony, nonetheless, her desire to be virtuous enables her to seek spiritual guidance, flee temptation, avoid the occasions of sin, and repel Nemours's advances.

She does not always succeed, however, in ridding her mind of Nemours, or even in suppressing indulgence in the pleasant thoughts of her love. When her mother lies so that Nemours will not think that he has influenced Mme de Clèves's decision not to attend the Maréchal de Saint-André's ball, the princess "sentit quelque espèce de chagrin que sa mère lui en eût entièrement ôté l'opinion" (64). Also, when Nemours takes her portrait, "elle fut bien aise de lui accorder une

faveur qu'elle lui pouvait faire sans qu'il sût même qu'elle la lui faisait" (92). In rewriting the letter with M. de Nemours, although her
husband was also present, "elle ne sentait que le plaisir de voir M. de
Nemours, elle en avait une joie pure et sans mélange qu'elle n'avait
jamais sentie" (117). Her ambivalent feelings make her proclaim at a
moment of deep anguish, "Je suis vaincue et surmontée par une inclination qui m'entraîne malgré moi. Toutes mes résolutions sont inutiles; je pensai hier tout ce que je pense aujourd'hui et je fais
aujourd'hui tout le contraire de ce que je résolus hier" (119). Finally,
in the famous scene charged with erotic symbolism in which the princess lies on a daybed wrapping ribbons around the duke's "canne des
Indes" (115), there can be no doubt that we have found her in a moment of solitary pleasure, "in a daydream of fetichistic sublimation."[13]
In more Salesian parlance, having made her exodus to Coulommiers,
the princess has been caught gorging herself on "la farine d'Egypte"
with little apparent concern for "la manne du ciel."

Saint François makes it clear that sins against chastity can be committed in the heart and mind as well as in the flesh. "La chasteté
dépend du coeur comme de son origine," he writes, "mais elle regarde
le corps comme sa matière; c'est pourquoi elle se perd par tous les
sens extérieurs du corps, et par les cogitations et désirs du coeur"
(168). And, of course, outside of marriage, "il n'est pas permis seulement d'y penser, d'une pensée voluptueuse volontaire et entretenue"
(164).

The princess, however, inhabits a world where, although human
acts remain free, human desires are determined. The Vidame de
Chartres notes, for example, that "l'on n'est pas amoureux par sa volonté" (109), and the narrator remarks toward the end of the novel
that Mme de Clèves "se faisait un crime de n'avoir pas eu de la passion
pour [son mari], comme si c'eût été une chose qui eût été en son
pouvoir" (165). Her task then is superhuman: not only to avoid committing adultery, but to suppress desirable and involuntary thoughts
about Nemours. Saint François recognizes that the latter task is for-
midable:

13. Nancy K. Miller, "Emphasis Added: Plots and Plausibilities in Women's Fiction,"
chap. 1 above, 29–30; hereafter cited parenthetically in the text. See too Michel Butor's
analysis of this scene in *Répertoire I* (Paris: Editions de Minuit, 1960), 74–78.

C'est chose bien aisée à un homme ou à une femme de s'empêcher de l'adultère, mais ce n'est pas chose si facile de s'empêcher des oeillades de donner ou recevoir de l'amour, de procurer des grâces et menues faveurs, de dire et recevoir des paroles de cajolerie. Il est bien aisé de ne point donner de corrival au mari ni de corrivale à la femme, quant au corps, mais il n'est pas si aisé de n'en point donner quant au coeur; bien aisé de ne point souiller le lit du mariage, mais bien malaisé de ne point intéresser l'amour du mariage. (267–68)

The princess never uses the word "sin," nor does anyone else in the novel. However, her repulsion for adultery and her insistence on her innocence of both sins of thought and deed could not be more manifest. "Moi, des crimes!" she cries out to her husband who, on his deathbed, has accused her of adultery, "la pensée même m'en est inconnue . . . je n'ai jamais fait d'action dont je n'eusse souhaité que vous eussiez été témoin" (162–63).

Saint François is a gentle, patient, compassionate, and loving taskmaster who insists only that human beings persist in the struggle to be virtuous and devout. "Faites profession ouverte de vouloir être dévote; je ne dis pas d'être dévote, mais je dis de le vouloir être" (316). And do not be surprised if you fall, he counsels, "puisque ce n'est pas chose admirable que l'infirmité soit infirme, et la faiblesse faible, et la misère chétive" (158). All one can do is to struggle against temptations, some of which last a lifetime (258). No matter what temptations come our way, "quelque délectation qui s'ensuive" (262), as long as the will remains steadfast and refuses consent both to the temptation and the pleasure, one is free of sin and God is not offended (262). No reader of *La Princesse de Clèves* would negate the persistent, if not heroic, struggle of the princess and, as Saint François reminds us, "C'est une heureuse condition pour nous en cette guerre, que nous soyons toujours vainqueurs pourvu que nous voulions combattre" (42).

Perhaps the major reason why critics have not written about Saint François de Sales or *L'Introduction à la vie dévote* in relation to *La Princesse de Clèves* is that we are never told, nor can we assume, that the princess ever practices, before her entrance into the convent at the end of the novel, any of the purely religious methods of devotion. Daily prayer, fasting, the sacraments of Holy Eucharist and penance, and the reading of the Scripture, all required by Saint François, are never mentioned in the novel. For this reason, perhaps, critics have not seen the network of devotional practices inscribed in the very fabric of the text.

But what about those critics who seem to delight in extinguishing any spark of religion in *La Princesse de Clèves?* There seems to have been a veritable campaign, ever since Auguste Comte, to negate the presence of God in Mme de Lafayette's masterpiece. "Ce qui m'a toujours frappé en lisant cette oeuvre éminente de l'esprit féminin, c'est l'absence complète de toute considération surnaturelle; le nom de Dieu n'y est pas même prononcé," writes Pierre Laffitte. Le Comte d' Haussonville concurs: "Le nom de Dieu . . . ne se trouve pas une seule fois dans toute l'oeuvre de Mme de La Fayette."[14] A modern critic too notes that "God plays no role in any of her works" (Haig, 53). If he means that God is not a protagonist, then, of course, we will have to agree, but in *La Princesse de Clèves,* in addition to other points that might be cited, the heroine is given an education in the Christian tradition and ultimately, thinking only of the things of "l'autre vie" (180), enters a convent, while her mother, although she does not speak about God, spends a good deal of time preparing to meet him. Given these facts, it would be difficult to maintain that God, absent from Mme de Lafayette's novels only in the sense that he is absent from his own works, plays no role here. It has been argued, and very well, by Helen Karen Kaps, that the absence of overt references to a Christian God or to a Christian doctrine shows perhaps above all Mme de Lafayette's "compliance with a code of propriety which excluded from fiction matters unsuitable by their extreme dignity as well as those unsuitable by their lack of it."[15] Moreover, we would add that the God of the novel, like his counterpart in the real world, if not present on the stage, is off somewhere in the wings, the *deus absconditus* of Mme de Lafayette's Augustinian friends of Port Royal.

Recalling Pascal, one might say that I wouldn't be looking for God, if I hadn't already found him; but found him I have in Mme de Lafayette's novel. In the final analysis, those critics are right to claim

14. Maurice Laugaa, *Lectures de Mme de Lafayette* (Paris: Armand Colin, 1971), 197, 188–203. Le Comte d'Haussonville, *Mme de La Fayette* (Paris: Hachette, 1891), 208.

15. Helen Karen Kaps, *Moral Perspective in "La Princesse de Clèves"* (Eugene: University of Oregon Press, 1968), 25.

that the name of God is not pronounced once in *La Princesse de Clèves,*
but only because it is pronounced at least twice. At two different
moments of excessive "tumulte" and "agitation" in the space of sev-
enty lines of the text, Mme de Clèves twice uses the name of God,
once when speaking to her husband and once to Nemours. First, when
pleading that her husband let her flee, if only to the solitude of her
room, she says, "Au nom de Dieu . . . trouvez bon que, sur le prétexte
de quelque maladie, je ne voie personne" (128). Then, when Nemours
begins to speak with her, the narrator notes, "Au nom de Dieu, lui
dit-elle, laissez-moi en repos" (129). To consider these expressions as
meaningless slips of the tongue or banalities without significance
would be to miss their importance as, if not proofs of the religious
spirit of the heroine, at least indicators or omens that prefigure the
religious ending of the novel. They also very neatly imply the ultimate
importance of solitude and "repos" in the novel.

I hope to have shown that the princess is imbued with the Christian
spirit throughout the novel and that, at the very least, her behavior
before the death of her husband depicts a secular rendition of Saint
François's *Introduction à la vie dévote.* Let us turn now to the final pages
of the novel, after the death of M. de Clèves, at a moment when the
relationship between the princess and Nemours no longer contains any
theological impediments, for I will not invoke, metaphorically, the
law that prohibited a woman from marrying her husband's mur-
derer.[16] The reader can then judge whether indeed the ending trans-
figures the events in which it was immanent.

After the death of her husband, the princess is in a state of severe
depression, full of guilt for not having loved him and loathing for
herself and Nemours. Her sole consolation is in her resolve to spend
the rest of her life as her husband would have wished had he still been
alive. When, several months later, she sees Nemours by chance in a
garden outside Paris, her sleeping passion has a violent reawakening
and shortly thereafter she is tricked by the Vidame de Chartres into
a meeting with Nemours where they finally speak to one another about
their passion. Despite her love for the duke, the princess persists in
her resolve not to marry him. The idea of "devoir," despite the at-

16. For opposing views, see Francillon, 170, and Kaps, 21.

tempts of critics to negate it, whether a phantom of the imagination or not,[17] always remains important,[18] as does her need for "repos," which would be severely violated by the nonpermanent nature of men's passion. The princess speaks of the certainty of no longer being loved by Nemours (173) and her inevitable subjection to the horrors and torments of jealousy. "Devoir" and "repos" combine to form the diptych of resistance: "Ce que je crois devoir à la mémoire de M. de Clèves serait faible s'il n'était soutenu par l'intérêt de mon repos; et les raisons de mon repos ont besoin d'être soutenues de celles de mon devoir" (175). Further protests from Nemours lead her to say, "Attendez ce que le temps pourra faire" (175); while this appears at the time merely an artifice to break off a conversation "qui [lui] fait honte" (176), as her "Adieu" (175) would indicate, later on, alone, she is still undecided: "la bienséance lui donnait un temps considérable à se déterminer" (177).

Finally, having judged that her reasons for not marrying Nemours are "fortes du côté de son devoir et insurmontables du côté de son repos" (178) and realizing that it would nonetheless be impossible to resist him face to face, she decides on the necessity of "absence" and "éloignement" (178) and flees to her estate in the Pyrenees. There she falls gravely ill and remains close to death for some time. This long illness and her reflections on the inevitability of death help her to attain the habit of distance and detachment from the things of this world. When she recovers, Nemours is still present in her heart but, despite her earlier statement to him—"les sentiments que j'ai pour vous seront éternels et . . . ils subsisteront également, quoi que je fasse" (175)—she finally succeeds in smothering the remains of her passion—"Il se passa un assez grand combat en elle-même. Enfin, elle surmonta les restes de cette passion qui était affaiblie par les sentiments que sa maladie lui avait donnés" (179). Having attained a higher and more detached vision (179) and determined not to return "dans les lieux où était ce qu'elle *avait* aimé" (179; my italics), she retires to a convent without giving a hint of any fixed intention of leaving the court. When Nemours tries to see her, he is told by another

17. "Where else would one expect to find a reproachful phantom?" asks Francis Lawrence in "*La Princesse de Clèves* Reconsidered," *French Review* 39 (1965): 20.

18. See 168, 171, 172, 175, 177, 178, 179, and 180, the final page of the novel.

that the princess has renounced the things of this world forever and only thinks of "l'autre vie" (180). The final paragraph of the novel relates the destiny of the two lovers. There we learn that Nemours's passion, "la plus violente, la plus naturelle et la mieux fondée qui ait jamais été" (180), finally dies away after several years, and that the princess "passait une partie de l'année dans cette maison religieuse et l'autre chez elle; mais dans une retraite et dans des occupations plus saintes que celles des couvents les plus austères; et sa vie, qui fut assez courte, laissa des exemples de vertu inimitables" (180).

Many readings of *La Princesse de Clèves* insist that the heroine's final decision is founded upon egoism.[19] What seems more applicable to the novel, however, is the theological distinction made by Marie-Odile Sweetser between "*amour propre*: faiblesse de la nature déchue et *amour de soi*: instinct moral mis en l'homme par Dieu pour lui permettre en connaissant sa propre valeur de s'élever."[20] It is this justifiable self-love predicated upon the notion of self-dignity and spirituality that motivates the princess's final decisions. Verisimilitude demanded and Mme de Lafayette very artfully succeeded in making both Nemours and M. de Clèves worthy of the heroine. However, despite the virtues of Nemours and his uncommon fidelity, the best case for egoism among the major characters can be made against him. He remains in large measure a Don Juan figure who commits numerous indiscretions that would have been unworthy of the lover in earlier literature. He tells the story of *l'aveu*, albeit with fictitious names, and when the princess has suspicions that her husband must have revealed her confession, Nemours "fut bien aise de les lui confirmer" (134). At a moment when the princess is suffering extreme anguish after *l'aveu*, we learn that Nemours "sentit pourtant un plaisir sensible de l'avoir réduite à cette extrémité" (126). Finally, at the end of the novel, he never uses "notre" to describe the happy union that he supposedly

19. These readings go from a simple La Rochefoucauldian connection made by Haig (82) to the scathing attack by Vigée (739–41). For opposing views, see Niderst (126) and Francillon, who stresses the providential character of the princess's illness and claims that it is the presence of divine transcendence in the final pages of the novel that saves the princess from the charges of "orgueil démesuré . . . égomanie monstrueuse ou . . . machiavélisme du coeur" (180).

20. Marie-Odile Sweetser, "*La Princesse de Clèves* devant la critique contemporaine," *Studi francesi* 52 (1974): 28.

wants between them—"Quel fantôme de devoir opposez-vous à *mon* bonheur. . . . Vous seule vous opposez à *mon* bonheur" (172, 175; my italics).

Another form of the egoism critique of the princess is sometimes linked to the widely held view that Mme de Clèves rejects Nemours in order to preserve her passion in its idealized state. In this respect, Harriet Allentuch writes, "Le trait de caractère fondamental de la princesse est l'égoïsme, le désir de posséder l'être aimé de façon permanente,"[21] while Sylvère Lotringer notes that "la princesse ne quittera pas la cour pour fuir la Passion, mais pour la conserver."[22] Nancy Miller's comments are more interesting and more challenging. "[The princess's] retreat to Coulommiers," she claims, "must be thought of not as a flight from sexuality but as a movement *into* it." This statement cannot, in my view, be refuted for the scene where we found her in solitary pleasure, but to see her final flight in the same light—"to preserve [desire] in and as fantasy,"[23] is to negate the final two pages of the novel. I have shown that after a great inner struggle the princess succeeds in conquering her passion for Nemours. She does not, finally, retreat to preserve her passion in any state but to destroy it. Ultimately, then, she rejects both the flesh-and-blood duke and the duke of the portrait upon whom she had gazed one night at Coulommiers. To imagine her fondling the duke's cane in the convent at a time when she is no longer interested in anything but "l'autre vie" is to miss the heroine's evolution.

The princess's desire to destroy rather than preserve her passion and her success in doing so should enable us to see the limits of the courtly

---

21. Harriet Allentuch, "Pauline and the Princesse de Clèves," *Modern Language Quarterly* 30 (1969): 175.

22. Sylvère Lotringer, "La Structuration romanesque," *Critique* 26 (1970): 517. See too Vigée, 731, and Hirsch, 83.

23. Miller, 43. Miller's article is perceptive and innovative. Her approach deals in the main with the female condition and, although the present study has a different focus, we converge on many issues, particularly in our defense of the princess and her authenticity. Miller's article and Michael Danahy's clearly depict the inadequacies of many of the deeply entrenched traditional interpretations. See Michael Danahy, "Social, Sexual and Human Spaces in *La Princesse de Clèves*," *French Forum* 6 (1981): 212–24, and A. Kibedi Varga, "Romans d'amour, romans de femmes, à l'époque classique," *Revue des sciences humaines* 168 (1977): 517–24.

readings of the text which form yet another critical stance that insists upon the permanence of passion in *La Princesse de Clèves*. "Ce n'est pas l'intérêt de son repos qui guide Mme de Clèves," writes Hipp, "ni la crainte devant la vie, mais bien plutôt cette recherche à la fois inconsciente et délibérée de l'obstacle, fondement de la conception occidentale de l'amour."[24] The novel, however, certainly has a more encompassing negative purview than is understood in the traditional love/marriage distinction[25] and, although Mme de Clèves tells Nemours that "les obstacles ont fait votre constance" (173), those obstacles fail to keep the love of either of them alive eternally. Despite the involuntary nature of the love of the princess and the duke, they are not for that Tristram and Isolde; the novel rejects rather than idealizes the notion of courtly love.

The princess has also been severely criticized for not being able to assert herself, for choosing the values of others, and for being a marionette of her mother. In this light, her final decision is seen to lack authenticity. Doubrovsky, who clarifies definitively the very real differences between *La Princesse de Clèves* and the theater of Corneille and Racine, rejecting the idea that the conflict in the novel is between its Racinian passion and its Cornelian characters, goes on to speak about "la mauvaise foi" of the heroine and to conclude that "le fond du problème, c'est un choix de valeurs, un choix déchirant entre les valeurs délibérément choisies d'un code aristocratique et les valeurs spontanément élues de la passion."[26] But this is a false dichotomy, or none at all, not only because the princess rejects them both, but because they are one and the same. Far more insightfully, Mme de La-

24. Marie-Thérèse Hipp, "Le Mythe de Tristan et Iseut et *La Princesse de Clèves*," *Revue d'histoire littéraire de la France* 65 (1965): 414. For the opposite view, "a debunking of the Tristan myth," see Lawrence, 21.

25. "Décrire le conflit nécessaire de la passion et du mariage en Occident, tel était mon dessein central" (Denis de Rougemont, *L'Amour et l'Occident* [Paris: Plon, 1939], 10).

26. Serge Doubrovsky, *"La Princesse de Clèves*: Une Interprétation existentielle," *Table ronde* 138 (1959): 42, 46. Kreiter too points to the "bad faith" of the princess: "Il est évident que cette retraite n'est pas de caractère religieux, mais plutôt une pratique purement formelle, improvisée comme un ultime moyen de sauvegarder son paraître" (Janine Kreiter, *Le Problème du paraître dans l'oeuvre de Mme de Lafayette* [Paris: Nizet, 1977], 183n.).

fayette depicts a princess who creates values of her own, unknown to the aristocrats in the novel who themselves choose "les valeurs spontanément élues de la passion."

Nowhere in the novel are the values ultimately chosen by Mme de Clèves shown to be those of the aristocracy. Nowhere are they seen as the prefabricated values of the aristocrats who populate Mme de Lafayette's universe. It would be impossible to substantiate the claim made by Jean Fabre that the princess's decision represents the triumph of "la bienséance,"[27] because Mme de Clèves rejects the social values of the world in which she lives, where ambition and gallantry are the soul of the court and where her desire for "repos" is met with her husband's riposte: "Le repos . . . n'est guère propre pour une personne de votre âge" (121). After the death of her husband, she speaks openly of her love for Nemours, for as she notes: "je le puis faire sans crime" (171). Yet she rejects that love despite the fact that it would not offend "la bienséance"—"je sais que vous êtes libre, que je le suis, et que les choses sont d'une sorte que le public n'aurait peut-être pas sujet de vous blâmer, ni moi non plus, quand nous nous engagerions ensemble pour jamais" (173).

The argument has been made, of course, that it is her mother she follows. "The mother's lesson is at the center of a nexus of scenes," writes Marianne Hirsch, "that reflect and echo one another, trapping the heroine in a structure of repetitions which ultimately preclude development and progression" (73). For Hirsch, the princess "exists only in relation to her mother's advice and admonitions" (78). Yet it must be noted that nothing her mother stood for would stand in the way of her marriage with Nemours. The duke tells her, "Vous seule vous imposez une loi que la vertu et la raison ne vous sauraient imposer" (175), and the narrator adds later that what she continues to resist is "une chose qui ne choquait ni la vertu, ni la bienséance" (178). Neither virtue nor decency would be offended by this marriage, nor would her mother's dictum that "le bonheur d'une femme . . . est d'aimer son mari et d'en être aimée" (41). And, it should be recalled, her mother's advice to flee the court was given at a time when M. de Clèves was still alive. The definitive stance of the princess, her

27. Jean Fabre, "Bienséance et sentiment chez Madame de Lafayette," *Cahiers de l'Association internationale des études françaises* 11 (1959): 54–55.

retreat and semiretirement to a convent, nowhere suggested by her mother, clearly show her development. This is a carefully crafted bildungsroman wherein the heroine, because of her own experience in relation to the teachings of her mentors, chooses a new way of life unparalleled in the novel, as the last word of the text, "inimitables," would suggest.

It will come as no surprise that my reading of the conclusion stresses its Salesian and Pascalian elements. Although the princess never takes the vow recommended for widows by Saint François and Saint Augustine, her life after the death of M. de Clèves depicts the "résolution inviolable de se conserver en l'état d'une chaste viduité" (244) recommended by the author of *L'Introduction à la vie dévote*. Once more, her saintly occupations, her rejection of worldly comforts, and her works of inimitable virtue manifest her desire to "contourner toutes ses affections en Dieu, et joindre de toutes parts son coeur avec celui de sa divine Majesté" (245).

In the preface to *L'Introduction à la vie dévote*, Saint François stresses the originality of his treatise:

Ceux qui ont traité de la dévotion ont presque tous regardé l'instruction des personnes fort retirées du commerce du monde, ou au moins ont enseigné une sorte de dévotion qui conduit à cette entière retraite. Mon intention est d'instruire ceux qui vivent ès villes, ès ménages, en la cour, et qui par leur condition sont obligés de faire une vie commune quant à l'extérieur; lesquels bien souvent, sous le prétexte d'une prétendue impossibilité, ne veulent seulement pas penser à l'entreprise de la vie dévote. (23–24)

At the end of the novel, the princess, while still in the world a part of the year, spends the other part in a convent. This should not be read as a failure of the Salesian method of devotion in society but rather as its highest fulfillment. Saint François had warned his pupil, "jusques à ce que Dieu vous élève plus haut, je vous conseille, Philothée, de vous retenir en la basse vallée que je vous montre" (86). A more complete and elevated way of devotion, therefore, would always be a possibility. Once more, the princess's flight to the convent and re-entry into the world are perfectly Salesian. When describing the overview of the fifth part of *L'Introduction à la vie dévote*, Saint François writes: "je la [Philothée] fais un peu retirer à part soi pour se rafraîchir, reprendre haleine et réparer ses forces, afin qu'elle puisse par

après plus heureusement gagner pays et s'avancer en la vie dévote"
(25–26). Absence and distance are Salesian strategies that lead to detachment from the things of this world and to the higher vision depicted at the end of the novel. The final paragraph demonstrates
conclusively that Mme de Clèves is, as it were, finally out of Egypt,
whether she is in or out of the world.

The ideal of "repos" in the novel is also Salesian.[28] As we have
noted, Saint François too contrasts "repos" with the tumult and agitation of the world in general and temptation and pride in particular—"Allons, ô ma chère âme, allons en ce repos infini, cheminons
à cette bénite terre qui nous est promise; que faisons-nous en cette
Egypte?" (62)—and uses it with all the nuances found in La Princesse
de Clèves.[29] In the novel, we find a fourfold use of the term which, as
it metamorphoses from one meaning to the next, depicts the evolution
of the soul of the heroine. The novel begins with the princess in possession of a "repos de l'innocence,"[30] but this prelapsarian state is
shattered when she falls in love with Nemours. From this moment
until the death of her husband, there is no "repos," only tumult,
violence, and agitation. After the death of her husband and several
months of solitude, she uses the term "triste repos" (166) to refer to
her state, a term that evokes the earlier use of "faux repos" (162) by
her husband to refer to his state after his marriage but before l'aveu.
Once again this "repos" is broken when she learns that Nemours is

28. The term "repos" is found everywhere in the seventeenth century, in secular and
religious contexts, as an ideal expressed by Stoics, Epicureans, and Christians. See Domna
Stanton (77–104) for an exhaustive yet readable survey of the ideal of "repos" in the literature of the period. See too Simone Fraisse, "Le 'Repos' de Madame de Clèves," Esprit
29 (1961): 560–67. In a letter written by the Abbé de Rancé to Mme de Lafayette in
1686, eight years after the publication of La Princesse de Clèves, we find the following
passage: "Vous demandez, Madame, les motifs qui m'ont déterminé à quitter le monde.
Je vous diray simplement que je le laissay parce que je n'y trouvay pas ce que j'y cherchois.
J'y voulois un repos qu'il n'estoit point capable de me donner" (Mme de Lafayette, Correspondance, 2 vols., ed. André Beaunier [Paris: Gallimard, 1942], 2:141). Finally, for an
account of how Mme de Lafayette turned to religion at the end of her life, almost a decade
after publishing La Princesse de Clèves, see Janet Raitt, Madame de Lafayette and "La Princesse
de Clèves" (London: George G. Harrap, 1971), 55–56.

29. See 61–65, 173, 277–78.

30. The term is used by Jean Rousset, in Forme et signification (Paris: José Corti,
1962), 24.

on her trail and her sleeping passion awakens. There follows a new period of tumult and agitation which, after a new flight and more time, is finally overcome when the princess succeeds in smothering the remains of her passion. The new sense of "repos" which lasts until the end of the novel is that of "inner peace" but a fourth sense is present, although it can only be realized in the future, that is "repos" as "repose," the eternal repose to which she aspires. Although we move from "repos" to "repos," the form of the work is not circular.[31] Indeed, it has been the affirmation of the novel's circularity that has imprisoned critics in the belief in its ultimate claustrophobia.

The claustrophobia is found by critics who view the ending as negative and the princess as the prisoner of her mother's admonitions. They see her imprisoned in the past rather than looking out toward the future.[32] Although I cannot subscribe to Georges Poulet's view of the ending of the novel as "une sorte de fixité sans désir,"[33] no one has more convincingly shown that the discontinuity of passion is rejected in the novel in favor of the continuity of existence. But this need of duration on the part of the princess, expressed clearly sixty pages before the end of the novel (119), should have encouraged critics to look for signs of the future as well as backtrackings toward the past. Even a literal reading of the text renders Doubrovsky's statement incomprehensible: "S'il n'y a aucune transcendance vers un avenir humain, il n'y a pas davantage de transcendance vers le Divin" (50). While it would be absurd to negate the tremendous importance of the past in the mind of the princess, it is equally absurd to suppress the importance of the future at the end of the novel. The heroine assumes the burden of the past and escapes the so-called claustrophobia of her condition not only by works of virtue in the world but in a convent whose doors open vertically both in time and space into a future of duration and repose.

In addition to the Salesian aspects of the conclusion, and of course there is overlap here, there are also some specifically Pascalian elements, most notably the ascension of the princess to the order of "la charité." Obviously the notion of charity is important in the work of

31. For an original and penetrating interpretation that holds for the novel's circularity but at the same time for the ascension of the heroine, see Sweetser, 29.

32. See, for example, Martin Turnell, 47.

33. Georges Poulet, *Etudes sur le temps humain* (Paris: Plon, 1950), 176.

Saint François—"la dévotion est la douceur des douceurs et la reine des vertus, car c'est la perfection de la charité" (36)—but at the end of the novel *caritas* has definitively replaced *eros*. In the Pascalian scheme of things, it is impossible to ascend to the order of charity without grace but the princess has worked very hard and in very Pascalian ways—her repeated attempts to "plier la machine" and her success in diminishing and ultimately extinguishing her passion—to make herself ready for its arrival. What Poulet writes about the temporal nature of the order of charity constitutes time at the end of the novel: "Dans l'ordre de la charité, le futur prend une signification transcendante. Ce n'est plus le futur du temps, c'est le futur-éternité" (118).

From our perspective then, despite the affirmations of critics,[34] there is no death wish or suicide here on the part of the princess. The best case for suicide among the major characters can be made against M. de Clèves.[35] Nor is there a death of desire as such.[36] What there is at the end of the novel is the death of mimetic desire on the part of the princess. The mimetic nature of the court—which, in the Pascalian perspective, is the locus of *divertissement*—is everywhere apparent. Every male tries to ape Nemours but fails—"[il avait] une manière de s'habiller qui était toujours suivie de tout le monde, sans pouvoir être imitée" (37). In addition, "Toutes [les] différentes cabales avaient de l'émulation et de l'envie les unes contre les autres" (45). Many of the characters evince "une sorte d'émulation qui allait jusqu' à la haine" (58) and the pale and bloodless emulation of the Duc de Guise is almost Shakespearian. The mimetic nature and contagion of love is even discussed theoretically and Nemours, the glass of fashion, is quoted: "plus [sa maîtresse] est admirée du public, plus on se trouve

---

34. Among many others, see Stanton, 97; Doubrovsky, 48; Haig, 123, 133.

35. Mme de Lafayette succeeds admirably in making M. de Clèves, despite his faults, worthy of the princess. Her portrayal of a sympathetic and worthy husband is not her least achievement when compared with earlier "courtly" literature. Nonetheless, his last words contain more of a death wish than anything attributed to the princess: "Je mourrai . . . mais sachez que vous me rendez la mort agréable . . . Que ferais-je de la vie? . . . Je me sens si proche de la mort que je ne veux rien de ce qui me pourrait faire regretter la vie" (162–63).

36. As asserted in Poulet's "une sorte de fixité sans désir" (176) and Stanton's remark that "Mme de Clèves achieves *la mort des désirs*" (96).

malheureux de n'en être point aimé" (62). The princess who wanted to be so different from others and whose education was designed to accomplish that end discovers in the throes of jealousy that she is exactly like everyone else.[37] It is precisely this fear of the mimetic triangle that enters into her refusal at the end of the novel: "Je ne saurais vous avouer, sans honte, que la certitude de n'être plus aimée de vous, comme je le suis, me paraît un si horrible malheur que, quand je n'aurais point des raisons de devoir insurmontables, je doute si je pourrais me résoudre à m'exposer à ce malheur" (173). This awareness counts heavily in her rejection of Nemours and the court, for it is only by transcending mimesis that she will be able to assert her difference. It should be clear that the assertion of that difference is not a form of egoism predicated upon a belief in her inherent difference from others, but, on the contrary, a justifiable love of self founded upon Mme de Clèves's belief in her fundamental similarity with others. In the final analysis, the charge of egoism leveled at the princess can be refuted by an affirmation of her humility.

Thirteen pages before the end of the novel when, after the death of her husband, the princess tries to fight off the return of her passion for Nemours by thoughts of duty toward M. de Clèves, Mme de Lafayette writes a sentence that, at first blush, might appear troubling for my thesis: "Elle [la princesse] s'abandonna à ces réflexions si contraires à son bonheur" (167). The sentence, at this point in the text, can only refer to her terrestrial happiness and, by the end of the novel, her acquisition of a new "breadth and depth of vision" (179) renders its contents completely outmoded. I am nonetheless inclined to consider it a slip of the pen, for even at this moment in the novel the princess has already demonstrated both her belief that the passions of men, particularly those like Nemours (119), are not durable and her knowledge of the horrors that await the women who love them (99). Although not for the same reasons that she puts forth, I agree with Nancy Miller when she writes that "the princess refuses to marry the duke not because she does not want to live happily ever after but because she does" (30–31).

The "conversion" at the end of the novel—a new beginning that

37. See René Girard, *Deceit, Desire and the Novel,* trans. Yvonne Freccero (Baltimore: Johns Hopkins University Press, 1965), 172–75, 299, 311–12.

characterizes the bildungsroman—marks a different relationship between the self and the other. That relationship can be seen above all in her saintly occupations, examples of inimitable virtue, and exemplary works of charity, but also in her final words for Nemours: "elle ne pensait plus qu' [aux choses] de l'autre vie et il ne lui restait aucun sentiment que le désir de le [Nemours] voir dans les mêmes dispositions où elle était" (180). The "breadth and depth of vision" that she finally achieves, put respectively in Pascalian and Girardian terms, is a movement from *eros* to *caritas* and from mimesis to *imitatio Dei*. There is no death wish here but, out of Egypt, the princess is no longer of the world. This "death" to the world as she remains in it living a life of virtue contains the promise of new life, duration, and repose.

9 Declining Dangerous Liaisons

The Argument against Love

FRANCIS L. AND MARY K. LAWRENCE

I N THE spring of 1663 Mme de Lafayette and Jean Corbinelli, the secretary of Bussy-Rabutin, dashed off extemporaneous compositions in which they developed a "raisonnement contre l'amour."[1] According to her correspondence with Huet, this spontaneous exercise took place during an excursion to the country (probably at Livry) during which the two seated themselves "sur le bout d'une table" to write their rival opinions. Such disputations were common amusements of the *précieux* circles in which they moved. Mme de Lafayette appeared in the 1661 Somaize *Dictionnaire des Précieuses* as Féliciane and Corbinelli as Corbulon. Only sparse references to Mme de Lafayette's most successful published works can be found in her correspondence, but she devotes one entire letter and part of another to the circumstances surrounding the unauthorized circulation of her extempore composition.

In a letter of May 15, 1663, she expostulates at length with the learned Huet, her literary counselor. His pique over having been shown her argument against love by a young woman from La Trousse (Mlle de Mery) is, its author assures him, groundless. She rebukes Huet for his hasty conclusion that her failure to send the work to him was a deliberate slight and a display of her lack of confidence in him. The piece in question was intended, she insists, for the eyes of Corbinelli alone. Without the author's permission or knowledge, he not

---

1. Madame de Lafayette, *Correspondance*, 2 vols., ed. André Beaunier (Paris: Gallimard, 1942), 1:193; hereafter cited parenthetically in the text.

only showed it to the young woman but allowed her to copy and display it. Here and in her next letter of June 11, Mme de Lafayette professes her annoyance, culminating in a frank avowal of her sentiments upon learning of Corbinelli's indiscretion in circulating an offhand composition that she had meant to burn: ". . . j'ay esté en colère" (1:194). André Beaunier, the editor of Mme de Lafayette's *Correspondance*, triumphantly produces his transcription of a manuscript that he believes to have been a youthful work on the same subject. This anonymous text, which he proposes as an earlier version of the lost composition of 1663, was preserved in the library of Sainte-Geneviève as manuscript 3213 under the title *Le Triomphe de l'indifférence*. In his *La Jeunesse de Madame de La Fayette,* Beaunier dates *Le Triomphe* around 1653. As Bernard Pingaud points out in his edition of *La Princesse de Clèves,* this dating is hardly credible in view of the fact that the manuscript contains a somewhat garbled quotation from *Le Misanthrope* (I,ii).[2] Since Molière's play was first performed in June 1666, *Le Triomphe* must have been written later, not earlier, than the argument mentioned in Mme de Lafayette's correspondence, though the unsigned manuscript could certainly predate *La Princesse de Clèves.* Pingaud thinks enough of *Le Triomphe* to reproduce six pages of it at the front of his edition, with this apology:

Il peut sembler paradoxal d'ouvrir une édition des oeuvres de Mme de Lafayette par un texte dont l'attribution est très douteuse. Mais le même "brouillard" qui entoure la vie privée de la comtesse règne aussi sur ce qu'elle a écrit. . . . Les pages suivantes, extraites du *Triomphe de l'indifférence,* qu'elles aient ou non pour auteur Mme de Lafayette, nous paraissent la meilleure introduction à son oeuvre tout entière consacrée à l'apologie du "repos." (3)

Both the uncertainty and the fascinating parallel must be acknowledged. While it is indeed far from certain that the author of *La Princesse de Clèves* wrote *Le Triomphe de l'indifférence,* the points of comparison between the discursive argument and the novel deserve to be explored. As Beaunier shrewdly observes in his preface to the anonymous manuscript, it is impossible to deny the thematic link with Mme de Lafayette's work, since "tous ses livres sont, en quelque façon, des raisonnements contre l'amour: des raisonnements appuyés sur des

2. Madame de Lafayette, *La Princesse de Clèves,* ed. Bernard Pingaud (Paris: Club du Meilleur Livre, 1957), 3.

faits ou des remarques, enfin des opinions: l'amour y est peint de couleurs sombres."[3] Although bitter complaints against cruel or fickle mistresses are common in love poetry and misogynistic portrayals of lustful women are plentiful in comic literature, arguments against love using the inconstancy of men as their base are relatively rare. The anonymous disputation and Mme de Lafayette's novel resemble one another in their common point of departure, which is also their common conclusion. The very paragraph in which Mme de Lafayette introduces Mlle de Chartres, the soon-to-be Princesse de Clèves, contains this daunting portrait of love and the perfidy of men: "Madame de Chartres . . . faisait souvent à sa fille des peintures de l'amour; elle lui montrait ce qu'il a d'agréable pour la persuader plus aisément sur ce qu'elle lui en apprenait de dangereux; elle lui contait le peu de sincérité des hommes, leurs tromperies et leur infidélité."[4] Mlle de St-Ange, the young woman who prosecutes the case against love in Le Triomphe, has a similarly low opinion of male lovers: "il n'est rien de si inconstant que les hommes en matière d'amour, quoy qu'ils en veuillent dire. On a toujours remarqué qu'ils ont changé les premiers" (48).

It must be pointed out that in both the treatise and the novel the arguments against love are made by a woman (Mlle de St-Ange in one, Mme de Chartres in the other) to a woman (Mlle de Tremblaye in the treatise, Mlle de Chartres in the novel). This is more remarkable than it may seem at first glance. Most warnings of this nature in fiction or didactic literature are delivered by men: husbands, fathers, and wise or jealous male advisors or guardians like Arnolphe of Molière's L'Ecole des femmes. But the warnings from men, whether serious or comic in tone, exude pure self-interest: "Gardez-vous d'imiter ces coquettes vilaines / Dont par toute la ville on chante les fredaines. . . . / Songez qu'en vous faisant moitié de ma personne, / C'est mon honneur, Agnès, que je vous abandonne."[5] The common theme

3. André Beaunier, ed., Le Triomphe de l'indifférence, Mesures (15 October 1937):4. Limited printing by José Corti. Future references are to this edition and will be inserted parenthetically in the text.

4. Madame de Lafayette, La Princesse de Clèves, ed. Antoine Adam (Paris: Garnier-Flammarion, 1966), 41; hereafter cited parenthetically in the text.

5. Molière, L'Ecole des femmes, in Oeuvres complètes, 2 vols., ed. Maurice Rat (Paris: Gallimard, 1959), vol. 1, III, ii, 94; hereafter cited parenthetically in the text.

underlying warnings to women on the dangers of love is not the effect upon the emotions and well-being of women but the damage to the feelings and rights of men. In crass terms, as Arnolphe's servant Alain, explains, "La femme est, en effet, le potage de l'homme / Et quand un homme voit d'autres hommes parfois / Qui veulent dans sa soupe aller tremper leurs doigts, / Il en montre aussitôt une colère extrême" (II,iii). The possessive male view of love epitomized in the "Maximes du Mariage" does appear in *La Princesse de Clèves* but it is not advanced by that paragon of husbandly virtue the Prince de Clèves. It is the consummate roué who would keep his lover for himself alone: "M. de Nemours trouve . . . que le bal est ce qu'il y a de plus insupportable pour les amants . . . il n'y a point de femme que le soin de sa parure n'empêche de songer à son amant; . . . lorsqu'elles sont au bal, elles veulent plaire à tous ceux qui les regardent; . . . quand elles sont contentes de leur beauté, elles en ont une joie dont leur amant ne fait pas la plus grande partie" (62). In the same vein, Arnolphe's eighth maxim warns: "Ces sociétés déréglées / Qu'on nomme belles assemblées / . . . on les doit interdire" (III,ii). Masculine suspicions of the woman's self-adornment are based upon similar grounds: "les soins de paraître belles / Se prennent peu pour les maris" (III,ii, Maxime III).

In the relationship between the Prince and Princesse de Clèves, the direction of this dramatic tension is reversed. It is the woman who seeks solitude while the man repeatedly demands that she take a greater part in society: when she retreats to the country after her mother's death, her husband must press her to return to Paris; shortly afterward, when he falls ill and she declares her desire to lead a more secluded life, he absolutely forbids her to do so; following the episode of the Vidame de Chartres's letter, she must beg to be allowed to go to the country. In fact, it is Mme de Clèves's "goût pour la solitude" that prompts her husband to the close questioning of her motives, leading to her famous confession (121ff.). The confession is actually the result of the Prince de Clèves's insistent suspicion and demands that the princess reveal to him the reasons that prompt what he regards as her unnatural taste for solitude. Subsequently M. de Clèves must beg his wife to return to the court and command her absolutely to go to the great festivities held at the Louvre in advance of the marriage of Madame Elisabeth.

But the great and central resemblance between *La Princesse de Clèves* and *Le Triomphe de l'indifférence* is, as we have already implied, not in form or even in the unconventional female point of view: it is the underlying absolute indictment of love as an emotion by its very nature blind and contrary to reason, implacably cruel, inconstant without exception, and inevitably unhappy. In the polemical treatise, this argument is first presented in full by Mlle de St-Ange under the guise of a fable. The amount of time that Cupid spent on Earth aroused the anger and jealousy of the gods and particularly of Venus, his mother. Although Cupid pointed out that his activities made his mother known and loved throughout the world, Venus decided, after consulting Juno, that she ought to allow Cupid to return to Earth only if he would consent to going back with wings so that he might return rapidly, bandaged eyes to prevent him from falling in love with a mortal, and arrows forged not by Felicity but by Saturn, out of iron, with only a light coating of sweetness. When Cupid protested these harsh conditions, Venus retorted that it was necessary that he be equipped to come and go swiftly to appease the gods. They were justly angered by his preference for mortal creatures and by the threat of Felicity to follow him to Earth. His bandaged eyes would calm the anger and jealousy of mortals, who would henceforth be able to attribute his conduct to chance or destiny. The cruelty of the iron arrows, Venus explained, was the result of the jealousy of the gods, who said that humans are too imperfect and ungrateful to merit the same love destined for divinities. To console her shocked and unhappy son, Venus said that mortals would not cease to love him. They would complain about his evident disregard for merit, but the sweetness with which his arrows would be coated would still make them passionately desired.

The goddess finished by declaring that such is the destiny of humans who, being naturally blind, inconstant, and unhappy, could only produce love like themselves. A vivid description of the Earth under siege by blind Cupid with his poisoned arrows ended the fable with a reflection on those unhappy lovers who run with all their might after objects who flee them and who, if by chance they come at last into the possession of the object of their passion, abandon it almost as soon as they believe themselves loved.

The debate is very nearly ended at its outset in the wake of this somber fable. Mlle de St-Ange asks if there is a madness to equal that of loving what one will soon hate; of running like a crazy person after an object that, as soon as attained, one will abandon forever; and of adoring charms and perfections that one will despise as soon as one is able to taste their sweetness. She declares herself so convinced of the truth of this portrait of the inevitable course of love that she finds it impossible to love even when she wishes to. Her opponent, Mlle de La Tremblaye, is so affected by the fable, and especially by the inconstancy of love, that she admits, "Cela seul seroit capable de me faire renonser à l'amour" (21). The fatal blow already delivered, Mlle de St-Ange insists nevertheless on conducting the full argument: "Je pourois de ce seul coup . . . donner la mort à l'amour sans mesme me donner la peine de combatre plus lontemps, mais quoyque je sache l'endroit par où je puis le blesser mortellement je veu par générosité, et pour vous convaincre plainement, le combatre celon toutes les reigles de l'art" (21).

As noted earlier, it is precisely with the dangers and miseries of inconstancy that Mme de Chartres begins her own discussions on love to her daughter: "elle lui contait le peu de sincérité des hommes, leurs tromperies et leur infidélité, les malheurs domestiques où plongent les engagements" (41). Even the strategy of the mother's instructions strongly recalls that of Mlle de St-Ange. Mme de Chartres, unlike most mothers, does not keep her daughter in ignorance in order to protect her from the dangers of gallantry: "elle faisait souvent à sa fille des peintures de l'amour: elle lui montrait ce qu'il a d'agréable pour la persuader plus aisément sur ce qu'elle lui en apprenait de dangereux" (41). In the same vein, Mlle de St-Ange declares resolutely, "Il n'est pas un endroit avantageux par lequel je ne l'aye fait voir; je l'ay montré dans sa plus brillante lumière. Il est juste à presant que je le dévoille et qu'au lieu d'un amour écléré, doux, constant et heureux, je vous le fasse voir un amour aveugle, cruel, inconstant et malheureux. Je vous ay montré ce qu'il devroit estre, je m'an vais maintenant vous faire voir ce qu'il est" (21). A fair summary of the illustrative technique of Mme de Lafayette's novel: she tells us what love ought to be in the ideals of Mme de Chartres and her daughter and shows us what it is in the histories of court intrigue and in the inner torment of the princess.

In both *Le Triomphe* and the novel, it is clear that the reasons for the actual failure of the ideal of love are rooted in the imperfection of human nature. As Mlle de St-Ange argues, "pour que l'amour peut rendre heureux, il faudroit qu'il eut les qualités que j'ay dites et c'est ce quy est impossible, parce que l'antandement humain estant aveugle le coeur infiniment mobile, et le sort des hommes malheureux" (25). As Venus tells Cupid, "Ceux qui seront les plus éclerez, les plus constant et les plus doux, produiront des amours plus parfaits et plus heureux, mais il s'an trouverra peu de ceux là" (19). Mme de Chartres speaking to her young daughter is gentler and more positive in her emphasis but hardly more encouraging about the extreme difficulty of controlling one's own impulses and adhering strictly to the path of perfect fidelity:

elle lui faisait voir . . . quelle tranquillité suivait la vie d'une honnête femme, et combien la vertu donnait d'éclat et d'élévation à une personne qui avait de la beauté et de la naissance. Mais elle lui faisait voir aussi combien il était difficile de conserver cette vertu, que par une extrême défiance de soi-même et par un grand soin de s'attacher à ce qui seul peut faire le bonheur d'une femme, qui est d'aimer son mari et d'en être aimée. (41)

The difficulties of loving the person one ought to love and remaining faithful to that person are so great, the way to achieving this perfect love so fraught with self-designed perils, that, from the beginning, readers of the treatise and the novel must regard the chances of happiness in love as very poor.

The blind fatality of love is as evident in Mme de Lafayette's novel as it is in Mlle de St-Ange's fable. The Prince de Clèves, who sees Mlle de Chartres in a shop shortly after her arrival in Paris, falls madly in love with her without even knowing who she is. Despite this romantic initial encounter and the obvious suitability of the match, she does not reciprocate his openly avowed passion. She is imperturbable even in the face of her mother's earnest efforts to impress upon her how much she owes this suitor who loved her at first sight and proposed marriage at a moment when everyone else avoided it. Her feelings for M. de Clèves both before and after marriage "ne passent pas ceux de l'estime et de la reconnaissance" (50). For Nemours, she feels almost immediately, even without being fully conscious of it, a love that defies reason and is against her own will as well as her moral sense. A remark by her mother reveals to her sentiments that "elle n'avait encore osé s[1] . . . avouer à elle-même" (65). The discovery is not only painful but degrading: "elle trouva combien il était honteux de les avoir pour un autre que pour un mari qui les méritait" (65). Following this discovery so repugnant to her, the princess learns that Mme de Chartres is seriously ill. From her mother's deathbed, Mme de Clèves receives her last solemn warning against love: "vous êtes sur le bord du précipice: il faut de grands efforts et de grandes violences pour vous retenir. . . . ne craignez point de prendre des partis trop rudes et trop difficiles, quelque affreux qu'ils vous paraissent d'abord; ils seront plus doux dans les suites que les malheurs d'une galanterie" (68).

As unsuitable and unwelcome as this love is to Mme de Clèves, it is also an unexpected and not altogether benign turn of fate for Nemours. The Chevalier de Guise, a disappointed suitor, reflects bitterly that the romantic first meeting between them is "un présage que la fortune destinait Monsieur de Nemours à être amoureux de Madame de Clèves" (54). Before meeting her, Nemours was preparing to visit England to try his luck with Queen Elizabeth, who had heard of him and was eager to meet him. His violent passion for Mme de Clèves causes him first to neglect his preparations, then to delay until Elizabeth begins to be offended, and finally to reject the entire scheme, although his chances for winning a crown seem excellent. All three of the major characters in this drama are victims of the misdirected arrows of the blind god of love.

Love is not only blind but, Mlle de St-Ange maintains, the cruelest of all evils, a compendium of every misfortune in the world. To illustrate her point, she cites an anecdote concerning a Mlle de La Fayette who served the queen of England. Unhappy lovers are miserable night and day. Torn between hope and despair, they are weighed down by trouble and buffeted by the storms of their passion. Even happy lovers when their satisfaction is achieved find that it vanishes quickly to be replaced by a lazy satiety that kills desire (39–44). In perfect harmony with these insights, the depiction of the love of the Princesse de Clèves for Nemours is primarily a portrait of pain in all its subtle variations. The fact that she needs protection against her feelings for M. de Nemours intensifies her grief over her mother's death. As Nemours makes veiled declarations to her, she is obliged to avoid him and falls into "une tristesse profonde" that is attributed to her recent loss.

After Nemours steals the miniature portrait of her, "elle fit réflexion à la violence de l'inclination qui l'entraînait vers Monsieur de Nemours; elle trouva qu'elle n'était plus maîtresse de ses paroles et de son visage" (93). A short time later, when she believes that she has in her hands a letter from another woman who has loved and been mistreated by Nemours, the princess "se trouvait dans une sorte de douleur insupportable, qu'elle ne connaissait point et qu'elle n'avait jamais sentie" (97). This new and unbearable pain is "la jalousie avec toutes les horreurs dont elle peut être accompagnée" (99). Her shame and remorse are so intense that she believes that she is entirely cured of her passion. When she is later able to reflect upon this episode, she realizes what she has experienced and asks herself, "Et veux-je . . . m'exposer aux cruels repentirs et aux mortelles douleurs que donne l'amour?" (119).

The subject of love's cruelty has already raised the greatest argument against it, the certainty of unfaithfulness, the cause of all jealousy. When Mlle de La Tremblaye asks timidly if by some great miracle one might find "un homme capable de discernement, de tandresse et de fidélité," Mlle de St-Ange responds dryly that "ce seroit un miracle plus rare que celuy qu'on raconte du Fenix [Phoenix]" (34). To Mlle de Tremblaye's weak protest, "Je sçait des gens quy se sont aimez toute leur vie," Mlle St-Ange counters grimly, "Leur vie n'a donc pas esté lonque" (46). One sees people die in the initial throes of love, but one never sees people who have loved violently for a long time. Both young women agree that men are far more often unfaithful than women. Mlle de la Tremblaye pursues the point to even greater lengths than her friend: "pour une femme qui change l'on trouve un million d'hommes non seulement qui change, mais qui joignent encore au changent la perfidie, le mépris, la haine et souvant l'outrage" (48). The reasons for this universal unfaithfulness have already been exposed by Mlle de St-Ange: "la privation yrite le désire et la possesion le fait mourir" (41).

In *La Princesse de Clèves* even that completely faithful spouse M. de Clèves acknowledges the uniqueness of his own devotion. He cries in pain, "Vous êtes ma femme, je vous aime comme ma maîtresse" (151). Mme de Clèves's cool analysis of this unparalleled persistence of love after marriage agrees with the theories expounded in *Le Triomphe*. After her husband's death, in her only direct discussion with Nemours, she explains: "Monsieur de Clèves était peut-être l'unique homme du monde capable de conserver de l'amour dans le mariage. Ma destinée n'a pas voulu que j'aie pu profiter de ce bonheur; peut-être aussi que sa passion n'avait subsisté que parce qu'il n'en aurait pas trouvé en moi" (173). As for Nemours, it is precisely her love for him that makes her anticipate nothing but unhappiness in marriage to him. She could not keep his love by her indifference. In this pursuit, it has been the obstacles that have kept him faithful: there was enough difficulty to inspire him to conquer, enough encouragement to give him hope. She is clear-sighted. Having established by rhetorical questions the general principles that men in love do not remain so eternally and that it would be unrealistic to hope for a miracle in her case, she goes on firmly to the particular. Nemours is attractive and gallant. He has had many love affairs and will have many more: "je vous verrais pour une autre comme vous auriez été pour moi. . . . Je vous croirais toujours amoureux et aimé, et je ne me tromperais pas souvent" (174). In this inevitable betrayal, she knows what her own suffering would be: "J'en aurais une douleur mortelle. . . . Dans cet état néanmoins je n'aurais d'autre parti que celui de la souffrance; je ne sais même si j'oserais me plaindre. On fait des reproches à un amant; mais en fait-on à un mari, quand on n'a qu'à lui reprocher de n'avoir plus d'amour?" (174).

The solution to this dilemma is the same in the treatise and the novel. Mlle de Tremblaye puts the objection succinctly: "Ce n'est pas un grand bonheur de ne rien aymer . . . car c'est ne vivre qu'à moitié" (54). Mlle de St-Ange is confident of her final riposte: "Ce n'est pas véritablement un grand bonheur en soy. . . . mais la paix et le repos dont il est accompagné le rend infiniment préférable aux amers douleurs de l'amour" (54). Her opponent concedes defeat. Just so Mme de Clèves avows the famous "intérêt de mon repos" (175). Considering and reconsidering her position, she finds that "Les raisons qu'elle avait de ne point épouser Monsieur de Nemours lui paraissaient fortes du côté de son devoir et insurmontables du côté de son repos. La fin de l'amour de ce prince, et les maux de la jalousie qu'elle croyait infaillibles dans un mariage, lui montraient un malheur certain où elle s'allait jeter" (178). This purely logical motive of self-preservation is enough to sustain her until, during a serious illness, she turns away from the things of the world, only to undergo a final victorious battle with her passion on her return to health. The greater spiritual under-standing and detachment from worldly concerns that she achieves in this final combat offers a hard-won peace that she preserves by divid-ing her time and good works between her home and a convent.[6] Unlike the novel, *Le Triomphe* suggests no final religious context for the peace achieved through determined rejection of love.

It must be left to individual readers to judge whether the sum of resemblances between Mme de Lafayette's novel and the anonymous treatise would justify an assumption of common authorship. It is enough here to note that the similarities exist not simply in a few common points but in the entire thrust of the argument and the con-clusion against love in both works.

6. For a review of scholarship and an analysis of the Christian humanism of *La Princesse de Clèves*, see the magisterial article by Marie-Odile Sweetser, *"La Princesse de Clèves* devant la critique contemporaine," *Studi francesi* 52 (1974): 13–29.

PART 4 Psychological Readings

10 The Princesse de Clèves's Will to Order

MICHAEL S. KOPPISCH

SHORTLY before Louis XIV's death, the Duc de Saint-Simon has a long conversation with his friend Philippe d'Orléans, who is about to become regent. Characteristically, the memorialist has plenty of advice to give Philippe about how he should conduct himself in his new role. Less characteristically, Saint-Simon praises the king and even proposes him as a model to be imitated for his "dignité constante et la règle continuelle de son extérieur." The first trait, he says, "présentait en tous les moments qu'il pouvait être vu une décence majestueuse qui frappait de respect; l'autre une suite de jours et d'heures, où, en quelque lieu qu'il fût, on n'avait qu'à savoir quel jour et quelle heure il était, pour savoir aussi ce que le Roi faisait, sans jamais d'altération en rien, sinon d'employer les heures qu'il passait dehors, ou à des chasses, ou à des simples promenades."[1] So rigidly structured was life at the court that Saint-Simon detects in its inhabitants a kind of "mécanique," which he recommends to Philippe: "en toutes choses la mécanique était bien plus importante qu'elle ne semblait l'être" (5:384). What is admirable about Louis XIV is that despite physical debilitation and its accompanying "décadence extérieure," he allows for no disruption of the well-established order of events that constitutes his day at court: "les journées étaient toujours les mêmes" (5:386). At a moment of poten-

I am grateful to Frieda S. Brown for her helpful reading of this chapter.

1. Louis de Rouvroy, Duc de Saint-Simon, *Mémoires*, 8 vols., ed. Yves Coirault (Paris: Gallimard, 1983–88), 5:381–82; hereafter cited parenthetically in the text.

tial upheaval, every detail of the king's comportment is calculated to maintain order, and his tactic works. If the courtiers' thoughts turn instinctively to concern for their own status in the new court—"chacun pensait à soi"—their urge to be done with the old order is held in check by "la terreur qu'on avait de ce monarque dépérissant à vue d'oeil" (5:386). Saint-Simon impresses upon Philippe the necessity that order always prevail. The new regent should trouble himself with details only insofar as they will help him "tenir tout en ordre et en haleine" (5:380). Lest his loss of interest "met bientôt les affaires en désordre" (5:384), he must limit his involvement in any task that seems at first important but will not, in the end, hold his attention. And Philippe would do best to abandon passion altogether. Failing this, he should at least avoid any prolonged affair with a single mistress whom he might, by force of habit, grow to love. For love is, by its very nature, inimical to an ordered existence, a fact well known to "certains prélats qui veulent conserver leur réputation par le secret profond de leur désordre" (5:384). Their lesson is one that Saint-Simon would have Philippe ponder. That the order created by appearances alone is factitious *in no way* diminishes the importance of its being preserved.

The ambiance into which Mme de Chartres introduces her daughter in the early pages of *La Princesse de Clèves* closely resembles the milieu depicted by Saint-Simon. Henri II's court seems a perfectly ordered world in which ideal characters play out their appointed roles. Exceptional human beings, the court's members are extraordinarily handsome, exquisitely polite, and always astute. They seem endowed with an inner sense of courtly protocol. Nothing that they do must interrupt the stately ceremonial that is court life. For the *magnificence* and *galanterie* of the novel's famous first line to be as pervasive as they are, there must exist some underlying order that regulates characters and events.[2] Confusion and anarchy are relegated to a place beyond the confines of the court. Recognizing this, Henri's queen, Catherine de Médicis, exercises over her most potent feelings an exemplary control. Although the king's legendary attachment to the beautiful Diane de Poitiers is openly acknowledged at court, the queen is careful not

---

2. Mme de Lafayette, *La Princesse de Clèves,* ed. Antoine Adam (Paris: Garnier-Flammarion, 1966), 35; hereafter cited parenthetically in the text.

to reveal her resentment of his infidelity. She surely realizes, as the narrator puts it, that by staying at the court and performing her functions as Henri's wife and queen, she actually facilitates his faithlessness: "La présence de la reine autorisait la sienne [Diane's]" (35). Yet, she never discloses her true feelings: "il semblait qu'elle souffrît sans peine l'attachement du roi pour la duchesse de Valentinois, et elle n'en témoignait aucune jalousie" (35). Of course, keeping such powerful sentiments as resentment and jealousy under wraps neither eliminates them nor saps them of their strength. It simply removes them to the realm of the unknown or the unrecognized, where they can act, often in secret, to wreak havoc on the prevailing order. No one really understands Catherine de Médicis: "elle avait une si profonde dissimulation qu'il était difficile de juger de ses sentiments, et la politique l'obligeait d'approcher cette duchesse de sa personne, afin d'en approcher aussi le roi" (35). What is easily mistaken—by both characters and readers—as an immutable order holding the court together turns out to be, for Catherine de Médicis at least, more like a strategy, a "politique" with all the impermanence that this implies.

Mme de Chartres understands the transitory quality of strategic alliances at the court but believes, nonetheless, that stability and, therefore, happiness are attainable. In her daughter's education, she emphasizes two principles essential to understanding the novel's protagonist. In the first place, Mlle de Chartres must be different from all other women. By her virtue, she will stand out, establish her superiority to others. Mme de Chartres teaches her daughter "combien la vertu donnait d'éclat et d'élévation à une personne qui avait de la beauté et de la naissance" (41). Since virtually everyone at court is wellborn and attractive, it is virtue that will distinguish Mlle de Chartres from others. The underlying order of court life, in Mme de Chartres's view, is an order founded on differences between individuals. This is a natural extension of the nobiliary hierarchy that in large measure determined courtiers' prestige. Very much attuned to this social hierarchy, Mme de Chartres decided to bring her daughter to court because, despite several proposals of marriage, "[elle] ne trouvait presque rien digne de sa fille" (41). What she inculcates in her daughter, however, is an internalized and highly personal version of this hierarchical order. Mme de Chartres's goal is to guarantee by her lessons both her daughter's place at court and, above all, the young woman's sense of her own preeminence. This Mlle de Chartres will acquire by heeding her mother's second great principle: "une extrême défiance de soi-même" (41). Mlle de Chartres must always be aware of her every thought and action, must always be on guard against the slightest temptation to falter in her adherence to that standard of virtue by which she will distinguish herself. She becomes her own staunchest adversary as she tries to achieve absolute self-mastery. The only acceptable life for her is one that conforms to the pattern her mother has set for it. No measure is too harsh for this woman who would become and remain "une personne où l'on ne pouvait atteindre" (52).

Latent in this ideal is the need for a private, inner certainty of self that will place the Princesse de Clèves above the turmoil caused by desire, jealousy, and rivalry. Permanent equilibrium among opposing factions at the court, which represents external reality, eludes the novel's characters. As Mme de Chartres seems to know, it cannot be realized in a place whose very soul is "l'ambition et la galanterie" (44). Not only do the various cliques that make up the court vie constantly with each other, but within each group jealousy among individuals is rampant: "Toutes ces différentes cabales avaient de l'émulation et de l'envie les unes contre les autres: les dames qui les composaient avaient aussi de la jalousie entre elles" (45). Beyond the superficial level of appearances, the closest approximation to order of which the court is capable is "une sorte d'agitation sans désordre" (45). Mme de Lafayette leaves little doubt that rivalry is at the root of this "agitation." What the Princesse de Clèves seeks is a tranquil existence in her own self-contained world, free from the turmoil of the court.[3] At stake are her personal independence and the distinction she wishes to maintain between herself and the rest of the court.

Marie-Odile Sweetser has argued tellingly that the Princesse de Clèves "se cherche, s'affirme, se crée dans une société qui tend à l'ab-

---

3. In "Bienséance et sentiment chez Madame de Lafayette" (*Cahiers de l'Association internationale des études françaises* 11 [1959]: 33–66), Jean Fabre contends that "avec tous les moralistes de son siècle, l'auteur de la *Princesse de Clèves* croit à une permanence de la nature humaine qu'il est possible et nécessaire de découvrir sous les apparences de la vie sociale" (62). Whether or not this is true, much in the novel undermines such a belief.

sorber, à en faire un être conforme à ses lois."[4] The heroine tries to find what John Lyons has called "a principle of coherence in human affairs."[5] At the end of the novel, she rejects Nemours in the name of both her duty and her *repos,* which Domna Stanton succinctly defines as "withdrawal from the movement and activities of the world to a retreat where man, relieved of disquieting passions and desires, could be spiritually reborn and enjoy uninterruptedly a stable, independent, and virtuous life."[6] Like other seventeenth-century characters—one thinks, for example, of Phèdre—Mme de Clèves adopts as her ideal a life from which disorder and its ravages are banished.

There is, however, a fundamental contradiction inherent in the Princesse de Clèves's quest for order and *repos.* Although she does, in fact, want to remove herself from the commotion of court life and more than once retreats to the country, her need to be different from other women, which her mother has taught her, subjects Mme de Clèves to precisely those conflicts she tries most desperately to avoid. In a state of *repos,* the character would gather up the strands of her existence, withdraw from the world, and live without reference to others. She would be true to herself, sufficient to herself. At least superficially, this is the life Mme de Chartres seems to have in mind for her daughter. She portrays for her child "quelle tranquillité suivait la vie d'une honnête femme" (41) and encourages her to find a faithful husband to whom she will remain permanently attached. Mlle de Chartres must at all costs avoid passion. It is a commonplace of seventeenth-century thought that passion is destructive of order and *repos.* Serge Doubrovsky, among others, believes that the intrusion of passion into the heroine's world is at the novel's center: "le thème essentiel du roman est l'irruption d'une passion fatale dans ce monde sûr de lui-même."[7]

4. Marie-Odile Sweetser, *"La Princesse de Clèves* et son unité," *PMLA* 87 (1972): 483.

5. John D. Lyons, *Exemplum: The Rhetoric of Example in Early Modern France and Italy* (Princeton: Princeton University Press, 1989), 222. Lyons also makes this case in his earlier essay, "Narrative, Interpretation and Paradox: *La Princesse de Clèves,*" *Romanic Review* 72 (1981): 383–400.

6. Domna Stanton, "The Ideal of 'Repos' in Seventeenth-Century French Literature," *L'Esprit créateur* 15 (1975): 102. In the same article, Stanton suggests that the Princesse de Clèves actually achieves "the virtuous, fixed, atemporal, and self-sufficient state" to which she aspires (101).

7. Serge Doubrovsky, *"La Princesse de Clèves:* Une Interprétation existentielle," *La Table*

Mme de Chartres's dying words to her daughter are a warning against the dangers of passionate love. Ironically, they also set Mme de Clèves on a path that leads inevitably away from *repos*. Mme de Chartres knows about her daughter's illegitimate love for Nemours and tells her, "vous êtes sur le bord du précipice" (68). So as not to fall from virtue, the Princesse de Clèves will have to exert great effort, engage in "de grandes violences" (68), fight fire with fire. Virtue here, however, is something of an abstraction. Mme de Chartres's real entreaty is that her daughter surpass other women. Doubting that a call to virtue alone can make her daughter honor a mother's last wish, Mme de Chartres declares that she prefers death to the spectacle of seeing her only child "tomber comme les autres femmes" (68). Earlier in the same passage, Mme de Chartres had exhorted her daughter to think about herself—"songez ce que vous vous devez à vous-même"— and, she adds in the same breath, "pensez que vous allez perdre cette réputation que vous vous êtes acquise et que je vous ai tant souhaitée" (68). In other words, the sign of the Princesse de Clèves's virtue is her reputation, the recognizable difference between herself and other women at the court. Her withdrawal—"retirez-vous de la cour," her mother counsels, "obligez votre mari de vous emmener" (68)—will distinguish her from others, as surely as success in some *galanterie* is a mark of distinction for other court inhabitants. In both cases, characters vie with each other to constitute their own individuality by establishing a difference between themselves and those others. The result of this rivalry is to usurp from individuals their independence. Much that they do and say is determined by those to whom they would be superior and those who might judge them so. Mme de Chartres does not want her daughter simply to leave the court. Her real wish is that the Princesse de Clèves not be confused with other women, not be like them. That would be the most devastating failure.[8]

---

ronde 138 (1959): 37. See also Louise K. Horowitz's excellent chapter on Mme de Lafayette in *Love and Language* (Columbus: Ohio State University Press, 1977), 51–72. There she writes that "the nature of passion, as portrayed in Mme de Lafayette's universe, is to ravage, to destroy the smooth continuum of existence, to alienate the self from its most intimate conception" (58).

8. The most interesting readings of the mother-daughter relationship in *La Princesse de Clèves* include William O. Goode, "A Mother's Goals in *La Princesse de Clèves*: Worldly and Spiritual Distinction," *Neophilologus* 56 (1973): 398–406; Marianne Hirsch, "A Moth-

At a crucial moment in the novel, Mme de Clèves, reflecting upon the way she has responded to her illicit love for Nemours, demonstrates explicitly that she has taken her mother's words to heart. In an extraordinary gesture, she confesses to her husband that she loves another man. Unbeknown to either her or M. de Clèves, their conversation has been overheard by Nemours himself, who divulges its subject to his friend the Vidame de Chartres. There are no secrets in the secretive world of the court, and word of the confession begins to spread. Mme de Clèves, naturally enough, accuses her husband of indiscretion. He replies that the strange adventure being recounted at court is surely not hers, but someone else's. Mme de Clèves emphatically rejects this possibility: "il n'y a pas dans le monde une autre aventure pareille à la mienne; il n'y a point une autre femme capable de la même chose. . . . on ne l'a jamais imaginée et cette pensée n'est jamais tombée dans un autre esprit que le mien" (136). The confession scene has, over the centuries, been variously interpreted as either a sign of the heroine's weakness of character or proof of her moral rectitude and truthfulness. Mme de Clèves herself thinks of her confession as a unique act, one that distinguishes her from all other women: she alone could have been capable of it. In terms that highlight this preoccupation with her own superiority, she also reproaches herself for having believed any man, even Nemours, capable of concealing what might enhance his prestige in the eyes of others: "C'est pourtant pour cet homme, que j'ai cru si différent du reste des hommes, que je me trouve comme les autres femmes, étant si éloignée de leur ressembler" (138). Her regret echoes her mother's last words to her. By allowing herself to love Nemours, the Princesse de Clèves has become like all other women. She has relinquished her status as an exceptional individual, different from others. She may appear not to resemble them, but in truth she does.

Her conversation with M. de Clèves shows both how tenaciously she holds on to her sense of difference from others *and* how passion reduces the characters to a state of conflict and, ultimately, chaos.

---

er's Discourse: Incorporation and Repetition in *La Princesse de Clèves*," *Yale French Studies* 62 (1981): 67–87; and Peggy Kamuf, "A Mother's Will: *The Princesse de Clèves*," in *Fictions of Feminine Desire* (Lincoln: University of Nebraska Press, 1982), 67–96. My own concern here is more with how Mme de Chartres's words illuminate the actions of her daughter than with the nature of the two women's relationship.

202 / Michael S. Koppisch

Their feelings and behavior are so similar that they begin to act and speak in identical ways. Afflicted with a "folle et violente passion" (138), Mme de Clèves "trouvait également impossible que son mari eût parlé et qu'il n'eût pas parlé" (137). Likewise, M. de Clèves is perplexed by what has transpired. He knows that he himself has not revealed the secret of his wife's confession; he believes her protestation of innocence; and yet what occurred is being discussed by others at court. Mme de Clèves's passion for Nemours and M. de Clèves's love of his wife leave them in a similar quandary. The only way M. de Clèves can imagine to resolve their dilemma—and it is no resolution at all—is by projecting it into the domain of appearances, *acting as if* the confession had not occurred: Mme de Clèves should present herself at court "comme à l'ordinaire" (138). Although the gap between appearances and real feelings is a source of anguish for her, she forces herself to follow her husband's wishes: "Elle se résolut donc de faire un effort sur elle-même" (138). By exercising self-control, she hopes to be able to close the painful breach, to become what she appears to be. The "extrême défiance de soi-même" (41) that Mme de Chartres has instilled in her daughter is an injunction against trusting her own instincts, and the Princesse de Clèves has answered it with an attempt to control her actions, words, and thoughts rationally. Not satisfied to manipulate appearances and, thereby, create in the eyes of others the desired image of herself, Mme de Clèves endeavors to make appearances and her true sentiments coincide. She thus rejects the superficial regularity of court life for a higher, more personal order that will give her own existence a perfect integrity. What separates the Princesse de Clèves from other characters is that her urge to control reality extends well beyond appearances to her own most intimate feelings. But she too is preoccupied with how others see her, for on this depends her reputation. She wants to be different, but she must also be seen as different. Ultimately, her inability to eliminate passion from her life puts her in danger of being like everyone else. Passion becomes a leveling force that violently undoes even the most resolute self-control.

To the extent that the Princesse de Clèves's self-control is motivated by her desire to be different from those around her, it actually has something in common with passion. For both these aspects of her being participate in the same structure of desire, both put her into rivalry with others. And, in the final analysis, both the urge to control herself and the will to be superior to others will make her resemble her opponents. Mme de Clèves's love for Nemours, much like her husband's love for her, is marred by recurring pangs of jealousy. She imagines that she is in competition with other women for Nemours's attention. What she desires, of course, is to be distinguished from them in his eyes, to be the only woman whom he loves. In this she is identical to M. de Clèves, who dies of jealousy, and to Nemours, who is tortured by his jealousy of other men, especially her husband. All three characters are driven by the obstacles to their desire. The Princesse de Clèves recognizes this characteristic in both the men who love her. She believes that her husband may have been the only man on earth capable of sustaining marital love, but wonders: "peut-être aussi que sa passion n'avait subsisté que parce qu'il n'en aurait pas trouvé en moi" (173). As to Nemours, "je crois même," she tells him, "que les obstacles ont fait votre constance" (173). In the eyes of Nemours, Mme de Clèves is in one way different from all other mistresses. He could marry her, certain of her everlasting fidelity, were it not for the obstacles with which she herself tries to block his love: "N'aurai-je envisagé, dis-je, une si grande félicité [marriage to her] que pour vous y voir apporter vous-même des obstacles?" (172). The nature of the impediments to love that she now creates—her duty and her "repos"—distinguishes her from women like Diane de Poitiers and Mme de Tournon, whose lovers are confronted, as M. de Clèves had been earlier in the story, with real rivals. That Mme de Clèves imposes obstacles to the full realization of love, however, identifies her with these women. And the Princesse de Clèves is, in any event, identical to both Nemours and her husband. All three are driven by the obstacles to their desire, rather than by some personal sentiment of love that is theirs alone without reference to others.

Wariness of real or imagined rivals fans the ardor of Mme de Clèves's passion at the same time that it heightens her awareness of the need for self-mastery. The internal conflict from which she suffers is extreme. When she thinks back on her acute feelings of jealousy at having believed, albeit mistakenly, that Nemours had been unfaithful to her, one part of her wants to reject love altogether. Having given him a sign of her love, she is "honteuse de paraître si peu digne d'estime aux yeux mêmes de son amant" (119). And what of her husband?

204 / Michael S. Koppisch

"Veux-je manquer à M. de Clèves? Veux-je me manquer à moi-même?" (119). With the latter question, she recognizes that love and jealousy are perilous to the integrity of her person. They, not she herself, control her: "je suis vaincue et surmontée par une inclination qui m'entraîne malgré moi" (119). Whence the irreconcilable conflict at the heart of her being: "Toutes mes résolutions sont inutiles; je pensai hier tout ce que je pense aujourd'hui et je fais aujourd'hui tout le contraire de ce que je résolus hier" (119). She struggles to control her own destiny, but passion has taken the upper hand. Jealousy reduces M. de Clèves to a remarkably similar frame of mind. Subject to "des sentiments violents et incertains dont je ne suis pas le maître," he questions whether he and his wife are still worthy of each other: "Je ne me trouve plus digne de vous; vous ne me paraissez plus digne de moi" (151). His psychic equanimity is destroyed by absolutely contradictory feelings: "Je vous adore, je vous hais, je vous offense, je vous demande pardon; je vous admire, j'ai honte de vous admirer" (151). Love in *La Princesse de Clèves* bedevils the characters it possesses with contradictory emotions that reduce them to utter confusion and turmoil.

Mme de Lafayette characterizes passion as "violente" in her novel; she uses the noun "violence" and its adjectival form frequently.[9] At a court fearful of the specter of disorder, overt violence is kept at bay. Desire and passion are not, for that, any the less violent. As if to create a context for the explosion of violent passion, the novel's first paragraph focuses attention on Henri II's "passion pour Diane de Poitiers," which, although of twenty years' standing, "n'en était pas moins violente" (35). Even after he has married Mlle de Chartres, M. de Clèves "conservait pour elle une passion violente" (52). In fact, despite Nemours's tendency to be something of a gallant, his passion for Mme de Clèves "fut d'abord si violente qu'elle lui ôta le goût et même le souvenir de toutes les personnes qu'il avait aimées" (60). This is a major change, brought about by violent passion. The Princesse de Clèves's love for Nemours is no less violent than his for her. Being "une personne de son humeur, qui avait une passion violente" (99), she suffers all the more from jealousy. Her husband's death strengthens

9. In his *Index du vocabulaire de "La Princesse de Clèves"* (Paris: Nizet, 1967), Jean de Bazin counts "violent" thirty-five times in the text and "violence" thirteen.

her resolve to reject love, but at the sight of Nemours, her "passion endormie se ralluma dans son coeur, et avec quelle violence!" (167). She recognizes that Nemours is a man "pour qui elle avait une inclination si violente qu'elle l'aurait aimé quand il ne l'aurait pas aimée" (167). Violence and passion are virtually synonymous in *La Princesse de Clèves*.

The effect of violence is a loss of the control characters can exercise over themselves and a concomitant breakdown of the differences among them upon which order is founded. What comes apart, of course, is not the court itself but the individual lives of the characters touched by the violence of passion. The Princesse de Clèves worries about her inability to control her passionate feelings, and the language of the text shows how much she becomes like others as passion overwhelms her. The order she has sought is a personal one. Its disintegration impinges most forcefully upon her as an individual. Realizing at one point that her jealous behavior must have revealed to Nemours her love for him, the Princesse de Clèves is no longer certain of who she is, of what her life represents: "elle ne se reconnaissait plus elle-même" (118). In an earlier conversation with Mme de Clèves, ostensibly about her mother's death, Nemours had spoken of himself in the very same terms: "Les grandes afflictions et les passions violentes . . . font de grands changements dans l'esprit; et, pour moi, je ne me reconnais pas depuis que je suis revenu de Flandre" (84). Two characters as different as the Princesse de Clèves and M. de Nemours are, in at least one way, identical: they both lose their clear sense of self in the wake of passion. This alienation is the direct result of passion's violence.

Mme la Dauphine, who understands the court perfectly and often uncovers the truth behind its inhabitants' intrigues and clandestine behavior, tells the Princesse de Clèves that Nemours's mistress confessed an illicit love to her husband because of "la peur qu'elle a eue de n'être pas toujours la maîtresse de sa passion" (132). Never were truer words spoken. They lay bare both the motivation of Mme de Clèves in confessing her love and the loss of her ability to restrain her own emotions. In a well-ordered personal universe, the rational must predominate over the irrational, reason and self-control over visceral feelings. However, as love overpowers Mme de Clèves, her husband, and Nemours, precisely the opposite occurs. They become subject to the irrational. Convinced that his wife has received Nemours in his absence, M. de Clèves asks her, "Comment pouviez-vous espérer que je conservasse de la raison? . . . je n'ai que des sentiments violents et incertains dont je ne suis pas le maître" (151). After the death of M. de Clèves, the Vidame de Chartres arranges for Nemours to meet with the Princesse de Clèves. Their encounter leaves him "si plein de joie, de tristesse, d'étonnement et d'admiration, enfin, de tous les sentiments que peut donner une passion . . . qu'il n'avait pas l'usage de la raison" (176). His frame of mind resembles that of his late rival. Mme de Clèves blames herself for her husband's death and just after it, "demeura dans une affliction si violente qu'elle perdit quasi l'usage de la raison" (164). The cause of M. de Clèves's death was "la passion qu'elle avait eue pour un autre," and, therefore, "la douleur de cette princesse passait les bornes de la raison" (164–65). As reason succumbs to violent passions, their victims become more and more alike.

In spite of their love, it would be hard to imagine two people more different than Nemours and the Princesse de Clèves. An aggressive suitor, Nemours is at times too bold. He spies on his mistress, imposes his presence upon her, and even steals her portrait while she looks on. But he also knows when to respect her privacy.[10] Nemours is the ideal courtier: so handsome that he is described as "un chef-d'oeuvre de la nature" (37), admired by men and women alike, ambitious, and calculating. Only passion could bring about in his character the changes it has wrought. His adeptness at the game of love is now mitigated by the influence of a violent passion, and he involuntarily reacts in ways foreign to the behavior of a knowing courtier. In a conversation with Mme la Dauphine and the Princesse de Clèves, for example, his reaction is physical and spontaneous when the princess rebuffs his attempt to be alone with her: "La douleur qu'eut ce prince . . . fut si violente qu'il en pâlit" (160). Her love can incite in Mme de Clèves a similar physical reaction at the mere mention of Nemours's name: "Le nom de M. de Nemours surprit Mme de Clèves

10. According to Jules Brody ("*La Princesse de Clèves* and the Myth of Courtly Love," *University of Toronto Quarterly* 38 [1969]: 105–35), "from beginning to end, the hero's behaviour will continue to present an ambiguous mixture of *respect* and *hardiesse*" (110).

et la fit rougir" (165). Passion penetrates to the core of its victims, robbing them of that control by which they try to maintain their individuality. It affects their minds and their physical beings, reducing them to its will, destroying their own. The Princesse de Clèves recognizes at the end of the novel that she cannot remove passion from her life. She still loves Nemours. Nor can she surrender to her love, for it is impossible to be certain that Nemours's love will endure. What has made her different from others and, therefore, given her a sense of her own individuality has been her will to preserve for herself an ordered life free from passion's disruptive reign. Her mother's lesson and her own bitter experience have taught her that passion and order cannot coexist. She also knows that the violence of passion can only be fought with another form of violence. Recovering her composure, Mme de Clèves makes a carefully reasoned decision "de ne se point remarier et de ne voir jamais M. de Nemours," even though "c'était une résolution bien violente à établir dans un coeur aussi touché que le sien" (177). The illness that brings her close to death is a "maladie violente" (178). She violently sacrifices a love that has done violence to her life and so regains control over her destiny. Both the violence of the sacrifice and that of her passion must be borne by the heroine. The last words of the novel—"et sa vie, qui fut assez courte, laissa des exemples de vertu inimitables" (180)—hark back to Mme de Chartres's command that her daughter be different from other women. Mme de Clèves would not, in the end, have disappointed her mother. There is, however, in the Princesse de Clèves's final victory no need for her to compare herself to others, to rival them in virtue.[11] The vision of her own death has given her the strength to conquer her passion: "Il se passa un assez grand combat en elle-même. Enfin, elle surmonta les restes de cette passion qui était affaiblie par les sentiments que sa maladie lui avait donnés" (179). Passion and the affairs of this world now seem to her "tels qu'ils paraissent aux personnes qui ont des vues plus grandes et plus éloignées" (179). The end of the Princesse de Clèves's life reveals that her urge to be exceptional could only be realized when its source was

11. I agree with Patrick Henry's conclusion in "*La Princesse de Clèves* and *L'Introduction à la vie dévote*" (chap. 8 in the present volume), 178, that "at the end of the novel *caritas* has definitively replaced *eros*" (95).

within herself. Her combat against passion had earlier been waged in the name of distinguishing herself from others. Her impending death permits her to fight the battle for herself and, thereby, to restore order to the short life remaining to her.

11 In Search of Selfhood

The Itinerary of the Princesse de Clèves

MARIE-ODILE SWEETSER

MONG recent critics who have given a well-informed, thoughtful, and sensitive analysis of *La Princesse de Clèves* and its main character, both Patrick Henry and Jean Mesnard use the technical term "bildungsroman" or "roman d'apprentissage."[1] This constitutes, in my view, the most apt definition of the novel and of the personal development of its eponymous character. This chapter will attempt to trace the psychological itinerary of the princess from her early education to her final decision, since Mme de Lafayette has given sufficient indications concerning the beginning and end of a life that she clearly intended to show as exemplary, a notion confirmed by the last sentences of the text. The social rank acquired at birth and the upbringing of young Mlle de Chartres are sketched in very precise, if succinct, terms. The novelist gives the reader the necessary background information that will lead to a well-rounded picture of the heroine's journey.

The offhand quip by Valincour, comparing young Mlle de Chartres to Agnès of *L'Ecole des femmes*, must be taken for what it is, a clever remark destined to entertain at the expense of a fair appraisal. Jean Mesnard, however, while cautioning against taking the quip at face value, sees in it a valuable insight: "Les deux héroïnes, l'une et l'autre

1. Patrick Henry, *"La Princesse de Clèves* and *L'Introduction à la vie dévote"* (chap. 8 in the present volume), 158; hereafter cited parenthetically in the text. Jean Mesnard, "Introduction" to his edition of *La Princesse de Clèves* (Paris: Imprimerie Nationale, 1980), 19; hereafter cited parenthetically in the text.

d'une très grande jeunesse, passent de l'ignorance à la connaissance, de l'ingénuité à l'autorité, du silence à la parole. Toutes deux sont à l'école, et à l'école de l'amour. Mais l'expérience de l'amour ne leur a pas livré le même enseignement. La plus romanesque des deux n'est pas l'héroïne du roman" (19). One must, in fact, acknowledge that, before learning from personal, direct experience, Mlle de Chartres, born in an aristocratic family, received, for the time represented in the novel, a most unusual education. She was raised by her mother, a woman of high principles and extraordinary virtue, who remained a widow in order to devote herself to the upbringing of her daughter, away from the court, a decision rather unusual in aristocratic circles where daughters were generally entrusted to governesses or sent to a convent before coming out in society and marrying to enhance the prestige and position of their family.[2] Mme de Chartres felt it was her duty to instill in her daughter the social and moral values of the aristocratic code. Among the latter, virtue is foremost, not presented in a repressive way, but rather in a positive way; it is desirable because it ensures true happiness for the virtuous wife:

mais elle ne travailla pas seulement à cultiver son esprit et sa beauté, elle songea aussi à lui donner de la vertu et à la lui rendre aimable. . . . elle faisait souvent à sa fille des peintures de l'amour; elle lui montrait ce qu'il a d'agréable pour la persuader plus aisément sur ce qu'elle lui en apprenait de dangereux. . . . et elle lui faisait voir, d'un autre côté, quelle tranquillité suivait la vie d'une honnête femme, et combien la vertu donnait d'éclat et d'élévation à une personne qui avait de la beauté et de la naissance.[3]

Her goal is not simply to make her daughter an attractive, marriageable heiress prepared to hold her rank in society and be an asset to an aristocratic husband and family, but also an individual aware of her moral duties, loving virtue for its own sake. This insistence on the attractive aspects of virtue has been shown to be part and parcel of Salesian thought by Patrick Henry.[4] Her upbringing can certainly be

2. Henry quite rightly remarks on this "atypical behavior for the seventeenth century" (158).

3. Mme de Lafayette, La Princesse de Clèves, ed. Antoine Adam (Paris: Garnier-Flammarion, 1966), 41; hereafter cited parenthetically in the text.

4. Henry quotes Saint François de Sales: "Les vertus ont cela d'admirable qu'elles délectent l'âme d'une douceur et suavité non pareille" (158).

qualified as open, enlightened, dedicated to a high ideal. Although no specific underpinning or religious principles are mentioned, it is easy to surmise that those moral values taught to the young Mlle de Chartres are upheld by Christian ethics, as several commentators have pointed out.[5] This interpretation is sustained within the text by the description of Mme de Chartres's death, which is that of a Christian woman whose only concern at the very end of her life is for the afterlife. It is typical of classical taste that references to religion should be implicit rather than explicit in works of fiction, thereby upholding a clear separation between writing for entertainment, on the one hand, and for edification, on the other.

While the mother shows herself to be open-minded and forward-looking in building up her daughter's commitment to virtue, she does not hide sin and corruption from her. Obviously, she intends to develop her moral judgment to enable her to distinguish between good and evil. Specifically, she warns her against the dangers of illicit, adulterous love affairs, "galanteries," so common in courtly society, pleasurable on the surface, destructive in their consequences. The ideal she presents to her daughter is that of the "honnête femme," a social model, and of the virtuous wife, an ethical one. The realization of that double-sided model brings the only true happiness to a woman, which is to love her husband and be loved by him: "ce qui seul peut faire le bonheur d'une femme . . . est d'aimer son mari et d'en être aimée" (41).

Here it seems that this concept of love and happiness in marriage should be defined. In a recent illuminating study, Christian Biet has

---

5. In a remarkable study, published twenty-five years ago, which has stood the test of time, Francis L. Lawrence stressed that mother and daughter were the only characters in the novel who unequivocally condemned adultery ("*La Princesse de Clèves* Reconsidered," *French Review* 39 [1965]: 19). He also seized the importance of the ending and Mme de Clèves's refuge in religion: "The step between detachment from things of this world to meditation on things eternal is hardly shocking in a 17th century Christian" (21). See also Henry, 169; Wolfgang Leiner, "La Princesse et le directeur de conscience: Création romanesque et prédication," in *La Pensée religieuse dans la littérature et la civilisation du XVIIe siècle en France,* ed. Manfred Tietz and Volker Kapp (Tübingen, Germany: Biblio 17-13, 1984), 47–49; Philippe Sellier, "*La Princesse de Clèves*: Augustinisme et préciosité au paradis des Valois," in *Images de La Rochefoucauld,* ed. Jean Lafond and Jean Mesnard (Paris: Presses Universitaires de France, 1984), 220.

masterfully shown the opposition between love consecrated by marriage—based on mutual esteem, respect, and affection, defined as "amicitia," a feeling that goes beyond friendship but is not a passionate, blind emotion—and *amour-passion,* an instinctive, irrational drive, an infatuation generally short-lived. In marriage, the partners must love each other in a deep, long-lasting fashion. They complement each other, each bringing a special contribution to the union. Specifically, in the context of seventeenth-century society, the wife is expected to bring physical and social assets and an irreproachable character, the husband matching physical and social assets, military valor, knowledge of the world, and wisdom.[6] M. de Clèves appears in complete accord with the mentality of his time and rank when he meets Mlle de Chartres, after having first been struck by her appearance without knowing her identity: "M. de Clèves sentit de la joie de voir que cette personne qu'il avait trouvée si aimable, était d'une qualité proportionnée à sa beauté; il s'approcha d'elle et il lui supplia de se souvenir qu'il avait été le premier à l'admirer et que, sans la connaître, il avait eu pour elle tous les sentiments de respect et d'estime qui lui étaient dûs" (43). The terms used in this passage are indeed significant: "aimable" (worthy of love), "qualité" (implying rank and noble birth), "beauté," "respect," and "estime." These terms are in exact conformity with the social and ethical ideal of the period, and could have led to a perfectly happy marriage under different circumstances. But the evolution of M. de Clèves's feelings for his bride into a one-sided, passionate, possessive love and her surge of passion for another man will upset this promising beginning.

Prior to this union, Mlle de Chartres had met no one capable of inspiring passionate feelings in her. Because other potential husbands encountered obstacles, M. de Clèves appeals to her directly to allow her freedom of choice before he speaks to her mother. The daughter immediately recognizes the nobility of his conduct and is moved by it: "Comme Mlle de Chartres avait le coeur très noble et très bien fait, elle fut véritablement touchée de reconnaissance du procédé du prince de Clèves" (49). The marriage proposal made by M. de Clèves is all

---

6. Christian Biet, "Droit et fiction: La Représentation du mariage dans *La Princesse de Clèves,*" in *Mme de La Fayette: "La Princesse de Montpensier," "La Princesse de Clèves,"* ed. Roger Duchêne and Pierre Ronzeaud (*Littératures classiques,* [1990, supplement]): 33–49; hereafter cited parenthetically in the text.

the more meritorious because the king and his favorite disapprove of the prospect of a match between Mlle de Chartres and a prince of royal blood, the oldest son of the Duc de Montpensier. In his well-informed study, Christian Biet traces the rise of the king's control in matrimonial alliances. The sixteenth century saw the evolution of marriage from a religious, sacramental, essentially private bond, founded on the consent of two individuals, to a secular, juridical institution, regulated by civil law and influenced by the monarch (Biet, 34–35). As a consequence of this transformation of marriage from a private, religious bond to a political, legal contract, the freedom of choice of the individuals concerned was greatly reduced. Thwarted in their personal freedom, individual noblemen and noblewomen sought and found compensation in illicit love affairs, so vividly evoked in the segments of the novel dealing with the court.

The young Mlle de Chartres, with her character and personality formed by a solid moral upbringing, finds herself in the midst of that courtly society, depicted at the outset in terms of beautiful appearances, but seething with unsavory passions, ambition, and "galanteries" underneath, that is, adulterous love, a hedonistic, egocentric drive geared to the conquest of the other. Court intrigues are an inextricable mixture of both passions. The queen, Catherine de Médicis, essentially an ambitious woman, is fully aware of the king's longstanding affair with Diane de Poitiers, Duchesse de Valentinois, but seems to accept the situation without complaining (35).

This long-lasting affair strikes young Mme de Clèves as very strange. Mme de Chartres uses it as an example of the irrational and demeaning nature of erotic love: Henri II, seduced in his youth by an older Diane who had been his father's mistress, continued to show her throughout his adult life the same passionate attachment in spite of her unfaithfulness and greed. The king thus is blamed for his lack of discrimination and his weakness, the duchess for her faithless, raw ambition, lack of devotion to the king, and total disregard for his reputation. Mme de Chartres states that a genuine fondness for the king on the part of the duchess would have made the affair more understandable, even excusable (55). This is simply an expression of the view commonly held; it does not mean that she condones adultery. As a Christian, she would condemn it, as her last advice to her daughter before she dies plainly shows.

At the most important moment in a young woman's life, that is, at the point of choosing a husband, Mme de Chartres acts according to the highest standards, both at the social and personal levels. As a lady of high birth, she attempts to secure a brilliant match for her daughter; as a virtuous woman and loving parent, she is concerned with the moral qualities of the suitor and the future happiness of her child whom she leaves free to accept or reject M. de Clèves's suit.[7] Twice, then, Mlle de Chartres has been given the opportunity of refusing. The first time, in the private conversation in which the prince consulted her before making a formal proposal to her mother, she was moved by gratitude and appreciation of the young man's delicacy of feeling. Now, although she admits in an intimate exchange with her mother that she does not feel any special attraction toward the young man, she agrees with her about the good personal qualities of the suitor: "Mme de Chartres lui dit qu'il y avait tant de grandeur et de bonnes qualités dans M. de Clèves et qu'il faisait paraître tant de sagesse pour son âge que, si elle sentait son inclination portée à l'épouser, elle y consentirait avec joie" (50). The nobility of character, also noted previously by Mlle de Chartres, the high-mindedness, and wisdom of the young man give the mother the fond hope that her daughter, although not spontaneously attracted to him, will soon grow to have for him the "amicitia," based on esteem and affection, that is the essence of conjugal love according to the views of the Christian tradition. Given her own experience of the prince's moral qualities and the warm approbation of her mother, Mlle de Chartres, in full freedom, agrees to marry him: "Mlle de Chartres répondit qu'elle lui remarquait les mêmes bonnes qualités: qu'elle l'épouserait même avec moins de répugnance qu'un autre, mais qu'elle n'avait aucune inclination particulière pour sa personne" (50). These feelings of esteem and gratitude on her daughter's part seem to Mme de Chartres a solid foundation for a happy marriage. She hopes that they will de-

7. On the importance of the education given by Mme de Chartres to her daughter, see Georges Forestier, "Mme de Chartres, personnage-clé de *La Princesse de Clèves*," *Lettres romanes* 34 (1980): 67–76. The critic perceives a contradiction between her social duty (a brilliant match for her daughter) and her moral principles (67). The two obligations are not mutually exclusive: as a matter of fact, M. de Clèves fulfills social and moral requirements. There is a hierarchy of values in Mme de Chartres's mind, the moral ones holding, obviously, the highest rank.

velop into an affectionate, loving relationship as the couple share common goals and common values. Hence the famous sentence: "elle ne craignit point de donner à sa fille un mari qu'elle ne pût aimer en lui donnant le prince de Clèves" (50).

These optimistic views could have been realized if a serious disproportion in the respective feelings of husband and wife had not affected their relationship from the start. The prince, passionately in love, notices the absence of a reciprocal feeling in his bride and suffers from it. Her mother, aware also of that situation, takes great care to show her daughter how indebted she is to the steadfast attachment of M. de Clèves: "elle prit de grands soins de l'attacher à son mari et de lui faire comprendre ce qu'elle devait à l'inclination qu'il avait eue pour elle avant que de la connaître et à la passion qu'il lui avait témoignée en la préférant à tous les autres partis, dans un temps où personne n'osait plus penser à elle" (51). This disproportion in the initial feelings of each partner could, perhaps, have been bridged if the princess had had the time and opportunity to get to know her husband better, and if she had not experienced the awakening of passion for another man. Her encounter at court at a festive occasion with the Duc de Nemours, an attractive and brilliant member of the king's inner circle, symbolizes the options faced by the princess at the start of her journey of self-discovery. She can follow the path of virtue in which she has been brought up and remain a faithful wife in spite of the strong attraction she now feels for another man, fighting the temptation to which most of the women of her milieu succumb. Or, she can follow in the footsteps of the ladies of the court, for whom adulterous love affairs are commonplace and usually condoned, if discreetly handled.

Her carefully programmed upbringing, the wise warnings of her mother about the social and moral degradation caused by an adulterous love affair, and the very nature and character of the princess—she is sincere, truthful, faithful to her engagements—weigh in favor of the first option, which in fact she chooses. Her behavior, inner thoughts, and decisions are fully in character up to the death of her husband. Suspense is maintained with a simple chain of events. Mme de Chartres's death leaves the heroine without her mentor, reduced to her own resources, keeping in mind, however, the last pathetic advice of her mother. When she mistakenly believes Nemours to be in love with another, she experiences the anguish and torments of jealousy. She then becomes aware of the dangers of her position, even when she finds out that the love letter that caused her sufferings was not addressed to the duke. Fabricating a duplicate of that letter with Nemours in order to protect her uncle, she feels guilty and ashamed at having enjoyed this moment of close companionship and thus of having deceived her husband: "elle trouvait qu'elle était d'intelligence avec M. de Nemours, qu'elle trompait le mari du monde qui méritait le moins d'être trompé, et elle était honteuse de paraître si peu digne d'estime aux yeux même de son amant" (119). These scruples are clearly those of a person with a very refined moral conscience, particularly since her husband was present at the letter writing, and its purpose was to be of service to the vidame.

Thus, in accordance with the last advice given by her dying mother, she comes to the conclusion that she must leave the court, since meeting M. de Nemours while she remains in Paris is unavoidable. Leaving the court is the best way to avoid temptation and the inner sufferings resulting from the struggle against it. The two worlds, court and country, are clearly contrasted. The court means temptation, passions, intrigues, hypocrisy, corruption. The country, represented by the residence at Coulommiers, amidst a park and flower gardens, is a haven, protected from the outside world, where the princess could find *repos,* the peace of mind and heart that she seeks.

To accomplish her plan of retreat in the country, the princess needs the consent of her husband. He is a courtier whose position depends on the king's favor, and he considers it his duty to attend court functions. He is, naturally, reluctant to grant her request, which he finds hard to understand and painful, since it would mean separation: "Vous avez depuis quelque temps un goût pour la solitude qui m'étonne et qui m'afflige parce qu'il nous sépare . . . je craindrais plutôt que vous ne fussiez bien aise d'être séparée de moi" (121). Confronted with suspicions on the part of her husband, Mme de Clèves decides, in spite of her previous hesitations, to speak up. She had, in fact, contemplated such a confession in her thoughts, expressed in a pressingly pathetic interior monologue: "Il faut m'arracher de la présence de M. de Nemours; il faut m'en aller à la campagne, quelque bizarre que puisse paraître mon voyage; et si M. de Clèves s'opiniâtre à l'empêcher ou à en vouloir savoir les raisons, peut-être lui ferai-je le mal, et à

moi-même aussi de les lui apprendre" (119). She is fully aware of the
potentially explosive and destructive nature of such a confession
which, however, is far from the result of a moment of panic. She does
remember her mother's advice: "Ayez de la force et du courage, ma
fille, retirez-vous de la cour, obligez votre mari de vous emmener; ne
craignez point de prendre des partis trop rudes et trop difficiles, quelque affreux qu'ils vous paraissent d'abord: ils seront plus doux dans
les suites que les malheurs d'une galanterie" (68). Her decision to
speak is also justified by the comments made by M. de Clèves himself
about the value of sincerity and the sympathy he would feel for a
woman who would appeal to his generosity: "la sincérité me touche
d'une telle sorte que si ma maîtresse, et même ma femme, m'avouait
que quelqu'un lui plût, j'en serais affligé sans en être aigri. Je quitterais le personnage d'amant ou de mari, pour la conseiller et pour la
plaindre" (76). These two statements, coming from loved and trusted
persons, were certainly decisive in her extraordinary and painful decision. She knows that she runs the risk of losing her husband's esteem, admiration, and possibly his love—feelings that he had so
clearly expressed on a former occasion: "mais les femmes sont incompréhensibles et, quand je les vois toutes, je me trouve si heureux de
vous avoir que je ne saurais assez admirer mon bonheur" (69). This
is precisely the point that Mme de Chartres had made before dying:
her daughter must not be like other women. The princess herself is
fully conscious of the fact that she is not like other women and does
not want to be like them, that is, ruled by passions instead of being
mistress of herself, guided by her judgment and will.[8] The fact that
she does decide to speak is unusual and unlikely but not irrational.
Most women would have avoided a painful confession, both for themselves and their husbands. She does insist on the courage required of
her while in the attitude of a penitent, but paradoxically innocent,
Magdalene:

Eh bien, monsieur, lui répondit-elle en se jetant à ses genoux, je vais vous faire
un aveu que l'on n'a jamais fait à son mari; mais l'innocence de ma conduite et
de mes intentions m'en donne la force. . . . Songez que pour faire ce que je fais,
il faut avoir plus d'amitié et plus d'estime que l'on en a jamais eu. . . . L'aveu

8. Descartes, *Les Passions de l'âme,* in *Oeuvres et lettres* (Paris: Gallimard, 1953), article
48, p. 720.

que je vous ai fait n'a pas été par faiblesse, et il faut plus de courage pour avouer
cette vérité que pour entreprendre de la cacher (122–23).

Several critics have recognized this "prise de parole" by the protagonist as a sign that she is in the process of acquiring the strength to
affirm herself. Although she requests help, understanding, guidance,
and affection from her husband, she is certainly taking a major initiative, a bold one involving major risks: "Elle trouva qu'elle s'était
ôté elle-même le coeur et l'estime de son mari et qu'elle s'était creusé
un abîme dont elle ne sortirait jamais. . . . La singularité d'un pareil
aveu, dont elle ne trouvait point d'exemple, lui en faisait voir tout le
péril" (125). Having second thoughts, however, she considers the
confession as a "remède," that is, a strong, cathartic medicine that
will save her from the worst. In the midst of her mental turmoil, she
sees her avowal as a proof of fidelity given to a husband who certainly
deserved it, as witnessed by the manner in which he received it (123).
She again considers her decision as setting her apart from other
women, although she finds her passion "unworthy of herself" (127).
These inner thoughts and feelings are indicative of her constant, progressive search for selfhood and prepare for the full posTesion of it at
the end.

M. de Clèves's first reaction after hearing his wife's confession is a
noble and generous one; he goes in the right direction by expressing
his trust and in giving her full freedom: "Je n'ai nulle inquiétude de
votre conduite, lui dit-il, vous avez plus de force et plus de vertu que
vous ne pensez" (127). He cannot, however, prevent himself from
experiencing curiosity about his rival or conceal his grief which, later,
combined with jealousy, unfounded suspicion, and incomplete information, will lead to his illness and death.

Because of Nemours's indiscretion, the extraordinary story of the
princess's avowal, anonymous but accurate, circulates at court; Mme
de Clèves's inner balance is then threatened. When questioned by the
duke, she invokes her *repos*: "Au nom de Dieu, lui dit-elle, laissez-
moi en repos!" (129). If Nemours had any delicacy of feeling or Christian charity, he would have realized how much his pursuit and indiscretion hurt the woman he claims to love. Later, she is shaken by
his hypocritical insinuation about M. de Clèves, according to which
he might have been guilty of having spread the story of the confession

made by his wife. This leads to a breach in the mutual trust between husband and wife, and their relationship is, from then on, damaged, to the great distress of the princess.

Mme de Clèves's anguish is all the more unbearable because she is led to suspect Nemours's indiscretion, a token of his vanity, his self-satisfaction at knowing he is loved (138–39). By speaking, even without mentioning names, he has forsaken the ideal of courtly love that requires the utmost discretion on the part of the lover in order to preserve the reputation of his lady. The princess thus becomes aware of the shortcomings of the man she loves, whom she had thus far considered a model gentleman and most respectful lover; she is also disappointed and hurt by her husband's growing suspicions, reproaches, and distress. When he apologizes in a letter for his outburst and assures her of his affection, she is comforted in her resolution of fidelity. She replies to him in her own letter, renewing her previous declarations of innocence. The mutual trust could still be restored and the marriage bond strengthened at this point if another grievous initiative by Nemours did not ruin this hope and bring about the prince's tragic end. The duke's attempt to see Mme de Clèves at Coulommiers where she is alone at night is reported to the prince who falsely interprets his presence as the sign of his wife's infidelity. The moral conscience of the princess will not allow her to forget that Nemours has indirectly caused the death of her husband.

The furtive appearance of the duke at Coulommiers during a warm summer night where he observes unseen the woman he loves in the intimacy of a private room furnished with a daybed and decorated with paintings of the siege of Metz in which he was a participant is one of the most poetic as well as dramatic scenes of the novel. The sitting room located in a garden pavilion opens up through French doors onto a flower garden. Mme de Clèves, lightly dressed in a négligé, with her hair flowing freely about her shoulders, is shown contemplating Nemours's portrait in the painting. She is also making bows with ribbons of the very color worn by the duke at the tournament around a cane that belonged to him. Her expression and her actions betray her feelings: she is obviously seeking communion with the man she loves through representation and symbolic signs. These should be seen in the context of archaic but still widely held beliefs in the magical power of objects belonging to a person or representing him or her.[9] The princess believes herself to be alone and does not utter a word or give any sign of having changed her resolutions. When she hears a slight noise and thinks she has seen Nemours, she rejoins her ladies in waiting in the next room. The attitude and gestures of Mme de Clèves are the celebration of a cult of love whose object is remote, idealized through representation.[10] The physical, real presence is refused. Thus her resolve is clearly reaffirmed and the final refusal subtly foreshadowed. The celebration of human love, idealized, sublimated to be sure, also foreshadows the final choice of an absolute, perfect love. The princess's itinerary is progressing in gradual stages, along a path that has been arduous and will, after her husband's death, prove even more so when she has complete freedom of choice and thereby complete responsibility for herself.

M. de Clèves's death represents a terrible ordeal for a virtuous wife, falsely accused of having been unfaithful and thus of having caused his death. She has, at least, in a dramatic conversation, the ultimate satisfaction of clearing his mind of doubts, of his thinking her an adulteress and a criminal: the word "crime" is used by her with horror (162). She succeeds in convincing him of her innocence and of the constancy of her affection for him. Her concerns are mostly for his welfare and for his life, which she attempts to save by making him see the truth; her generosity and nobility of soul are very much in evidence: "S'il n'y allait que de mon intérêt, je souffrirais ces reproches; mais il y va de votre vie. Ecoutez-moi, pour l'amour de vous-même: il est impossible qu'avec tant de vérité, je ne vous persuade mon innocence" (163).

The princess's grief is extreme at the death of her husband, carrying her to the edge of a mental breakdown. Not only has she lost a person for whom she had great esteem and affection; also, she considers herself responsible for his untimely death: "Mme de Clèves demeura dans une

9. Béatrice Didier, "Le Silence de la Princesse de Clèves," in L'Ecriture-femme (Paris: Presses Universitaires de France, 1981), 81–82, 90. The interpretation centered on magic seems convincing in seventeenth-century terms. The psychoanalytical one definitely belongs to a twentieth-century mentality.

10. Marie-Odile Sweetser, "La Littérature et les femmes," in Le Langage littéraire au XVIIe siècle: De la rhétorique à la littérature, ed. Christian Wentzlaff-Eggebert (Tübingen, Germany: Gunter Narr, 1991), 51–65.

affliction si violente qu'elle perdit quasi l'usage de la raison. . . .
Quand . . . elle vit quel mari elle avait perdu, qu'elle considéra qu'elle
était la cause de sa mort, et que c'était par la passion qu'elle avait eue
pour un autre qu'elle en était cause, l'horreur qu'elle eut pour elle-
même et pour M. de Nemours ne se peut représenter" (164). In a
telling reversal, it is no longer her husband who falsely accuses her of
a crime; the princess now believes that she and the duke are responsible for his death. The anaphora of "mourant" is evocative of the
relentless remorse that shakes her soul and that she will never, in her
uprightness, be able to expunge: "Ce mari mourant, et mourant à
cause d'elle et avec tant de tendresse pour elle, ne lui sortait point de
l'esprit. Elle repassait incessamment tout ce qu'elle lui devait, et elle
se faisait un crime de n'avoir pas eu de la passion pour lui, comme si
c'eût été une chose qui eût été en son pouvoir" (165).

She is keenly aware of what she owes her husband. Georges Forestier
pertinently remarks that the notion of "devoir" comes up most often
in the last pages of the novel, far more often than those of "repos"
and "vertu."[11] In a previous study, I pointed out the intensity and
duration of the princess's grief as opposed to the few tears in her eyes
at her last interview with Nemours: the disproportion is indeed striking,[12] indicative of her true, deepest feelings and of the ensuing commitment to enduring fidelity to the man who gave her true love and
single-minded devotion: "pourrais-je m'accoutumer [au malheur] de
croire voir toujours M. de Clèves vous accuser de sa mort, me reprocher de vous avoir aimé, de vous avoir épousé et me faire sentir la
différence de son attachement au vôtre?" (174).

The other fundamental aspect of her character comes out strongly
in the last interview with Nemours: her sincerity, her straightforward
speech. It is, in fact, another avowal scene, made this time to the
person she loves and from whom she does not want to hide her
thoughts and feelings. Again she tells Nemours that this lack of ar-

11. Forestier, 74–75. One could then conclude that moral duty is the most important
value in the choice of Mme de Clèves. The author's argument, however, is that this notion
is the legacy of Mme de Chartres whose lessons have suffused her daughter's thinking. He
admits that duty is at least as important as the fear of seeing Nemours fall out of love,
and therefore as important as "repos" in her final decision.

12. Marie-Odile Sweetser, "La Princesse de Clèves et son unité," PMLA 87 (1972):
487.

tifice, this truthfulness distinguishes her from other women. She is keenly conscious of being apart and that constitutes her concept of selfhood and leads to the decision of acting on that newly acquired certitude. Thus it is, as Jean Lafond has so powerfully demonstrated in his splendid essay, a choice for what is best in her, an expression of authenticity from a free and responsible individual. She realizes, as Lafond indicates, "la passion morale du vrai, de l'authentique contre l'aliénation des passions—son existence est une existence réussie, esthétiquement et moralement réussie."[13] It is in this second avowal that she reaches the full autonomy that the first one had begun to establish. At this point, it exists on a personal, human basis resting on her desire and resolution to be true to herself, including the marriage vows freely consented to and to which she intends to remain faithful: "il faut que je demeure dans l'état où je suis et dans les résolutions que j'ai prises de n'en sortir jamais" (174). The choice of retreat and solitude will at the same time protect and enhance the realization of this imperative need: to be herself, to belong to herself. A contemporary American novelist has praised, for the same reasons, the "Benefits of the Solitary Life," as a way to find the self.[14] For a seventeenth-century aristocratic lady, retreat from court life and the turmoils of passion was the natural solution, the accepted way to realize herself fully. As Roger Duchêne judiciously points out:

L'auteur ne condamne pas cette éducation. La dernière phrase du roman montre au contraire sa réussite. Peu importe que la vertu ait coûté cher à Mme de Clèves puisqu'elle n'a pas de prix. Ces idées nous choquent. Nous pensons au contraire que. . . . la Princesse de Clèves est passée à côte du bonheur, puisqu'elle a refusé l'amour. Mais les contemporains. . . . étaient quasi unanimes à dénoncer le caractère destructeur des passions et les mérites de la paix intérieure de ceux qui en étaient exempts ou libérés.[15]

13. Jean Lafond, "Mme de Lafayette et le repli sur l'être," *Bulletin de la Société des Professeurs français en Amérique* (1987–88): 35.

14. May Sarton, "Rewards of a Solitary Life," *The Literary Eye* (*New York Times*, 140, 30 September 1990; reprint of 8 April 1974): "the moment comes when the world falls away, and the self emerges again from the deep unconscious, bringing back all I have recently experienced to be explored and slowly understood, when I converse again with my own hidden powers, and so grow, and so be renewed, till death do us part."

15. Roger Duchêne, "Les Deux *Princesses* sont-elles d'un même auteur?" in *Mme de la Fayette, Littérature classique* (1990, supplement): 14.

It is later, after the experience of illness and the brush with death, that the princess will be able to go beyond her purely human odyssey and eventually find, along with her true self, the ideal, lasting love that she was seeking but knew could not be found in human relationships.

Generally, probably because of later biographical data concerning the life of Mme de Lafayette, scholars have stressed the Pascalian and Augustinian attitude and beliefs that they have found implicitly present in the last stage of Mme de Clèves's life: Jean Lafond, Jean Mesnard, Alain Niderst, and Philippe Sellier are among the foremost specialists to address the topics. Other scholars have significantly contributed toward redressing the balance. Patrick Henry and William Marceau have clearly shown the Salesian elements of this spiritual itinerary.[16] Wolfgang Leiner also has brought new light to the question in demonstrating that Mme de Clèves's conduct and itinerary can be explained in the context of Christian morality as preached by well-known, mainstream Jesuit and Jesuit-educated theologians, Bourdaloue and Bossuet, for example, the first a Jesuit, the other raised in a Jesuit "collège" in Dijon.[17] This important study led me to a reexamination of the final stage of Mme de Clèves's personal and spiritual itinerary, when she chooses retreat from the court and pious occupations without, however, entering a convent and committing herself to a religious life. The final stage of the princess's spiritual itinerary should be read in the light of statements made by Ignace de Loyola about the election of a suitable path according to individual needs and freedom:

Quand, l'âme étant tranquille, quelqu'un, après avoir considéré le but pour lequel il est créé (c'est-à-dire la gloire de Dieu et son salut), choisit tel genre de vie existant à l'intérieur de l'Eglise catholique comme une sorte de moyen lui per-

16. See Jean Mesnard's recent study, "Morale et métaphysique dans *La Princesse de Clèves*," *Littératures classiques* (1990, supplement): 65–74; William Marceau, "The Christianity of Madame de Lafayette" and Patrick G. Henry, "Comments," in *Literature and Spirituality in Seventeenth-Century France. Papers on French Seventeenth-Century Literature* 17 (1990): 171–88.

17. In this respect, Wolfgang Leiner notes: "Les appels pressants de Mme de Chartres à sa fille de ne jamais perdre de vue l'idéal de la vertu et de ne jamais oublier ses devoirs sont comme des échos reprenant les exhortations de morale chrétienne prêchée par les Jésuites" (50).

mettant de tendre plus facilement et sûrement à sa fin. On reconnait qu'il y a cette tranquillité chaque fois que l'âme n'est agitée par aucun des divers esprits et *exerce librement ses capacités naturelles*. M'étant mis devant les yeux la fin de ma création. . . . ne pencher pour aucune solution, ni de prendre ni de refuser la chose en question, mais plutôt demeurer comme dans une position médiane et en équilibre, prêt à me porter tout entier sur le champ à la solution que j'aurai reconnue devoir correspondre mieux à la gloire divine et à mon salut.[18]

The translator and commentator makes a pertinent remark on this point, stressing human freedom:

Il n'y a pas de modèle tout fait ou objectif de la perfection. . . . D'une certaine façon, Ignace fait sienne l'affirmation que l'on a tant reprochée à son contemporain Erasme que 'la vie monastique n'est pas la perfection', en ce sens du moins que la perfection n'est liée *a priori* à aucune manière particulière de vivre, qu'elle ne se mesure pas à la fidélité à des normes préétablies et objectivement repérables, mais à l'intériorité de la fidélité de l'homme aux exigences que la Parole de Dieu fait naître en lui. ("Introduction," *Exercices,* 23–24)

This is precisely the state that the princess reaches after her illness that brings her close to death, an eventuality that Ignace had considered the perfect hypothetical point for choosing a suitable way of life: "Me demander, en outre, si j'étais sur le point de mourir, quel parti je préférerais avoir pris dans la délibération présente. Aussi je comprendrai facilement que je dois le choisir maintenant" (*Exercices,* 103n186).

From these considerations, drawn from moral and spiritual works of the Counter-Reformation, one can conclude that far from being an extinction, the solution chosen by the princess, again in full freedom, is a true elevation, a heightening of the gifts bestowed upon her at the outset, cultivated by a wise and virtuous mother at first, then by herself alone amidst trials and tribulations, ending in an exaltation, discreetly and succinctly sketched by an author who, like her heroine, practices classical restraint but, like her again, through her very simplicity of expression and truthfulness, reaches the sublime.

18. Saint Ignace de Loyola, *Exercices spirituels,* trans. and ed. Jean-Claude Guy (Paris: Seuil, 1982), 101n177, 102n179, my italics. Hereafter cited parenthetically in the text.

12 The Power of Confession

The Ideology of Love in *La Princesse de Clèves*

JANE MARIE TODD

La Princesse de Clèves is about the insertion of a female subject into a system of social relationships that define her as wife, and about the ideology, in the process of being elaborated, that supports marital love and monogamy as the social ideal. It is, moreover, the story of a woman's rebellion against this new ideology, but a rebellion that takes an unusual form: it consists of embracing that ideology, but only as an impossible ideal, of remaining faithful to a husband who is dead and idealized, idealized *because* dead, and even dead *because idealized,* capable of existing only in absolute terms, only in a world within or a world beyond. "M. de Clèves était peut-être l'unique homme du monde capable de l'amour dans le mariage,"[1] the princess explains to the Duc de Nemours, in a passage that marks her first real departure from her mother's teachings about love.

In order to assess the princess's ultimate decision to renounce love and society (and ultimately life itself), it is necessary to understand her motivations in relation to the ideologies of love elaborated throughout the novel. That is, it is important to understand not only her psychology but the way in which her psychology, and psychological discourse itself, are related to instances of *power.* In his *Histoire de la*

1. Madame de Lafayette, *La Princesse de Clèves,* ed. Antoine Adam (Paris: Garnier-Flammarion, 1966), 173; hereafter cited parenthetically in the text.

sexualité, Michel Foucault notes that, in the history of the West, "l'individu s'est longtemps authentifié par la référence des autres et la manifestation de son lien à autrui . . . ; puis on l'a authentifié par le discours de vérité qu'il était capable ou obligé de tenir sur lui-même. L'aveu de la vérité s'est inscrit au coeur des procédures d'individualisation par le pouvoir."[2] Introspection, and the complex psychological discourse of ambivalent feelings and hidden motivations that resulted from it, became the hallmark of modern subjecthood or, as Foucault puts it, of "subject-ion" (*assujettissement*) to power.

This interiorization or psychologization of power developed over the centuries, beginning in the Middle Ages and continuing, in different forms, to the present. The etymology of the term *aveu* reflects the shift in the source of the individual's "authenticity": "de l''aveu,' garantie de statut, d'identité et de valeur accordée à quelqu'un par un autre, on est passé à l''aveu,' reconnaissance par quelqu'un de ses propres actions ou pensées" (Foucault, 78). It is precisely at the time of the writing of *La Princesse de Clèves* that this shift in meaning was occurring.[3] Foucault views the confession as a particularly modern phenomenon, and as one of the foremost ways that the instances of power insinuated themselves into the most private recesses of the individual, in order to regulate the subject from within. Indeed, it might be more accurate to say that power *created* these private recesses. For before there can be confession, there must be introspection: the subject internalizes power's dictates in order to confess the desires or impulses that deviate from the moral code in place.

Foucault even links this shift in the exercise of power, and therefore in the nature of the subject, to a "metamorphosis" in literature: "d'un plaisir de raconter et d'entendre, qui était centré sur le récit héroïque ou merveilleux des 'épreuves' de bravoure ou de sainteté, on est passé à une littérature ordonnée à la tâche infinie de faire lever du fond de soi-même, entre les mots, une vérité que la forme même de l'aveu fait miroiter comme l'inaccessible" (80). *La Princesse de Clèves* would seem to occupy a key place in this history. Not only does it enjoy the canonical status of being the first modern psychological novel, but an

2. Michel Foucault, *Histoire de la sexualité: 1. La Volonté de savoir* (Paris: Gallimard, 1976), 78–79; hereafter cited parenthetically in the text.

3. See Joan DeJean's discussion of this term in chap. 2 of this volume, 63–64.

unheard-of confession, that of the princess to her husband, is central to the plot. The *invraisemblance* of this confession, noted both within the novel and by its contemporary readers, suggests that it marks an important inroad in the progression of psychologization. "Il n'y a que vous de femme au monde qui fasse confidence à son mari" (116), Mme la Dauphine tells the princess. The princess and her mother—who provides her moral education—would seem to represent the vanguard in the *manie d'avouer.*

In fact, the moral code that Mme de Chartres instills in her daughter differs both in its content and in the form of its enforcement from that in place at the court when mother and daughter make their appearance. The world they enter at the beginning of the novel is a world of surfaces, of social appearances. In the first pages, the narration floats along that surface, admiring the "bien fait," the "plein d'esprit," the "chef[s]-d'oeuvre de la nature," the "personne[s] parfaite[s]." Even "galanterie," a term used pejoratively throughout the novel, in particular by Mme de Chartres, appears in the first sentence as the affirmation of a courtly value: "La magnificence et la galanterie n'ont jamais paru en France avec tant d'éclat que dans les dernières années du règne de Henri second" (35). *Galanterie* here refers to a courtly code of behavior rather than to the indiscretions of individual members of the court that the princess's mother finds so objectionable.

The narration distinguishes Mme de Chartres's pedagogical method from that currently in fashion in the following terms:

La plupart des mères s'imaginent qu'il suffit de ne parler jamais de galanterie devant les jeunes personnes pour les en éloigner. Mme de Chartres avait une opinion opposée; elle faisait souvent à sa fille des peintures de l'amour; elle lui montrait ce qu'il a d'agréable pour la persuader plus aisément sur ce qu'elle lui en apprenait de dangereux; elle lui contait le peu de sincérité des hommes, leurs tromperies et leur infidélité, les malheurs domestiques où plongent les engagements; et elle lui faisait voir, d'un autre côté, quelle tranquillité suivait la vie d'une honnête femme, et combien la vertu donnait d'éclat et d'élévation à une personne qui avait de la beauté et de la naissance; mais elle lui faisait voir aussi combien il était difficile de conserver cette vertu, que par une extrême défiance de soi-même et par un grand soin de s'attacher à ce qui seul peut faire le bonheur d'une femme, qui est d'aimer son mari et d'en être aimée. (41)

The mother's strategy to produce a discourse about sexuality achieves two aims: first, it promotes the ideology of romantic love, understood as limited to marriage; and second, it introduces the *distrust* of oneself, and therefore the necessity of attending to one's interior life, one's penchants and desires, that is, the precondition for the very possibility of confession. (It is a sign of the power of the ideology of interiority that the princess feels compelled to confess not any actual misdeed or indiscretion, but rather a mere *inclination* that she has discovered in herself.) In a word, the mother's discourse sets out the various erotic possibilities in order that one—monogamy—might be promoted and protected.[4]

In this vein, Foucault writes: "C'est par l'isolement, l'intensification et la consolidation des sexualités périphériques que les relations du pouvoir au sexe et au plaisir se ramifient. . . . Prolifération des sexualités par l'extension du pouvoir; majoration du pouvoir auquel chacune de ces sexualités régionales donne une surface d'intervention" (66). In the case of *La Princesse de Clèves*, we have not a multiplicity, but a simple dichotomy of sexual practices (*galanterie/fidélité*); nevertheless, the deployment of power is the same. Introspection will lead to confession and confession makes possible the intervention by an agent of power—in this case, the prince and his spy.

The context of the mother's lesson to her daughter is also significant. In Madame de Lafayette's vision, the instruction on love takes place away from the court, in isolation, between a mother and daughter whose relationship is uninterrupted by a male presence—the princess's father is dead—and whose communication is pure. In what is undoubtedly an idealized view of the domestic, female realm, the mother, *in fact* the representative of a new ideology about to take hold, is presented as presiding exclusively over her daughter's happiness.

Even after Mme and Mlle de Chartres are integrated into courtly society, the communication between them, in bypassing the deceitfulness of language in favor of the *gaze,* does not fall victim to the misunderstandings that so often propel the plot. When the princess goes to her mother to confess her attraction to Nemours, for instance, she finds that her confession is unnecessary. Her mother tells her,

4. For an insightful discussion of the mother's pedagogical techniques and their effects, see Peggy Kamuf, "A Mother's Will: *La Princesse de Clèves*," in *Fictions of Feminine Desire* (Lincoln: University of Nebraska Press, 1982), 67–96.

"Vous avez de l'inclination pour M. de Nemours; je ne vous demande point de me l'avouer. . . . Il y a déjà longtemps que je me suis aperçue de cette inclination" (67). Nothing could better convey the *specular* nature of ideal love as it is presented in the novel than this passage: for if, as Foucault argues, the confession is that which is elicited by power and necessary to it, then the superfluity of confession is a sign both of the mother's absolute power and of her absolute love. No confession is needed because the mother already knows; the daughter's feelings do not have to pass through the world or through language in order to be understood.

The mother's power *is* absolute, all the more so because she dies: "Si quelque chose était capable de troubler le bonheur que j'espère en sortant de ce monde," she laments on her deathbed, "ce serait de vous voir tomber comme les autres femmes; mais, si ce malheur vous doit arriver, je reçois la mort avec joie, pour n'en être pas le témoin" (68). These words, and the guilt they speak to, haunt Mme de Clèves and make the mourning for her mother particularly painful: "Mme de Clèves était dans une affliction extrême . . . ; quoique la tendresse et la reconnaissance y eussent la plus grande part, le besoin qu'elle sentait qu'elle avait de sa mère, pour se défendre contre M. de Nemours ne laissait pas d'y en avoir beaucoup" (68). This mourning serves to internalize further the mother's interdiction, and increases the mother's power over her daughter.

In idealizing the relation between mother and daughter as pre- or extrasocial, as a specular communication, Madame de Lafayette manages to convey the contradictions inherent between the ideology of love that the mother espouses and the real social (and patriarchal) modes of reproduction existing in the court. While her view of the mother/daughter relation is undoubtedly utopian, and a by-product of the very contradictions in the social world she is depicting, that utopian vision does set in relief certain social realities.

We see the first contradiction at the time of Mlle de Chartres's introduction into the court and the system of kinship. It is at this point that the *name* and its relation to male relatives come into play: "Elle était de la même maison que l[a] vidame de Chartres et une des plus grandes héritières de France" (41). While the mother's ideology dictates that she find her daughter a husband whom she loves (or *could* love), it is clear that this individualist approach fails to consider overriding social realities. While it is impossible to explain why Mme de Chartres, given her view of marital love, consents to the engagement with the prince, even after her daughter has told her that she has "aucune inclination particulière pour sa personne" (50), this mystery is partly illuminated by the haste and near panic in which the agreement is reached, as a result of the many broken engagements that have preceded it and the disgrace that accompanies them. That is, the mother is obliged to bow to the code of the court when seeking a husband for the princess, since alliances depend not only on questions of birth, wealth, and rank, but also on all the complicated political intrigues and personal animosities that structure courtly life. Such are the elementary rules of kinship, and they have very little to do with the model of specular love.

It should be no surprise, then, that when the prince replaces the mother as the princess's confessor, the specular relationship is destroyed and a mediated one introduced. Even the permission to confess is given through indirection: the prince relates to the princess a conversation he had had with Sancerre during which he revealed to the latter that "si ma maîtresse, et même ma femme, m'avouait que quelqu'un lui plût, j'en serais affligé sans en être aigri. Je quitterais le personnage d'amant ou de mari, pour la conseiller et pour la plaindre" (76). As in much of the novel, the meaning of this statement is blurred by a problem of address or of destination: originally a hypothetical statement addressed to a distraught friend, it is only through the princess's act of interpretation that it becomes an invitation to transfer the role of confessor from mother to husband. In a novel whose plot is advanced primarily through intercepted letters, mistaken identities, and overheard conversations, the deceitfulness and, indeed, the *faithlessness* of language is everywhere apparent. In contrast to the relation between daughter and mother, the princess's relation to her husband depends upon a language that is rarely trustworthy.

In fact, in *La Princesse de Clèves*, specular, maternal love is the model for "true," monogamous, heterosexual love. Because she loves the Duc de Nemours, the princess is "tuned in" to his feelings: "Il prit une conduite si sage et s'observa avec tant de soin que personne ne le soupçonna d'être amoureux de Mme de Clèves . . . et elle aurait eu peine à s'en apercevoir elle-même si l'inclination qu'elle avait pour lui ne lui eût donné une attention particulière pour ses actions" (61). But, while the princess's face and actions are entirely legible to those who love her, those not attached to her by love inevitably fail to read them: "Si Mme la Dauphine l'eût regardée avec attention, elle eût aisément remarqué que les choses qu'elle venait de dire ne lui étaient pas indifférentes" (82). Of course, Madame la Dauphine does not notice, because this mode of communication (and it is flawless) is reserved for those who love.

The model for pure love and pure communication, because it is a maternal one, is one that the prince cannot live up to. Once the mother dies, the princess is cast adrift in a language whose power over her increases, despite or because of the unreliability of its reference and destination. While the prince accurately "reads" the princess's physiognomy on a number of occasions—he knows, for example, that the princess does not love him, and he contrives to learn the identity of her beloved by watching her responses to the hypothetical scenarios he presents to her—the fact that he requires the supplement of confession to know of the princess's "sin" indicates that nonlinguistic communication is incomplete in this instance. The confession itself, we recall, is not only elicited in the indirect manner discussed above, but, unknown to both parties, is also mediated by a third, the Duc de Nemours, who overhears it from his hiding place.

The princess's critical silence regarding the *name* of her lover— here, as in the case of the princess's marriageability and, in fact, that of the Vidame de Chartres's unsigned and unaddressed letter, the name represents social authority and linguistic identity—leads directly to the prince's machinations to discover her lover and his distrust regarding the completeness of her confession. Similarly, the duke's third-person account of the conversation and his own doubts about whether he is in fact the beloved designated in the confession lead to both the prince's suspicions and the duke's presence in the garden at Coulommiers. Finally, because, in the absence of the princess, the prince trusts the spy's account of the events at Coulommiers (an account rendered incomplete by the interrupted gaze, in that the spy cannot see beyond the garden wall), the prince believes in his wife's infidelity and dies as a result of this belief. Thus, while the confession clearly functions according to the model set out by Foucault—far from protecting the princess, it sets in motion a series of actions whose consequences further intensify the ideology's hold on her—its functioning depends in part on the "untethered" nature of language: the spy's account mediates what should have been a direct communication between prince and princess, while rumor attaches to a confession deprived of a proper name. One might say that Madame de Lafayette presents a Foucauldian theory of power grafted onto a Derridean theory of language.

One might argue, of course, that the agent of power, the prince, hardly fares better than its object—or subject, in the Foucauldian sense. After all, he dies of grief after being convinced that his wife has been unfaithful. There are two responses to this assertion. In the first place, the prince is himself subject to power: it is because he has internalized the ideology of monogamy that the thought of his wife's infidelity deals him a death blow. In the second place, like the mother, the prince is never more powerful than when he is dead: the princess finally forsakes the duke, society, and even life itself only after the prince has died. The combination of her idealization of his fidelity and love and the guilt she feels at having indirectly been the cause of his death brings about the princess's final decision to remain faithful to his memory forever.

This is not, however, the final stage of the princess's moral development. The Princesse de Clèves falls ill as a result of her emotional conflict and difficult mourning and is close to death for a long time. "Cette vue si longue et si prochaine de la mort fit paraître à Mme de Clèves les choses de cette vie de cet oeil si différent dont on les voit dans la santé" (179). In other words, the princess embraces not merely her dead mother and her dead husband, but finally death itself. Her education has come full circle, for death is simply another version of the ideal presocial existence that she had enjoyed with her mother. In death, if not in life, true fidelity is possible.

It is virtually a commonplace of criticism indebted to Foucault that power "relentlessly produces and recontains subversion so that . . . 'any apparent site of resistance ultimately serves the interests of power.'"[5] What La Princesse de Clèves illustrates is virtually the opposite. In embracing, without mimicry or parody, but in all ear-

5. Carolyn Porter, "Politics, Aesthetics, and the New Histories," Pacific Coast Philology 25 (1989): 26. The author is quoting Walter Cohen.

nestness, the ideology in its absolute form, she also guarantees that it will have no hold on her. In a world of few options, the princess, by remaining true to her dead mother, her dead husband, and finally to death itself, manages to weaken society's hold on her and, perhaps, to remain true to herself.

The question remaining concerns the relation between a literary text and the ideologies represented within it. In the passage from *Histoire de la sexualité* cited earlier, Foucault claims that the psychological novel is a "littérature ordonnée à la tâche infinie de faire lever du fond de soi-même, entre les mots, une vérité que la forme même de l'aveu fait miroiter comme l'inaccessible" (80). He suggests that literary discourse is continuous with ideological formations, or that literary genres express or espouse the dominant ideologies. But an analysis of *La Princesse de Clèves* demonstrates that the situation is far more complicated. At different moments in the novel, Madame de Lafayette *expresses, represents,* and *critiques* the ideology of interiority in question.

The text *expresses* it when it adopts the point of view of the mother and suggests that the princess's happiness depends upon her distrust of self and her faith in the protection by her mother or her husband that a timely confession would ensure. In a sense, what Foucault views as a literary historical event (the shift from the *chanson de geste* to the psychological novel) occurs in *La Princesse de Clèves* as a narrative event: the introduction of Mme de Chartres and her ideology of romantic marital love into courtly society. But in representing this shift as a microevent, and one initiated by the *mother* exclusively with her daughter's happiness in mind, the novel of course blurs the ideological issues involved and overlooks the larger ramifications of this historical shift, including its relation to patriarchy, which Foucault himself overlooks. In this respect, understanding *La Princesse de Clèves* as a tale about power and ideology necessarily involves reading "against the grain."

Nevertheless, the novel *represents* ideology *as* ideology when it foregrounds the contradictions inherent in the princess's social world that make the carrying out of the mother's instructions virtually doomed to failure. This representation, however, entails constructing a counterideology, an ideal world of pure (maternal) love and faultless communication, a world free from deceit and intrigue where marriage would be based only on love and love would guarantee understanding. In contrast to this utopia, real social relations are shown to be based upon intrigue, political and familial power, and a language that misleads and misdirects. As such, marriage based solely on love (without consideration of duty, family ties, or social rank) is virtually impossible and confession as a means of protecting oneself from sin opens one to the dangers of rumor and misunderstandings.

Finally, *La Princesse de Clèves critiques* the ideology of interiority when it shows the dire consequences of confession and when it has the princess turn away from the social world in the recognition that the mother's ideology cannot function as she would wish in that world. Nevertheless, it remains a *partial* critique in that the princess rejects the *world* rather than the ideology per se. Given her circumstances, however, the princess's decision may be her best defense.

Epilogue

JOHN D. LYONS

CAN an epilogue to these studies of *La Princesse de Clèves* be a conclusion? Conclusiveness seems impossible both because of the uniquely surprising and elliptical nature of the novel's own conclusion and because of the diversity and the lively interaction of the views presented here. This volume shows that the study of Lafayette's masterpiece, more than three centuries after its publication, is as animated as ever. Rather than attempt closure, I take the position of a reader with the privilege of joining the debate at the moment when it takes its next turn in the tradition, the moment when we confront the often sharply divergent views of sociocritics, feminists, ethicists, psychologically oriented readers, historians of knowledge, and others. The different ways of understanding key elements of the novel may at first appear overwhelming: does the heroine retreat from the court to seek religious peace and eternal salvation? To maintain an outmoded aristocratic ethic? Or to enjoy continued sexual fantasy? Is the heroine's mother a model of Christian virtue? A proponent of romantic love above all? Or the defender of the value of appearances? Does the novel propose a flawless visual feminine communication in opposition to a failed masculine verbal code, or does it propose a new verbal form, an elliptical *écriture féminine*? I imagine myself moderating a seminar in which other readers, like myself, are determining how the experience of these twelve studies will affect their own understanding of *La Princesse de Clèves*.

I will not attempt to recapitulate the careful and subtle analyses that have been presented to support the positions thus summarily and simplistically juxtaposed, nor will I claim a privilege as final arbiter to select readings that I consider the "correct" ones. Since this collection will stimulate rather than halt debate about *La Princesse de Clèves,* an epilogue might best serve as a magnifier of difference, as an instrument to focus attention on interpretive divergences, and as a guide to the occasional points where initially opposed methodological assumptions lead to similar readings. As a simple means of getting a comparative view of the dozen articles in this volume, I suggest looking at opinions of three moments of the novel that attract the attention of most of the contributors: the mother's lesson, the confession or confessions, and the heroine's retreat after her final conversation with her suitor Nemours.

THE MOTHER'S LESSON

Mme de Chartres raised her daughter away from the court and according to educational principles very different from those of other mothers. Readers have different views of the content of the lesson, of the princess's understanding of it, and of the importance of the form in which the mother's lesson is imparted. For Albanese, the mother intends to impress upon the heroine a form of virtue based on "utter self-reliance and self-restraint" (93) through which the princess will attempt to achieve "physical and moral perfection" for the purposes of appearing socially superior to others at court. In short, for Albanese the mother represents values of aristocratic distinction. In this account of the princess's education the only element of the mother's pedagogical method that is mentioned is the place. The princess is raised away from the court, presumably because the court is seen as the collective form of the global enemy or rival. Such a view of the heroine's upbringing stresses the consistency of values expressed in the single word *gloire.* The princess's subsequent conduct is rooted in the outmoded nobiliary values of the mother.

A radically different view of this education, presented by Kuizenga, holds that the mother, far from stressing individual heroic preeminence, represents the "tradition that prioritizes the public and social over the individual" (79). If the public and the private are thus distinguished and pitted against one another, then the aristocratic model fits with some difficulty into this scheme. As I understand Albanese's description, the individual is not important per se, but only as representative of an hereditary elite, one for which there is no real privacy but for which the public would serve as both rival and audience. In seeking *gloire* as an aristocratic performer, the princess needs the public precisely to distinguish herself from others. Kuizenga presents the mother's lesson as the formation of a "moral woman" (79) who refuses passion as a hindrance to performance of a social function within the institution of marriage, itself a unit of the larger social order "based on rank, wealth, and proximity to power" (79). Albanese, on the other hand, situates virtue within all those qualities that give the heroine "a status of exceptionality unknown to all other females at court" (94). In other words, one reading (Kuizenga's) sees the mother's education as leading to conformity and submission, while the other (Albanese's) sees this education as leading to a refusal of conformity to the prevailing public standards. Kuizenga agrees that the princess at least partly revolts against her social function, but argues that this revolt is caused by the heroine's misunderstanding of what her mother meant by love (79–80).

The princess's education appears also to Koppisch as a stimulation to rivalry with others. Like Albanese, Koppisch stresses the aristocratic basis of the mother's lesson. The courtly system is based on differences between individuals, and Mme de Chartres wants her daughter to have a "sense of her own preeminence" (198). Koppisch, however, makes a major contribution to understanding the contradictory nature of this education by pointing out the way the princess will be required to compare herself constantly to others. In Koppisch's terms, this lesson is "a natural extension of the nobiliary hierarchy that in large measure determined courtiers' prestige" (197). The key term here may well be "extension," for constant comparison, and thus, in successful cases, repeated distinction from other nobles can only occur in proximity, as at court. This shift in reference is a result of the physical and geographic shift from a decentralized feudal landed aristocracy to a centralized monarchical system with vestiges of aristocratic privilege. Aristocracy, as played out on the narrow stage of the court, produces the peculiar performance that is "une sorte d'agitation sans désordre."[1] As Koppisch shows, the mother prevents her

1. Mme de Lafayette, *La Princesse de Clèves*, ed. Antoine Adam (Paris: Garnier-Flammarion, 1966), 45; hereafter cited parenthetically in the text.

daughter from reaching tranquility by impressing on her the importance of a comparative, rather than an absolute, system of values: "her
need to be different from other women, which her mother has taught
her, subjects Mme de Clèves to precisely those conflicts she tries most
desperately to avoid" (199). Linked to the mother's deathbed conversation with the heroine, Mme de Chartres's teaching prior to arrival
at the court does indeed appear to be cast in relativistic terms. Mme
de Clèves should not "tomber comme les autres femmes" and risk
losing "cette réputation que vous vous êtes acquise et que je vous ai
tant souhaitée" (68; Koppisch, 200). Like Albanese, Koppisch argues
that the mother's lesson is based on the value of appearances, but like
Kuizenga he sees this educational system as fundamentally contradictory, rather than consistently built on the sole foundation of *gloire*.

A major challenge to these readings comes from the two chapters
devoted to the relation between *La Princesse de Clèves* and religious
doctrines and practices of the seventeenth century. Leiner bases his
argument on the implicit presence and acceptance of Roman Catholicism by both narrator and characters. This approach raises the thorny
issue of how to weight unspoken ideological assumptions (which I will
discuss below), but it also involves the issue of determination and
overdetermination of narrative events. Is it significant that Leiner pays
greater attention to the mother's contact with her daughter after she
is already tempted by the attentions of Nemours? For Leiner, the
mother's "system of values is based on two key concepts: virtue and
duty" (143). Leiner does not entertain any hesitation about the strictly
Christian nature and source of this duty, and therefore it appears that
for him no other cultural influences codetermine this educational position: neither neoclassical stoicism nor epicureanism, with their emphasis on detachment and tranquility, is mentioned.

Although Henry also views the novel as based primarily on contemporary Roman Catholic doctrine, his approach is quite different
from Leiner's since it stresses a different intertext (a handbook of
Christian life rather than sermons) and accentuates a type of discursive
practice represented in the novel rather than implicit, the heroine's
dialogue with her mother and husband. Henry compares this relationship to the practice of seeking out a director of conscience,
whether a layperson or a person in religious orders. Although most
of Henry's discussion is devoted, like Leiner's, to later sections of the

novel, he points out similarities between the mother's goal—"lui donner de la vertu et la lui rendre aimable" (41; Henry, 158)—and François de Sales's insistence on the sweetness, *la douceur,* of virtue.

In the most detailed consideration of the mother's lesson, Todd views this education as having two aims. One of these is the distrust of self on which many other contributors have commented. The other is "the ideology of romantic love, understood as limited to marriage" (228). In this view, the mother's lesson is comparative insofar as it selects from among erotic behaviors a single one that is recommended, monogamy, in anticipation of a comportmental and emotional concept not yet dominant: "the mother, *in fact* the representative of a new ideology about to take hold, is presented as presiding exclusively over her daughter's happiness" (228). The term "romantic love" is apparently not used loosely here but intentionally and pointedly to indicate a doctrine usually identified with a cultural movement of the following centuries. Yet while Mme de Chartres compares monogamous love with its inferior alternatives, her lesson does not, as in the descriptions presented by Albanese and Koppisch, create in her daughter the constant comparative exercise through which she maintains her superiority over others.

In Todd's view the princess strives for an absolute form of love rather than a merely superior courtly performance or reputation. The attainment of this monogamous happiness is, however, impossible from the start, for the mother's educational aim is the preservation of the pedagogic instance itself. The educational process in which mother and daughter are engaged is not merely a means to endow the heroine with a specific doctrine or ideology but to provide a model for the object of the heroine's desire. For this reason one might even refer to Mme de Chartres herself as an "inimitable example," for after this idealized relationship with her mother there are no other examples of an entirely satisfactory love object. The subsequent failure of the princess's marriage—neither husband nor wife is happy in their relationship—can be traced to the unattainable model of love provided by the mother: "specular, maternal love is the model for 'true,' monogamous, heterosexual love" (230). Neither the Prince de Clèves nor Nemours is equivalent to Mme de Chartres. The basis for the failure of heterosexual love is due to the absence of a common mode of communication between female and male characters.

This description of the princess's upbringing and its consequences will surely be controversial, but Todd's interpretation of the mother's pedagogy has even broader and more challenging implications for the novel's semiological conceptions. The mother-daughter relationship is described by Todd as "specular." This entails a primacy accorded to visual over verbal semiosis. The communication between the two women, which bypasses "the deceitfulness of language in favor of the *gaze,* does not fall victim to the misunderstandings that so often propel the plot" (228). There are reasons to pause at this assertion, or at least to circumscribe it quite narrowly. For one thing, as Todd points out, visual understanding not only fails between men and women but fails among women. Therefore, while the *"faithlessness* of language is everywhere apparent" (230), it is hard to sustain the faithfulness of the visual, which even lets down the usually perspicacious dauphine. What Todd is arguing becomes at some point an understanding based on the sympathy of "those who love" (231, cf. the conclusion of La Fontaine's fable "L'Oeil du maître") rather than on the simple visual/ verbal distinction. For another thing, language is far from excluded from the mother's educational strategy. While third-person accounts in language do lead to many misunderstandings—not the least of which is the Prince de Clèves's belief that his wife has been unfaithful—such language-mediated accounts are the distinguishing feature of the mother's educational practice. In a passage cited by several readers in this volume, the narrator of *La Princesse de Clèves* writes, "La plupart des mères s'imaginent qu'il suffit de ne parler jamais de galanteries devant les jeunes personnes pour les en éloigner. Mme de Chartres avait une opinion opposée; elle faisait souvent à sa fille des peintures de l'amour; elle lui montrait ce qu'il a d'agréable pour la persuader plus aisément sur ce qu'elle lui en apprenait de dangereux; elle lui contait le peu de sincérité des hommes" (41). Since the heroine and her mother are far from court, the visualizing expressions ("peinture," "faisait voir," "montrait," and so forth) must be secondary or figurative. They refer to the vividness of the accounts given by the mother in language, for the court and the libertine conduct it manifests are not physically or visually present. Moreover, far from being an education based on silence, Mme de Chartres's approach differs from that of other mothers precisely because she *does* speak and does use narrative in a situation in which most mothers are silent. One could argue that the princess has been initiated into sexual understanding through an excess of language.

THE CONFESSION

It is hardly surprising that the *aveu* that the princess makes to her husband in telling him of her inclination for another man should receive so much attention in the present volume. After all, not only was it much debated at the very moment of the novel's publication, but, like the mother's educational method, the confession is characterized in the novel itself as highly unusual. Among the issues on which contributors differ are whether the *aveu* is a confession at all, how many confessions the princess actually makes, why she tells her husband what she does, and finally, what are the effects and the moral responsibilities consequent to the *aveu*.

The *aveu* is not called a confession within *La Princesse de Clèves* itself; that is, the alternate French term *confession* is not used to refer to the heroine's statement to her husband about her feelings for another man. This fact was ignored by the scholarship on Lafayette's novel until DeJean's important article in which the older sense of *aveu* is adduced as an appropriate understanding of the rhetorical position the princess assumes in dealing with the Prince de Clèves. In DeJean's view, the *aveu* here awakens resonances of the earlier meaning of the term, defined as an oath of feudal loyalty by which a vassal pledges fidelity in return for the grant of land from a lord (63–64). This interpretation enabled a number of insights that remained unavailable with earlier readings of *aveu* simply as "confession." The princess does indeed give a mark of fidelity rather than a recognition of misconduct. The heroine also, as DeJean notes convincingly, seeks the kind of grant—land, the right to remain on the estate at Coulommiers—that lords grant their vassals. While recognizing the persuasive and useful quality of this renewed interpretation of the *aveu*, we see that both within the novel and in many current readings of Lafayette's text this *aveu* and others are treated very much as confessions. As DeJean points out, the Prince de Clèves seems unable to resist considering what his wife has told him as constative rather than performative. That is, whereas avowal in the feudal sense performs the speech acts (and thus legal and social acts) of submission and promise and is thus performative in Austin's sense, "confession" links the performative with the constative by providing significant amounts of information about previous events. The husband cannot refrain from emphasizing the informational, constative aspect of what she says. He sees her statement as the *beginning* of a confession, rather than as an entirely completed utterance. As DeJean says so well, "He attempts, as the novel's readers have done from the first, to turn her promise of future loyalty, an as yet unwritten narrative, into a confession, the completed accounting for past guilt" (64). The Prince de Clèves behaves, in this respect, very much like the jealous lovers of Lafayette's earlier *Zayde,* for whom no amount of information about the beloved woman's amorous experiences is ever sufficient. In this way, as DeJean points out, the transformation of *aveu* into confession is enacted in *La Princesse de Clèves* itself and is not an extraneous accretion but a demonstration, on the novelist's part, of a difference between the princess's understanding of what she has done and the understanding of her two hearers.[2]

Not only is the *aveu*'s function as a confession debated here, but the number of "confessions" is an issue raised by a reading of this collection of studies. Miller writes of three confessions: the first, the princess's statement to her husband (the *aveu*); the second, the princess's enjoyment of her emotion for Nemours in the pavillion at Coulommiers when she believes she is alone but is in fact again observed by Nemours; and the third, the heroine's frank conversation with Nemours after her husband's death. In this way of counting confessions we are faced with an approach quite the opposite of DeJean's. From no confession we reach three, through a very broad use of the term "confession." What exactly does Miller mean by this term? She seems to consider as confession any symbolic manifestation of what is usually repressed, regardless of the intention of the person carrying out this manifestation or the presence or absence of a receiver. While Nemours is present on all three occasions and thus receives information about

---

2. The verb *avouer* and the noun *aveu* are also used elsewhere in the novel in the more simple, modern sense of the transfer of information without the pledge of a vassal's loyalty (though certainly with some sense of an abiding relationship of trust), and without the connotation of guilt. The vidame, for instance, curious about the anonymous woman who is reported to have told her husband about her feelings for another, suspects that the "other man" is Nemours and "le pressa extrêmement de le lui avouer" (126).

the princess's feelings for him, the episode of the "canne des Indes," widely regarded as autoerotic fantasy, does not constitute confession in the sense of a deliberate transmission of information about one's acts to another person. Indeed, the princess's reverie in the pavillion is not even the kind of event sometimes described as "confessing something to oneself" (*s'avouer quelque chose*), since there does not seem to be the kind of self-analytic presence of mind in this passage that occurs in other moments when the princess mentally reviews her acts and feelings. On the other hand, by placing these three episodes together, Miller's reading permits us to appreciate the significant difference between information and speech act. As Nemours says during the third confession, "quelle différence de . . . savoir par un effet du hasard ou de l'apprendre par vous-même, et de voir que vous voulez bien que je le sache!" (171). Nemours, unlike M. de Clèves earlier, distinguishes between the factual information contained in the princess's utterance, on the one hand, and her will to communicate it specifically to him, on the other. This second aspect, to which Nemours refers with such delight, is the princess's speech act of "confession." Quite remarkably, the outcome of this juxtaposition is to reveal that Nemours finally appreciates what the Prince de Clèves (in DeJean's study) has so much difficulty realizing: that the princess is really making a gesture of loyalty, an *aveu,* rather than transmitting information. The princess uses precisely this term for both statements, "Je vous fais cet aveu" (171).

Defining and counting the confessions are first steps in understanding the significance and powerful attraction of these passages for readers. As Henry points out, the confession at Coulommiers resembles a religious confession in several respects. Indeed, the parallel with a penitential confession reinforces the outrage that the princess feels on learning that her story has been divulged, since church confessions are meant to be sealed forever. The confession exemplifies in the most aggravated form the tendency of language to wander, to fall into the possession of those not intended to receive it, even though paradoxically, this act is intended (e.g., Koppisch 205, Kuizenga 82) to maintain or restore the princess's control over herself or her story. Koppisch cites the words of the dauphine to the effect that the unknown woman who confided in her husband did so for "la peur qu'elle a eue de n'être pas toujours la maîtresse de sa passion" (132; Koppisch,

205), and for DeJean it is a way to wrest the initiative from "all those seeking to control the plot of her life" (63).

Desan would probably not disagree that the confession is an attempt by the princess to gain a certain control or dominance by speaking, but his view of the relationship between language and acts differs from several other interpretations expressed here. For example, Desan sees the princess as guilty rather than innocent by traditional standards: "the princess has sinned, for she is indeed guilty of her thoughts" (115), her claim about "l'innocence de ma conduite et de mes intentions" (122) notwithstanding. Like Albanese, Desan describes the heroine as a representative of an archaic morality. In this description of the confession, the princess seems to place undue weight on thoughts, whereas in the modern mercantile world only acts count. And in this instance speech acts appear to be separated from other kinds of acts.

In Rendall's reading of the final confession, the heroine's last conversation with Nemours, an even stricter ethical standard is applied by the princess herself. Rendall, however, perceives this ethical standard as applying to effects and perceptions rather than to thoughts (including intentions): "The question posed by the novel is whether, or to what extent, we can be held morally responsible for the consequences of other people's *perceptions* of our behavior" (127). Rendall finds that the novel distinguishes between a more relaxed, indulgent standard implied by the narrator's account of the princess's actions, and the heroine's own assessment. His ingenious and productive exploration of the relationship between conduct codes (*bienséances*) and knowledge codes (*vraisemblance*) in seventeenth-century French literature shows that the heroine and her husband both tacitly accept the system of plausibility. Thus the princess accepts guilt, in her final confession, for inferences that can be drawn from descriptions, even flawed and partial ones, based on her conduct.

In this debate, in which many descriptions of confessions or *aveux* stress the errant quality of language, differences of interpretation concern the degree to which (or whether) the princess makes a deliberate statement of her own improper conduct and whether her statement concerning her feelings and intentions can return control of language (and the perceptions it awakens) to the heroine herself. The extremes in this debate seem to be DeJean, for whom the first *aveu* is not an admission of guilt but one attempt to assert a woman's active authorial role over the male appropriation of her narrative, and Rendall, who presents the final confession as the heroine's submission to dominant codes of attributed moral responsibility. However, both of these readings have in common a recognition of the dangers of language gone astray.

RETREAT

The conclusion of *La Princesse de Clèves* is probably the most hotly debated part of the novel. For readers taking a Christian perspective, the princess's decision not to marry Nemours provides an example of Christian virtue as defined and taught by the Roman Catholic church. Moreover, as Leiner, Henry, and Sweetser all argue, Christian virtue is not conceived simply as denial or mortification but as a means of acquiring greater and more lasting happiness than that offered by worldly love. A rather different view appears in the studies by Albanese and Koppisch, who describe the heroine's rivalry with other aristocrats for distinction and superiority. In their emphasis on the heroine's quest to be different from other women, these readings point toward a less optimistic evaluation of the story's ending. Koppisch sees in the very end an abandonment of the struggle for distinction, and, despite the term "victory" in this description, the princess's retreat is motivated by the realization that the game of distinction is simply of little importance. The princess becomes exceptional only by ceasing to try to be exceptional and thus mimetic desire (as Henry also points out) and mimesis itself as a concept are abandoned. Despite the proximity of Koppisch's and Albanese's views of the impetus toward difference, Koppisch sees the princess as ultimately successful. Albanese, though concurring that the princess is "beyond mimesis" (103), portrays an aristocrat who has outlived her class. Perhaps implied in this view is the belief that the princess is no longer engaged in mimetic activity, not because she has acquired the wisdom to transcend it, but simply because there are no other authentic partners available for mimetic rivalry. If so, melancholia rather than happiness appears to be the princess's lot, a nostalgia described by Desan as "the waning of passion and morality from a bygone epoch" (124).

A third, radically different, view of the conclusion can be found in readings inspired by feminism. Miller, Kuizenga, and DeJean see the heroine's retreat as a defiance of the patriarchal order. Whereas the Christian and class-oriented readings, as well as Koppisch's combination of social and psychological interpretation, all point to the princess's decision as largely determined by, and in accord with, existing social institutions, feminist readings generally see the heroine as primarily concerned with gender differences, rather than with class or religious practice. Mme de Clèves's decision not to marry Nemours and not to stay at court is thus the refusal of patterns of conduct arranged to fit male ideas of what is good, pleasurable, or discursively (and even grammatically) correct.

Religious conversion of a radical sort is thus rejected (Kuizenga, 81) and religious modes are adopted only partially and with an emphasis on full realization of the self in a secular sense. For DeJean, the princess functions very much as a representative of Lafayette's critical or metadiscursive view of narrative fiction within the seventeenth-century publishing context: "The princess comes to realize that to control her story she must suppress it" (66). Miller, in emphasizing the implausibility of the ending, points to a lack of verisimilitude as a way of reacting against male assumptions about women's desire, the assumption that women are creatures of desire and must yield to it. Not yielding to it, Miller argues in part, is a way for the heroine to preserve her desire as fantasy. There is a rather distant similarity between Miller's feminist reading and Albanese's and Desan's sociocritical readings, for they all emphasize the heroine's decision to perform or to play a certain game according to rules of her own, despite the anachronism of those rules. Miller sees the solitary preservation of desire as a forward-looking act most aptly compared to women's fiction of the nineteenth century. Albanese and Desan see the princess as attempting to play the solitary game of aristocratic honor when that game has become obsolete and there are no surviving partners worthy of her competition.

These three readings (Miller, Albanese, and Desan) have in common with several others (DeJean and Todd) that they open *La Princesse de Clèves* to description as partially utopian. Whether the term is used—as when DeJean calls the heroine's retreat a movement into a "utopian 'elsewhere'" (70)—or not, the princess's detachment from the society around her can be seen as creating or aspiring to a differently organized society. In DeJean's case, the term utopian is connected with its original sense of place: little is known about the "grandes terres qu'elle avait vers les Pyrénées" (178) and the "maison religieuse" (180) between which she divides her time. What is important is that they constitute the "noncourt" which she has chosen. The term utopia can be used somewhat freely to apply to a reading such as Albanese's to the extent that the aristocratic values acted on by the heroine have *no place* in the court, or, indeed, any place except in the princess's mind.

Todd describes the novel's conclusion as a return to the "ideal presocial existence that [the princess] had enjoyed with her mother" (232). She goes on to say that the novel "entails constructing a counterideology, an ideal world of pure (maternal) love and faultless communication, a world free from deceit and intrigue where marriage would be based only on love and love would guarantee understanding" (233–34). The relationship between the education represented in the novel as actually taking place in a location outside the court and this "ideal world" is not dealt with in detail by Todd, who identifies the mother's pedagogy with death itself. Are the mother's lesson and the "ideal presocial existence" two separate things—that is, does the reader (and the princess) construct an ideal world nostalgically out of the real presentations made by the mother as presented by Lafayette? Is this part of a counterideology absent from the text but created, as a negative image, in the reader's mind? One of the most interesting possibilities opened by this line of reasoning is the interpretation of *La Princesse de Clèves* as a parody. Todd explicitly disowns this term and this consequence, but the argument that the reader creates a counterideology to the one(s) presented in the novel leads, at the very least, to an impression that irony is an important component of the reader's response to Lafayette's text. Moreover, Todd argues further that the princess frees herself from ideology by adopting it absolutely: "In embracing, without mimicry or parody, but in all earnestness, the ideology in its absolute form, she also guarantees that it will have no hold on her" (232–33). It is hard to see how such an earnest and complete acceptance of ideology can constitute liberation from that ideology except in two ways. First, if one attempts to assume the point of view of the heroine, one might claim that the princess is simply without any consciousness of ideology and is thus free from a sense of dividedness or irony. Second, one might take the point of view of a very ideologically aware reader, and say that a complete acceptance of an ideology on the part of a character functions as a kind of reductio ad absurdum, or (I would submit) a parody. Though this view does not seem to be Todd's, I suggest that it can be derived from her remarks and that it would open a provocative discussion of the conclusion of *La Princesse de Clèves* as either absurd or as wrong. This leads to an issue on which a great deal of our understanding of Lafayette's novel must turn: our assumptions about the relationship between the Princesse de Clèves and *La Princesse de Clèves*.

EPONYMITY AND IDEOLOGY

To what extent do the thoughts, acts, and words of the Princesse de Clèves reflect the ideas of the text's narrator and/or of its author? Can we assume that the text endorses what she thinks and does and proposes her as an entirely valid and trustworthy model? Should we assume that she is a form of antiheroine, or should we suppose that the princess occupies some middle ground, being neither entirely endorsed nor entirely criticized and ridiculed?

For two critics, DeJean and Miller, the princess becomes so closely identified with the concept of a woman writer that it seems as if the heroine is an author herself, or at least a fictive equivalent for the author in an ideal and not a biographical sense. They argue the importance of seeing *La Princesse de Clèves* as a text standing on its own, independent of quarrels of attribution and beyond the reductive interpretations that would resolve problems of significance by appealing to Lafayette's biography (e.g., Miller, 32). On the other hand, Miller's comments on women's tradition in literature suggest that the heroine's demands are so closely related to decisions on a stylistic or narrative approach that author and heroine are engaged in a common pursuit, which Miller calls italicization (32), "the extravagant wish for a *story* that would turn out differently." This union of heroines and authors is not surprising, in Miller's reading, since the plots of women's literature are not about life, "They are about the plots of literature itself" (36). DeJean even more specifically describes the princess's actions as comparable to the actions of a writer, who may be the author of *La Princesse de Clèves*: "the princess's story is simultaneously a sentimental education and an authorial apprenticeship" (60). DeJean's interpretation is strongly supported by the princess's collaboration in writing a fictive replacement for the woman's letter lost by her uncle the vidame. This portion of the novel is a *mise-en-abyme* that mirrors the historical situation of the seventeenth-century woman writer. In addition to this scene of writerly production, DeJean finds a figurative correlation between Lafayette's use of the concise and even elliptical expression criticized by certain male contemporaries and the princess's removal of her story from public view by her decision to leave the court and Nemours. This ellipsis links the heroine and the author in a common enterprise of suppression at both verbal and narrative levels. "The 'chez elle' [180] to which the princess withdraws is the actual as well as the utopian 'elsewhere' that seventeenth-century French women novelists delimited as the estate of *écriture féminine*" (70).

The readings by Leiner, Sweetser, the Lawrences, and Henry concur that the author and heroine share common values, but these readers do not describe the heroine as herself assuming an authorial position. Instead they consider the heroine as a character exemplary of Christian virtue and social virtue (*honnêteté*). As Leiner writes, "The Princesse de Clèves serves without doubt as a model of Christian virtue" (152), and it is clear from Leiner's description, as from Henry's, that this model character has no rival in the text for our admiration. Albanese and Desan do not offer such clear-cut assessments of the author's endorsement of the heroine. Albanese, however, seems to suggest that the novel as a whole, and not only the heroine, has a wistful view of the aristocratic ethos, what he calls "unapologetic nostalgia for aristocratic splendor" (101), and that the novel champions the heroine's struggle against the degraded values of a tamed courtly aristocracy. Desan seems to distinguish between the enlightened views of the princess at the end of the novel—that is, during her final meeting with Nemours—and earlier, more naive views that motivated her confession to her husband (121ff). The author and the heroine tend to converge as the novel draws to its conclusion; both are at least partially disabused of the obsolete aristocratic modes of exchange and discourse. Therefore, in concluding, Desan adopts a position close to DeJean's and Miller's. The success of the novel depends on the success of the heroine, who thinks of herself as an exemplary character for posterity: "Because her strict adherence to this moral code aims to leave behind 'des exemples de vertu inimitables' [180] . . . , the novel can be considered a success" (123–24).

Despite the tendency to treat *La Princesse de Clèves* and the Princesse de Clèves as bearing the same values, Rendall and to some extent Todd call into question the basis of such readings by devoting attention to the narrator as distinguished both from the heroine and the author. Rendall's ethical study persuasively locates divergences between the narrator and the character at several points. Generally, in this view, the narrator has a more indulgent moral standard than the princess and often indicates that the heroine is unreasonable in her ethical positions. This suggestion that the princess may be in some ways the representative of inappropriate values may very well be seen as an attack on the novel itself by some of those who equate the perfection of the heroine and the perfection of the text itself. Rendall, however, gives no indication that he intends a negative evaluation of Lafayette's writing. In fact, by separating narrator and character he allows for a much freer and broader reading of authorial intention, one that could permit readers the option of constructing the kind of "counterideology" mentioned by Todd. Kuizenga, like Rendall, sees a difference between *La Princesse de Clèves* and the Princesse de Clèves as a mark of the novel's quality. With an opinion of the princess's success contrary to Desan's, Kuizenga points to the final sentence, with its remark about examples of virtue, to argue that it is the very difference between the heroine and a perfect model that is the proof of the excellence of Lafayette's text—the heroine's *failures,* in other words, demonstrate the complexity of represented existence: "Precisely because the novel does not deal in simplified formulae, and indeed works constantly to show the margin of uncertainty that passion introduces into the behavior of even those who most strive for coherence and virtue, at the end Mme de Clèves is not the incarnation of virtue, but one who leaves some examples of it" (82).

As only one among the many who will read this volume, I cannot know which of the many interwoven debates contained here will attract the greatest and most productive attention. For me, however, the issue of the relationship between Mme de Clèves and *La Princesse de Clèves* is an area of study that takes on special importance in view of these twelve studies. DeJean, with her classic article on anonymity, has raised the issue of suppression of name in such a persuasive way that many of the scholars included herein have referred to that significant ellipsis. One of the effects produced by this ellipsis is a shift in the role played by the heroine, the eponymous princess. Even as we resist the tendency to reduce the novel's text into a direct projection of the novelist's biography or personal ideological choices, we may find ourselves in need of a person, a subject, to whom to attribute them. The dynamic of attribution, coupled with the reader's tendency to identify with the heroine as solitary subject, can create an extension of the heroine's identity over the whole novelistic universe she inhabits. The ellipsis of the author's name and the elliptical style may tempt us to elide author and narrator and even to forget that the princess is only a part of the fictive world represented in the text, not a separate entity that can be used to gauge the rest of her society as if the relationship between "her" and "it" were not thoroughly dialectical and interactive. Todd's statement that the novel expresses, represents, and critiques seventeenth-century ideology is one way, a welcome way, of resisting the temptations thrown in front of us by eponymity.

In dealing both with the character, the Princesse de Clèves, and with the novel *La Princesse de Clèves,* we must confront the system within which each act, each gesture, each word, and even each name operates in a network of causes and effects. This system can be called, globally, ideology, if by ideology is understood that which is so completely assimilated as to be taken for granted, generally called the plausible or, in seventeenth-century France, the *vraisemblable.* Ideology as the "taken-for-granted," the assumptions about what is so obvious it is not worth discussing, should be distinguished from simple rule or precept. Studies of *La Princesse de Clèves* show that ideology, like pitch in music, is perceptible almost exclusively through contrast. What is *vraisemblable,* as Genette points out, is unspoken, for it does not need justification.[3] In Lafayette's text the norm does not slide in-

3. Gérard Genette, "Vraisemblance et motivation," in *Figures II* (Paris: Seuil, 1969), 71–99. Genette also shows that a story completely lacking in verisimilitude may be told without explanation and justification. In both cases, apparently, the reader is expected to compare the story pattern to assimilated norms. *La Princesse de Clèves* is a "motivated" story in that the question of ideological norms and deviations is not left solely to the reader but is indicated in the text.

visible or unspoken into the background. Ideology manifests itself in explanatory comments usually provoked—and this is the insight that confers a deep unity to the studies in the present volume—by the heroine's deviation from the norm. Whether the princess be considered a Christian woman contrasted with the nonobservant or even pagan courtiers, a true aristocrat set against a fallen, tamed and essentially bourgeois court nobility, a woman struggling against a male society, the heroine is, as Leiner says, a *Kontrastfigur* (149) whose difference is noted verbally either directly by the narrator or through the words of other characters. However, this contrast and the discourse it generates within Lafayette's text is only one level of the ideological questioning and display. The level that contains such explicit narrative comparisons as that between Mme de Chartres's explicit educational method and the normal mother's silent or implicit way of teaching about men could be called the horizontal contrastive approach. It sets character against character, especially the Chartres-Clèves family against the larger population of the novelistic world.

Another set of ideological fractures or contrasts is vertical. Here we find the much thornier problem of the relationship between narrator and heroine and between author and narrator. Some contributors locate meaning in the close identification of narrator and heroine and see their shared ideology as important to our understanding of the novel. This is the dominant view among the contributors, even ones approaching the text from points of view as different as Henry, Koppisch, and Miller. This does not mean that all would claim that narrator and heroine are in agreement at every moment of the narrative. The stronger the critic's stress on *La Princesse de Clèves*'s relation to the bildungsroman concept, the more likely he or she is to find an initial divergence of narrator and character, followed by an ultimate convergence. Bildungsroman as genre generally supposes that the main character will pass from ignorance to enlightenment, as that latter state is determined by the ideological values held by the narrator. Koppisch's reading gives an excellent example of textual closure provided by final—indeed, in extremis—ideological union. The princess, haunted by her mother's stress on competitive differentiation from other characters, realizes that this struggle itself is the greatest obstacle to true self-fulfillment. The narrator signals agreement with this position by identifying the heroine's opinions about the world with such "personnes qui ont des vues plus grandes et plus éloignées" (179). Such vertical contrast and the subsequent merger of views invites us to detect ideology as much as do the horizontal contrasts. If ideology is that which is taken for granted, then the princess's final acceptance of a view that she had not earlier maintained must make us aware that her earlier position on the issue of personal distinction cannot be accepted as indisputably and automatically true. When the novel is viewed as a progressive enlightenment of the heroine, the early divergence between narrator and character is the marker that the final position cannot be taken for granted—that it cannot be considered natural or automatic—but that it is a way of defining the earlier, untested views of the heroine as ideologically inferior.

Final convergence, however, is not the only pattern that narrator-character values can adopt. In Leiner's study the princess seems at all points a model of Christian virtue. While the heroine may be tempted, she does not succumb, and therefore it is not her values that change but only her situation. If this understanding of Leiner's article is correct, then there is no progressive convergence in ideology between character and narrator but merely a harmonious demonstration of the variety of applications of Christian virtue to phases of a woman's life. Another pattern is that traced by Rendall, who finds not progressive convergence but varying degrees of difference between the values of narrator and character. This disparity does not provide the unified ideological outlook that Leiner and Henry find in Christian ethics, and the lack of sequential convergence prevents closure of the bildungsroman type.

This leads to still another level of the vertical ideological distinctions made in La Princesse de Clèves: the division between author and narrator. Rendall's reading, first of all, strongly emphasizes the appeals to verisimilitude made by characters and narrator. He points out both horizontal contrast in the assumptions made by the princess and, for instance, her suitor Nemours, and vertical contrast in assumptions made by the princess and the narrator. Seeing the final conversation with Nemours as displaying the behavioral assumptions conveyed in three voices—the princess, Nemours, and the narrator—he sees the narrator as holding values closer to Nemours's than to the princess's (137–38). The vertical ordering of values comes into play at this point, for the narrator's position may not be the correct one. Since the characters and the narrator rely on judgments of plausibility, and since plausibility is shown to be a highly fallible instrument for conjecturing what has happened (and thus, arguably, as a dubious guide to what will happen in the future), the narrator as well as the characters are on shaky epistemological ground. Rendall remarks that the "narrator does not acknowledge the role played by such appeals to *vraisemblance* in her narrative . . . so that their functioning, highlighted in her analysis of the characters' thought and discourse, remains occulted in her own" (138). By acknowledgment seems to be meant here that the narrator does not display a critical awareness of the weakness of these appeals while showing several times the mistakes made by the characters when using similar concepts. Thus the fallibility of *vraisemblance* within the world of the characters provides readers with an example that corrodes their trust in the narrator. This arrangement is attributable to the author: "the implicit critique of judgments based on verisimilitude undermines the authority of the narrator's appeals to them and thus opens, or widens, an ironic gap between implied author and narrator" (138). Despite—or rather, through—the narrator's blindness to her ideological assumptions, the novel's author lays bare the danger of such uncritical beliefs. For Rendall, then, *La Princesse de Clèves* is a novel critical of its heroine and its narrator. Unlike many of the other readers who find that such tensions are not constructed deliberately by the author (e.g., Todd, who states that one must read the novel "against the grain" to understand that it is a "tale about power and ideology" [233]), Rendall makes the case that an ideological critique set forth by its author can be detected by the authorial audience attentive to the vertical fractures of the text's value structure.[4] The Princesse de Clèves as eponymous character is thus meant to be at least in partial contradiction to the ideological position of *La Princesse de Clèves*.

The modern reader of *La Princesse de Clèves* is confronted by a series of interpretive choices now wider than ever. The studies presented here show that Lafayette's novel stands up well to a representative spectrum of today's approaches to reading and describing narrative literature.

4. The term "authorial audience" is taken from Peter Rabinowitz's influential article, "Truth in Fiction: A Reexamination of Audiences," *Critical Inquiry* 4 (1977): 121–41.

To say that the novel stands up to these approaches is to affirm that no one reading is able to provide a totally irresistible and definitive interpretation. It is not the least of Lafayette's merits to have constructed such a *piège à critiques,* such a brief and apparently simple tale, readable by a high school student of French, which can still reward the sustained attention of the most subtle and informed scholars.

These twelve readings will not simplify our task of reading *La Princesse de Clèves.* But that is not their aim, nor was it the aim of the novel's author. Three centuries later, this brief text is still testing the frontiers of literary criticism.

Bibliography

Adam, Antoine. *Histoire de la littérature française*, vol. 4. *L'Apogée du siècle: La Fontaine, Racine, La Rochefoucauld, Mme de Sévigné*. Paris: Editions Domat, 1954.

———. *Histoire de la littérature française au XVIIᵉ siècle*. 5 vols. Paris: Editions Mondiales, 1958.

———. *Romanciers du XVIIᵉ siècle*. Paris: Gallimard, 1962.

Allentuch, Harriet. "Pauline and the Princesse de Clèves." *Modern Language Quarterly* 30 (1969): 171–82.

———. "The Will to Refuse in *La Princesse de Clèves*." *University of Toronto Quarterly* 44 (1975): 185–98.

Arland, Marcel. *Les Echanges*. Paris: Gallimard, 1946.

———. "Sur la Princesse de Clèves." *Nouvelle revue française* 55 (1941): 603 et seq.

Ashton, Harry. "Essai de bibliographie des oeuvres de Mme de Lafayette." *Revue d'histoire littéraire de la France* 13 (1913): 899–918.

———. "L'Anonymat des oeuvres de Madame de Lafayette." *Revue d'histoire littéraire de la France* (1914).

—. *Madame de La Fayette: Sa vie et ses oeuvres*. Cambridge: Cambridge University Press, 1922.

Astorg, Bertrand d'. "Le Refus de Madame de Clèves." *Esprit* 31 (1963): 655–62.

Baldensperger, Fernand. "A propos de l'aveu de la Princesse de Clèves." *Revue de philologie française* 15 (1901): 26–31.

Bastaire, Jean. *Madame de Clèves: "Tragédie en cinq actes."* Paris: José Corti, 1980.

Bazin, J. de. *Index du vocabulaire de "La Princesse de Clèves."* Paris: Nizet, 1967.

Beasley, Faith E. *Revising Memory: Women's Fiction and Memoirs in Seventeenth-Century France*. New Brunswick, N.J.: Rutgers University Press, 1991.

Beaunier, André. *La Jeunesse de Mme de La Fayette*. Paris: Flammarion, 1921.

———. *L'Amie de La Rochefoucauld*. Paris: Flammarion, 1927.

Béguin, Albert. Préface à *La Princesse de Clèves*. Lausanne, Switzerland: Editions Rencontre, 1967.

Bénichou, Paul. *Morales du grand siècle*. Paris: Gallimard, 1948.

Beugnot, Bernard. "Y a-t-il une problématique féminine de la retraite?" In *Onze études sur l'image de la femme dans la littérature française du dix-septième siècle*, edited by Wolfgang Leiner, 25–40. Tübingen, Germany: Gunter Narr, 1984.

Biet, Christian. "Droit et fiction: La Représentation du mariage dans *La Princesse de Clèves*." In *Mme de La Fayette: "La Princesse de Montpensier," "La Princesse de Clèves,"* ed. R. Duchêne, P. Ronzeaud, 33–49. *Littératures classiques* (Suppl. 1990).

Boixareu, Mercédès. *Fonction de la narration du dialogue dans "La Princesse de Clèves."* Archives des Lettres Modernes, vol. 239. Paris: Lettres Modernes, 1989.

258 / Bibliography

Boorsch, Jean. "Madame de Lafayette and the Manipulation of History." *American Society of Legion of Honor Magazine* 46 (1975): 97–109.

Bordeaux, Henri. *Les Amants d'Annecy—Anne d'Este et Jacques de Nemours.* Paris: Plon-Nourrit, 1921.

Boursier, Nicole. "Une Lecture de *La Princesse de Clèves.*" *Les Lettres romanes* 33 (1979): 61–72.

Bray, René. *La Formation de la doctrine classique en France.* Paris: Hachette, 1927.

Brody, Jules. "*La Princesse de Clèves* and the Myth of Courtly Love." *University of Toronto Quarterly* 38 (1969): 105–35.

Brooks, Franklin. "Madame de Lafayette et le XVIᵉ siècle: Marie Stuart." *Papers on French Seventeenth-Century Literature* 10 (1978–79): 121–37.

Brooks, Peter. *The Novel of Worldliness.* Princeton: Princeton University Press, 1969.

Burkart, R.-M. *Die Kunst des Masses in Mme de La Fayette "Princesse de Clèves."* Bonn, Germany: L. Röhrscheid, 1932.

Busson, H. *La Religion des classiques.* Paris: Presses Universitaires de France, 1948.

Bussy-Rabutin, Roger de, Comte de. *Correspondance.* 6 vols. Edited by Ludovic Lalanne. Paris: Charpentier, 1858.

Butor, Michel. "Sur *La Princesse de Clèves.*" In *Répertoire I*, 74–78. Paris: Editions de Minuit, 1960.

Camus, Albert. "L'Intelligence et l'échafaud." In *Théâtre, récits, nouvelles.* Paris: Gallimard, 1962.

Carré, Marie-Rose. "La Rencontre inachevée: Etude sur la structure de *La Princesse de Clèves.*" *PMLA* 87 (1972): 475–82.

Cavillac, Cécile. "Apparence et transparence dans *La Princesse de Clèves.*" *L'Information littéraire* 40 (1988): 23–29.

Chamard, H., and G. Rudler. "La Couleur historique dans *La Princesse de Clèves.*" *La Revue du seizième siècle* 5 (1917–18): 1–20.

———. "Les Épisodes historiques." *La Revue du seizième siècle* 2 (1914): 289–321.

———. "Les Sources historiques de *La Princesse de Clèves.*" *La Revue du seizième siècle* 2 (1914): 92–131.

———. "L'Histoire et la fiction dans *La Princesse de Clèves.*" *La Revue du seizième siècle* 5 (1917–18): 231–43.

Charnes, Jean-Antoine de. *Conversations sur la critique de "La Princesse de Clèves."* Paris: Claude-Barbin, 1679.

Cherbuliez, Victor. "L'Ame généreuse: *La Princesse de Clèves.*" *Revue des deux mondes* 56 (1910): 274–98.

Colombat, André P. "*La Princesse de Clèves* et l'épouvantable vérité du désir." *Papers on French Seventeenth-Century Literature* 17 (1990): 517–29.

Coman, Colette. "Noms propres et durée dans *La Princesse de Clèves.*" *French Review* 51 (1977): 197–203.

Cordelier, Jean. "Le Refus de la Princesse." *XVIIᵉ siècle* 108 (1975): 43–57.

Coulet, Henri. *Le Roman jusqu'à la Révolution,* 1:244–69. Paris: Armand Colin, 1967.

Cuénin, Micheline. "La Mort dans l'oeuvre de Mme de Lafayette." *Papers on French Seventeenth-Century Literature* 10 (1978–79): 89–119.

Dallas, Dorothy. *Le Roman français de 1660 à 1680.* Paris: J. Gamber, 1932.

Danahy, Michael. "Social, Sexual, and Human Spaces in *La Princesse de Clèves.*" *French Forum* 6 (1981): 212–24.

Dédéyan, Charles. *Mme de Lafayette*. Paris: Société d'Edition de l'Enseignement Supérieur, 1955.

DeJean, Joan. "Classical Reeducation: Decanonizing the Feminine." In *The Politics of Tradition*, edited by Joan DeJean and Nancy Miller, 103–8. *Yale French Studies*, Vol. 75 (1988).

———. "Female Voyeurism: Sappho and Lafayette." *Rivista di letterature moderne e comparate* 40 (1987): 201–15.

———. "Lafayette's Ellipses: The Privileges of Anonymity." *PMLA* 99 (1984): 884–902.

———. *Libertine Strategies: Freedom and the Novel in Seventeenth-Century France*. Columbus: Ohio State University Press, 1981.

DeJongh, William de. "La Rochefoucauld and *La Princesse de Clèves*." *Symposium* 13 (1959): 271–77.

Delacomptée, Jean-Michel. *La Princesse de Clèves: La Mère et le courtisan*. Paris: Presses Universitaires de France, 1990.

Delhez-Sarlet, Claudette. "*La Princesse de Clèves*: Roman ou nouvelle?" *Romanische Forschungen* 80 (1968): 53–85, 220–38.

———. "Les Jaloux et la jalousie dans l'oeuvre romanesque de Mme de la Fayette." *Revue des sciences humaines* 29 (1964): 279–309.

———. "Style indirect libre et 'point de vue' dans *La Princesse de Clèves*." *Cahiers d'analyse textuelle* 6 (1964): 70–80.

Deloffre, Frédéric. *La Nouvelle en France à l'âge classique*. Paris: Didier, 1967.

Dens, Jean-Pierre. "*Thanatos* et mondanité dans *La Princesse de Clèves*." *Papers on French Seventeenth-Century Literature* 15 (1988): 431–39.

Didier, Béatrice. "Le Silence de la Princesse de Clèves." In *L'Ecriture-femme*. Paris: Presses Universitaires de France, 1981.

Doubrovsky, Serge. "*La Princesse de Clèves*: Une Interprétation existentielle." *La Table ronde* 138 (1959): 36–51.

Duchêne, Roger. "La Conversion de Mme de La Fayette." In *L'Intelligence du passé: Les Faits, l'écriture et le sens*," edited by Pierre Aquilon, Jacques Chapeau, François Weil, 303–10. Tours, France: Université de Tours, 1988.

———. "La Veuve au XVIIe siècle." In *Onze études sur l'image de la femme dans la littérature française du dix-septième siècle*, edited by Wolfgang Leiner, 165–81. Tübingen, Germany: Gunter Narr, 1984.

———. *Madame de La Fayette*. Paris: Fayard, 1988.

Duchêne, Roger, and Pierre Ronzeaud, eds. *Mme de La Fayette: "La Princesse de Monpensier," "La Princesse de Clèves."* *Littératures classiques* (Supplement 1990).

Durry, Marie-Jeanne. "Le Monologue intérieur dans *La Princesse de Clèves*." In *La Littérature narrative d'imagination*, 86–93. Paris: Presses Universitaires de France, 1961.

———. *Madame de La Fayette*. Paris: Mercure de France, 1962.

Ehrmann, Jacques. *Un Paradis désespéré: L'Amour et l'illusion dans l'Astrée*. Paris: Presses Universitaires de France, 1963.

Fabre, Jean. "Bienséance et sentiment chez Mme de La Fayette." *Cahiers de l'Association internationale des Etudes françaises* 2 (1959): 33–66.

———. "L'Art de l'analyse dans *La Princesse de Clèves*." In *Travaux de la Faculté des lettres de l'Université de Strasbourg*, 261–306. Paris: Les Belles-Lettres, 1946.

Fontaine-Bussac, Geneviève. "L'Ethique dans *La Princesse de Clèves.*" *Revue d'histoire littéraire de la France* 77 (1977): 500–506.

Fontenelle, Bertrand le Bovier de. "Lettre d'un géomètre de Guyenne." *Mercure galant* (1678): 56–64.

Forestier, Georges. "Madame de Chartres: Personnage-clé de *La Princesse de Clèves.*" *Les Lettres romanes* 34 (1980): 67–76.

Fraisse, Simone. "Le 'Repos' de Madame de Clèves." *Esprit* 29 (1961): 560–67.

France, A. *Préface à "La Princesse de Clèves."* Paris: L. Conquet, 1889.

Francillon, Roger. *L'Oeuvre romanesque de Madame de Lafayette.* Paris: José Corti, 1973.

François, Alexis. "De *l'Heptaméron* à *La Princesse de Clèves.*" *Revue d'histoire littéraire de la France* 49 (1949): 305–21.

Friedrich, Klaus. "Mme de Lafayette in der Forschung (1950–65)." *Romanistiches Jahrbuch* 17 (1966): 112–49.

Frolich, Juliette. "*La Princesse de Clèves* ou la magie du conte." *Orbis Litterarum* 34 (1979): 208–26.

Gaillard, Roger. *Approche de "La Princesse de Clèves."* Paris: Edition de l'Aleï, 1983.

Garaud, Christian. "Le Geste et la parole: Remarques sur la communication amoureuse dans *La Princesse de Clèves.*" *XVIIe siècle* 121 (1978): 257–68.

Genette, Gérard. "Vraisemblance et motivation." In *Figures II,* 71–99. Paris: Seuil, 1969.

Girard, René. *Deceit, Desire and the Novel.* Translated by Yvonne Freccero. Baltimore: Johns Hopkins University Press, 1965.

———. *Mensonge romantique et vérité romanesque.* Paris: Grasset, 1961.

Godenne, René. *Histoire de la nouvelle française aux dix-septième et dix-huitième siècles.* Geneva: Droz, 1970.

Goldin, Jeanne. "Maximes et fonctionnement narratif dans *La Princesse de Clèves.*" *Papers on French Seventeenth-Century Literature* 10 (1978): 155–76.

Goode, William O. "A Mother's Goals in *La Princesse de Clèves*: Worldly and Spiritual Distinction." *Neophilologus* 56 (1973): 398–406.

Green, Frederich. *French Novelists: Manners and Ideas from the Renaissance to the Revolution.* New York: Appleton, 1928.

Gregorio, Laurence A. "Husserl, History and Historiography: A Phenomenological Approach to *La Princesse de Clèves.*" In *Actes de Columbus,* edited by Charles G. S. Williams, 209–16. Tübingen, Germany: PFSCL, 1990.

———. *Order in the Court: History and Society in "La Princesse de Clèves."* Saratoga, Calif.: Anma Libri, 1986.

Guers, Simone. "La Religion dans *La Princesse de Clèves.*" *Cahiers du dix-septième siècle* 2 (1988): 133–41.

Haase-Dubosc, Danielle. "La Filiation maternelle et la femme-sujet au 17ème siècle: Lecture plurielle de *La Princesse de Clèves.*" *Romanic Review* 78 (1987): 432–60.

Haig, Sterling. *Madame de Lafayette.* New York: Twayne, 1970.

Harth, Erica. *Ideology and Culture in Seventeenth-Century France.* Ithaca: Cornell University Press, 1983.

Haussonville, Le Comte d'. *Madame de La Fayette.* Paris: Hachette, 1891.

Henriot, Emile. "L'Histoire de Mme Henriette d'Angleterre est-elle de Mme de La Fayette?" *Le Temps,* 16 March 1926.

———. "Ménage et Mme de La Fayette." *Le Temps,* 10 August 1926.

————. "Mme de La Fayette et Madame." *Revue hebdomadaire*, 3 January 1925.

Henry, Patrick. *"La Princesse de Clèves* and *L'Introduction à la vie dévote."* In *French Studies in Honor of Philip A. Wadsworth*, edited by Donald W. Tappan and William A. Mould, 79–100. Birmingham, Ala.: Summa, 1985.

Hipp, Marie-Thérèse. "Le Mythe de Tristan et Iseut et *La Princesse de Clèves." Revue d'histoire littéraire de la France* 65 (1965): 398–414.

————. *Mythes et réalités: Enquête sur le roman et les mémoires.* Paris: Klincksieck, 1976.

Hirsch, Marianne. "A Mother's Discourse: Incorporation and Repetition in *La Princesse de Clèves." Yale French Studies* 62 (1981): 67–87.

Hoog, Armand. "Sacrifice d'une princesse." *La Nef* 6 (1949): 16–25.

Horowitz, Louise K. *Love and Language.* Columbus: Ohio State University Press, 1977.

Houppermans, Sjef. "La Princesse et la mort." *Studi francesi* 98 (1989): 219–28.

Hullot-Kentor, Odile. "Clèves Goes to Business School: A Review of DeJean and Miller." *Stanford French Review* 13 (1989): 251–66.

Hyman, Richard J. "The Virtuous Princesse de Clèves Revisited." *French Review* 38 (1964): 15–22.

Joran, Théodore. "La Princesse de Clèves ou une pseudo-héroïne de la piété conjugale." *Revue bleue* (1925): 510–15.

Judovitz, Dalia. "The Aesthetics of Implausibility: *La Princesse de Clèves." Modern Language Notes* 99 (1984): 1037–56.

Kamuf, Peggy. "A Mother's Will: *La Princesse de Clèves."* In *Fictions of Feminine Desire*, 67–96. Lincoln: University of Nebraska Press, 1982.

Kaplan, David. "The Lover's Test Theme in Cervantes and Madame de Lafayette." *French Review* 26 (1953): 285–90.

Kaps, Helen Karen. *Moral Perspective in "La Princesse de Clèves."* Eugene: University of Oregon Press, 1968.

Kassaï, Georges. "L'Indirect dans *La Princesse de Clèves." Les Lettres nouvelles* (1970): 123–32.

Kibédi, Varga A. "Romans d'amour, romans de femmes à l'époque classique." *Revue des sciences humaines* 168 (1977): 517–24.

Knox, Edward C. *Patterns of Person: Studies in Style and Form from Corneille to Laclos.* Lexington, Ky.: French Forum, 1983.

Köhler, Erich. *Madame de La Fayette: "La Princesse de Clèves." Studien zur Form des klassischen Romans.* Hamburg, Germany: Cram, de Gruyter, 1959.

Koppisch, Michael S. "The Dynamics of Jealousy in the Works of Madame de Lafayette." *Modern Language Notes* 94 (1979): 757–73.

Krailsheimer, Alban John. *Studies in Self-Interest from Descartes to La Bruyère.* Oxford: Oxford University Press, 1962.

Kreiter, Janine Anseaume. *Le Problème du paraître dans l'oeuvre de Mme de LaFayette.* Paris: Nizet, 1977.

Kuizenga, Donna. *Narrative Strategies in "La Princesse de Clèves."* Lexington, Ky.: French Forum, 1976.

Kusch, Manfred. "Narrative Technique and Cognitive Modes in *La Princesse de Clèves." Symposium* 30 (1976): 308–24.

Lafond, Jean. *La Rochefoucauld: Augustinisme et littérature.* Paris: Klincksieck, 1977.

————. "Madame de Lafayette et le repli sur l'être." *Bulletin de la Société des Professeurs français en Amérique* (1987–88): 31–40.

La Harpe, Jean-François de la. *Cours de littérature.* Paris: Firmin-Didot, 1851.

Lalanne, Ludovic. *Brantôme et "La Princesse de Clèves."* Paris: Renouard, 1898.

Langlois, Marcel. "Quel est l'auteur de *La Princesse de Clèves?" Mercure de France* (15 February 1939): 58 et seq.

Lanson, Gustave. *Histoire de la littérature française.* Paris: Hachette, 1909.

Lapointe, René. "La Princesse de Clèves par elle-même." *Travaux de linguistique et de littérature* 6 (1966): 51–58.

Lasalle, Thérèse. "Enonciation de la fatalité et structure du récit: Quelques remarques sur *Les Désordres de l'amour* et *La Princesse de Clèves." Cahiers de littérature du XVIIe siècle* 6 (1984): 293–300.

Lathuillère, Roger. *La Préciosité: Etude historique et linguistique.* Geneva: Droz, 1966.

Laudy, Bernard. "La Vision tragique de Madame de La Fayette, ou un jansénisme athée." *Revue de l'Institut de Sociologie de l'Université libre de Bruxelles* 3 (1969): 449–62.

Laugaa, Maurice. *Lectures de Mme de Lafayette.* Paris: Armand Colin, 1971.

Lawrence, Francis L. "*La Princesse de Clèves* Reconsidered." *French Review* 39 (1965): 15–21.

Lebeau, Jean. "De *La Modification* de Michel Butor à *La Princesse de Clèves." Cahiers du Sud* 51 (1964): 284–91.

Lebois, André. "Blonde et folle Princesse de Clèves." In *XVIIe Siècle: Recherches et portraits,* 291–309. Blainville-sur-Mer, France: L'Amitié par le livre, 1966.

Le Breton, André. *Le Roman au XVIIe siècle.* Paris: Hachette, 1890.

Leiner, Wolfgang. "La Princesse et le directeur de conscience: Création romanesque et prédication." In *La Pensée religieuse dans la littérature et la civilisation du XVIIe siècle en France,* edited by Manfred Tietz and Volker Kapp, 45–68. Tübingen, Germany: *Papers on French Seventeenth-Century Literature,* 1984.

———. "Mme de Lafayette and La Princesse de Clèves." *Journal of European Studies* 3 (1973).

Leov, Nola M. "Sincerity and Order in the *Princesse de Clèves." Journal of the Australasian Universities Language and Literature Association* 30 (1968): 133–50.

Lever, Maurice. *Le Roman français au XVIIe siècle.* Paris: Presses Universitaires de France, 1981.

Lotringer, Sylvère. "La Structuration romanesque." *Critique* 26 (1970): 498–529.

———. "Le Roman impossible." *Poétique* 3 (1970): 297–321.

Lyons, John D. *Exemplum: The Rhetoric of Example in Early Modern France and Italy.* Princeton: Princeton University Press, 1989.

———. "Narrative, Interpretation and Paradox: *La Princesse de Clèves." Romanic Review* 72 (1981): 383–400.

———. "Speaking in Pictures, Speaking of Pictures: Problems of Representation in the Seventeenth Century." In *Mimesis: From Mirror to Method, Augustine to Descartes,* edited by John D. Lyons and Stephen G. Nichols, Jr., 166–87. Hanover, N.H.: University Press of New England, 1982.

Maclean, Ian. *Women Triumphant.* Oxford: Clarendon Press, 1977.

MacRae, Margaret J. "Diane de Poitiers and Mme de Clèves: A Study of Women's Roles, the Victim and the Conqueror." *Papers on French Seventeenth-Century Literature* 12 (1985): 559–73.

Magendie, M. *Le Roman français au XVIIe siècle, de l'Astrée au Grand Cyrus.* Geneva: Droz, 1932.

Magne, Emile. *Le Coeur et l'esprit de Madame de LaFayette.* Paris: Emile Paul Frères, 1927.

————. *Le Vrai Visage de La Rochefoucauld.* Paris: Ollendorf, 1925.

————. *Madame de La Fayette en ménage.* Paris: Emile Paul Frères, 1926.

Magny, Claude-Edmonde. *Histoire du roman français.* Paris: Editions du Seuil, 1948.

Malandain, Pierre. "Ecriture de l'histoire dans *La Princesse de Clèves.*" *Littérature* 36 (1979): 19–36.

————. *Madame de Lafayette: "La Princesse de Clèves."* Paris: Presses Universitaires de France, 1985.

Malraux, Clara. "Autour de Mme de Lafayette." *Confluences* 15 (1942): 442–45.

Marceau, William C. "The Christianity of Mme de Lafayette." *Papers on French Seventeenth-Century Literature* 17 (1990): 171–84.

Marks, Elaine. "Women and Literature in France." *Signs* 3 (1978): 832–42.

Mathet, Marise-Thérèse. "Une Princesse dans la forêt des songes, la Princesse de Clèves." *L'Information littéraire* 42 (1990): 22–26.

May, Georges. "L'Histoire a-t-elle engendré le roman?" *Revue d'histoire littéraire de la France* 55 (1955): 155–76.

McBride, Robert. "*La Princesse de Clèves*: A Tale of Two Ethics." *Studi francesi* 87 (1985): 468–82.

Mercier, Michel. *Le Roman féminin.* Paris: Presses Universitaires de France, 1976.

Miller, Nancy K. "Emphasis Added: Plots and Plausibilities in Women's Fiction." *PMLA* 96 (1981): 36–48.

————. "Introduction" to *The Princess of Clèves.* Translated by Walter J. Cobb. New York: New American Library, 1989.

————. *Subject to Change: Reading Feminist Writing.* New York: Columbia University Press, 1988.

Molino, Jean. "Qu'est-ce que le roman historique?" *Revue d'histoire littéraire de la France* 75 (1975): 195–234.

Moore, Ann M. "History and Temporal Structure in *La Princesse de Clèves.*" *Proceedings of the Eighth Annual Meeting of the Western Society for French History* 8 (1981): 131–46.

————. "Temporal Structure and Reader Response in *La Princesse de Clèves.*" *French Review* 56 (1983): 563–71.

Moore, Will G. *French Classical Literature.* Oxford: Oxford University Press, 1961.

Morel, Jacques. "Sur l'histoire de la lettre perdue dans *La Princesse de Clèves.*" *Papers on French Seventeenth-Century Literature* 19 (1983): 701–9.

Moriarty, Michael. "Discourse and the Body in *La Princesse de Clèves.*" *Paragraph* 10 (1987): 65–86.

Mortimer, Armine Kotin. "Narrative Closure and the Paradigm of Self-Knowledge in *La Princesse de Clèves.*" *Style* 17 (1983): 181–95.

Mouligneau, Geneviève. *Mme de Lafayette romancière?* Brussels: Université de Bruxelles, 1980.

Moye, Richard H. "Silent Victory: Narrative, Appropriation, and Autonomy in *La Princesse de Clèves.*" *Modern Language Notes* 104 (1989): 845–60.

Nicolich, Robert. "The Language of Vision in *La Princesse de Clèves*: The Baroque Principal of Control and Release." *Language and Style* 4 (1971): 279–96.

Niderst, Alain. *"La Princesse de Clèves" de Madame de Lafayette.* Paris: Nizet, 1977.

———. *"La Princesse de Clèves": Le Roman paradoxal*. Paris: Larousse, 1973.

———. "Traits, notes et remarques de Cideville." *Revue d'histoire littéraire de la France* 69 (1969): 822–31.

Nurse, Peter. *Classical Voices*. London: George G. Harrap, 1971.

Paulson, Michael G. "Gender, Politics and Power in Madame de La Fayette's *La Princesse de Clèves*." *Papers on French Seventeenth-Century Literature* 15 (1988): 57–66.

———. "The Equality of the Two Sexes in *La Princesse de Clèves*." *Cahiers du dix-septième siècle* 2 (1988): 57–66.

Peyre, Henri. *Literature and Sincerity*. New Haven: Yale University Press, 1963.

Picard, Raymond. *De Racine au Parthénon: Essais sur la littérature et l'art à l'âge classique*. Paris: Gallimard, 1977.

Pingaud, Bernard. *Mme de La Fayette par elle-même*. Paris: Editions du Seuil, 1959.

Pizzorusso, Arnaldo. *La Poetica del romanzo in Francia (1660–1685)*. Rome: Edizioni Salvatore Sciascia, 1962.

Poizat, Valentine. *La Véritable Princesse de Clèves*. Paris: La Renaissance du Livre, 1920.

Poulet, Georges. "Madame de Lafayette." In *Etudes sur le temps humain*, 122–32. Paris: Plon, 1950.

Rabinowitz, Peter. "Truth in Fiction: A Reexamination of Audiences." *Critical Inquiry* 4 (1977): 121–41.

Raitt, Janet. *Madame de Lafayette and "La Princesse de Clèves."* London: George G. Harrap, 1971.

Ratner, Moses. *Theory and Criticism of the Novel in France from "L'Astrée" to 1750*. New York: De Palma, 1938.

Raynal, Marie A. *La Nouvelle française de Segrais à Mme de La Fayette*. Paris: Picart, 1927.

———. *Le Talent de Mme de La Fayette*. Paris: Picart, 1927.

Redhead, Ruth Willard. "Images of Conflict in the Fictional Works of Mme de Lafayette." *Papers on French Seventeenth-Century Literature* 17 (1990): 481–516.

———. *Themes and Images in the Fictional Works of Madame de Lafayette*. New York: Peter Lang, 1990.

Relyea, Suzanne. "Elle se nomme: La Représentation et la lettre dans *La Princesse de Clèves*." In *Onze études sur l'image de la femme dans la littérature française du dix-septième siècle*, edited by Wolfgang Leiner, 109–19. Tübingen, Germany: Gunter Narr, 1984.

———. "*Se manquer ou se prononcer*: Presence and Self-Possession in *La Princesse de Clèves*." *Papers on French Seventeenth-Century Literature* 10 (1983): 35–46.

Rémy, Jean-Charles. *Madame de Lafayette*. Lausanne, Switzerland: Editions Rencontre, 1967.

Respaut, Michèle. "Un Texte qui se dérobe: Narrateur, lecteur et personnages dans *La Princesse de Clèves*." *L'Esprit créateur* 19 (1979): 64–73.

Reynier, Gustave. *Le Roman réaliste au XVIIᵉ siècle*. Paris: Hachette, 1914.

———. *Le Roman sentimental avant "l'Astrée."* Paris: Armand Colin, 1908.

Richardson-Viti, Elizabeth. "The Princesse de Clèves: The 'Euphoric' Disphoric Heroine." *Wascana Review* 21 (1986): 3–16.

Rougemont, Denis de. *L'Amour et L'Occident*. Paris: Plon, 1939.

Rousseau, Jean-Jacques. *Les Confessions*. Edited by J. Voisine. Paris: Garnier Frères, 1964.

Rousset, Jean. "Echanges obliques et 'paroles obscures' dans *La Princesse de Clèves*." In *Littérature, histoire, linguistique*. Lausanne, Switzerland: 1973.

———. "La Princesse de Clèves." In *Forme et signification*, 17–44. Paris: José Corti, 1962.

———. "Monologue et soliloque." In *Ideen und formen*, 203–13. Frankfurt, Germany: Klostermann, 1965.

———. "Sur la composition de *La Princesse de Clèves*." In *Studi in onore di Carlo Pellegrini*, 231–42. Turin, Italy: Società editrice internazionale, 1963.

Roy, Claude. "Le Roman d'analyse." *La Nef* 16 (1959): 61–66.

Russo, Paolo. "La Polemica sulla *Princesse de Clèves*." *Belfagor* 16 (1961): 555–602.

Sainte-Beuve, Charles-Augustin. *Critiques et portraits littéraires*. Paris: 1839.

———. "Madame de La Fayette." In *Portraits de femmes*, 249–87. Paris: Garnier, 1869.

Sakharoff, Micheline. "La Sous-Conversation dans *La Princesse de Clèves*, un anti-roman." *French Forum* 2 (1977): 121–33.

Salomon, Charles. "La Doctrine morale dans *La Princesse de Clèves*." *Revue universitaire* 7 (1898): 1–11.

Sarlet, Claudette. "La Description des personnages dans *La Princesse de Clèves*." *XVII* siècle 44 (1959): 186–200.

———. "Le Temps dans *La Princesse de Clèves*." *Marche romane* 2 (1959): 51–58.

Scanlan, Timothy M. "Maternal Mask and Literary Craft in *La Princesse de Clèves*." *Revue du Pacifique* 2 (1976): 23–32.

———. "Silence in *La Princesse de Clèves*." *Nottingham French Studies* 19 (1980): 1–13.

Schor, Naomi. "The Portrait of a Gentleman: Representing Men in (French) Women's Writing." In *Misogyny, Misandry, and Misanthropy*, edited by R. Howard Block and Francis Ferguson, 113–33. Berkeley and Los Angeles: University of California Press, 1988.

Scott, James W. "Le Prince de Clèves." *Modern Language Review* 52 (1957): 339–46.

———. *Madame de Lafayette. A Selective Critical Bibliography*. London: Grant and Cutler, 1974.

———. *Madame de Lafayette: "La Princesse de Clèves."* London: Grant and Cutler, 1983.

———. "The 'Digressions' of *La Princesse de Clèves*." *French Studies* 11 (1957): 315–22.

Sellier, Philippe. *"La Princesse de Clèves*: Augustinisme et préciosité au paradis des Valois." In *Images de La Rochefoucauld*, edited by Jean Lafond and Jean Mesnard, 217–28. Paris: Presses Universitaires de France, 1984.

———. "L'Inclination dans *La Princesse de Clèves*." *Journées de Port-Royal* (1982).

Sévigné, Mme de. *Correspondance*, 3 vols. Edited by Roger Duchêne. Paris: Gallimard, 1972–78.

Shaw, David. *"La Princesse de Clèves* and Classical Pessimism." *Modern Languages* 63 (1982): 222–31.

Singerman, Alan J. "History as Metaphor in Mme de Lafayette's *La Princesse de Clèves*." *Modern Language Quarterly* 36 (1975): 261–71.

Stanton, Domna. "The Fiction of Préciosité and the Fear of Women." *Yale French Studies* 62 (1982): 107–34.

———. "The Ideal of *Repos* in Seventeenth-Century French Literature." *L'Esprit créateur* 15 (1975): 79–104.

Stempel, Ilse. "Desillusionierung und Kritik: Madame de Lafayette und die Entzauberung des höfischen Helden." In *Die französische Autorin vom Mittelalter bis zur Gegenwart.* Wiesbaden, Germany: Athenaion, 1979.

Stewart, Philip. "La Princesse de Clèves." In *Rereadings: Eight Early French Novels,* 51–87. Birmingham, Ala.: Summa, 1984.

Stoll, Christiane. "Les Murailles conventuelles de *La Princesse de Clèves.*" *Europe: Revue mensuelle littéraire* (1984): 159–66.

Stone, Harriet. "Exemplary Teaching in *La Princesse de Clèves.*" *French Review* 62 (1988): 248–58.

Styger, Flora. *Essai sur l'oeuvre de Mme de La Fayette.* Zurich: J. Weiss, 1944.

Sweetser, Marie-Odile. "La Littérature et les femmes." In *Le Langage littéraire au XVIIe siècle: De la rhétorique à la littérature,* edited by Christian Wentzlaff-Eggebert, 51–65. Tübingen, Germany: Gunter Narr, 1991.

———. "*La Princesse de Clèves* devant la critique contemporaine." *Studi francesi* 52 (1974): 13–29.

———. "*La Princesse de Clèves* et son unité." *PMLA* 87 (1972): 483–91.

Taine, H. *Essais de critique et d'histoire.* Paris: Hachette, 1920.

Thibaudet, A. *Réflexions sur le roman.* Paris: Gallimard, 1938.

Thomas, Ruth P. "Light and Darkness in *La Princesse de Clèves.*" *Kentucky Romance Quarterly* 28 (1981): 75–104.

Tiefenbrun, Susan W. "Analytische Dialektik in der *Princesse de Clèves.*" *Poetica* 5 (1972): 183–90.

———. *A Structural Stylistic Analysis of "La Princesse de Clèves."* The Hague: Mouton, 1976.

———. "Big Women." *Romanic Review* 69 (1978): 34–47.

———. "The Art of Repetition in *La Princesse de Clèves.*" *Modern Language Review* 68 (1973): 40–50.

Tocanne, Bernard. *L'Idée de nature en France dans la seconde moitié du XVIIe siècle.* Paris: Klincksieck, 1978.

Turnell, Martin. *The Novel in France.* New York: Vintage, 1958.

Valincour, Henri du Trousset de. *Lettres à Madame la Marquise * * * sur le sujet de "La Princesse de Clèves."* Paris: Mabre-Cramoisy, 1678.

Vigée, Claude. "*La Princesse de Clèves* et la tradition du refus." *Critique* 159–60 (1960): 723–54.

Viollis, A. *La Vraie Mme de La Fayette.* Paris: Bloud et Gay, 1926.

Virmaux, Odette. *Les Héroïnes romanesques de Madame de LaFayette.* Paris: Klincksieck, 1981.

Voltaire. *Le Siècle de Louis XIV.* In *Oeuvres historiques.* Paris: Gallimard, 1957.

———. *Le Temple de Goût.* In *Mélanges.* Paris: Gallimard, 1961.

Weinberg, Kurt. "The Lady and the Unicorn, or M. de Nemours à Coulommiers: Enigma, Device, Blazon and Emblem in *La Princesse de Clèves.*" *Euphorion* 71 (1977): 306–35.

Weinstein, Arnold. *Fictions of the Self: 1550–1800.* Princeton: Princeton University Press, 1981.

Weisgerber, J. *L'Espace romanesque*. Paris: L'Age d'homme, 1978.

Weisz, Pierre. "Tragédie et vérité romanesque: *La Princesse de Clèves*." *L'Esprit créateur* 13 (1973): 229–40.

Williams, Charles G. S. *Valincour: The Limits of "honnêteté."* Washington, D.C.: The Catholic University of America Press, 1991.

Wilson, Katharina, and Frank J. Warnke. *Women Writers of the Seventeenth Century*. Athens: University of Georgia Press, 1989.

Woshinsky, Barbara R. *"La Princesse de Clèves": The Tension of Elegance*. The Hague: Mouton, 1973.

Zumthor, Paul. "Le Sens de l'amour et du mariage dans la conception classique de l'homme: Mme de La Fayette." *Archiv für das Studium der neuren Literaturen und Sprachen* 181 (1942): 97–109.

Notes on Contributors

RALPH ALBANESE, JR., is professor of French and chairman of the Department of Foreign Languages and Literatures at Memphis State University. He is the author of *Le Dynamisme de la peur chez Molière: Une Analyse socio-culturelle de "Dom Juan," "Tartuffe," et "L'Ecole des femmes"* (1976), *Initiation aux problèmes socio-culturels de la France au XVIIème siècle* (1977), and assorted articles on seventeenth-century French literature. His *Molière à l'Ecole républicaine: De La Critique universitaire aux manuels scolaires (1870–1914)* has recently been published by Stanford French and Italian Studies.

PHILIPPE DESAN is associate professor of French at the University of Chicago. He has advanced degrees in sociology and literature from France and the United States. In addition to numerous articles and several edited books and journal issues, he has written *Naissance de la méthode: Machiavel, La Ramée, Bodin, Montaigne, Descartes* (1987), *Les Commerces de Montaigne: Le Discours économique des "Essais"* (1992), and *L'Imaginaire économique de la Renaissance* (1992).

PATRICK HENRY is professor of French at Whitman College and coeditor of *Philosophy and Literature*. He is the author of *Voltaire and Camus* (1975) and *Montaigne in Dialogue* (1987). He is currently editing *Approaches to the Teaching of Montaigne's "Essays"* for the Modern Language Association of America.

JOAN DEJEAN is trustee professor of French at the University of Pennsylvania. She has written extensively on French women writers and is the author of *Tender Geographies: Women and the Origins of the Novel in France* (1991) and *Fictions of Sappho, 1546–1937* (1989). She has edited, with Nancy K. Miller, *Displacements: Women, Tradition, Literatures in French* (1990).

MICHAEL S. KOPPISCH is professor of French and associate dean of the College of Arts and Letters at Michigan State University. He has published numerous articles on seventeenth-century French literature and is the author of *The Dissolution of Character: Changing Perspectives in La Bruyère's "Caractères"* (1981).

DONNA KUIZENGA is chair of the Department of Romance Languages at the University of Vermont. She has taught at the University of Wisconsin-Madison, the Universität des Saarlandes, and the University of Missouri at Columbia, where she also served as acting director of the Women's Studies Program. She received her Ph.D. from the Graduate Center of the City University of New York and is the author of

Narrative Strategies in "La Princesse de Clèves" (1976), and articles on Racine, La Fontaine, Lafayette, Le Moyne, and Scudéry.

FRANCIS L. LAWRENCE is president and university professor of Rutgers, The State University of New Jersey. He has written extensively on seventeenth-century French poetry and theater. His publications include *"La Princesse de Clèves* Reconsidered," *French Review* (1965); *Molière: The Comedy of Reason* (1968); *"Dom Juan* and the Manifest God"; "Molière's Antitragic Hero," *PMLA* (1978); and "Love in Molière" in *Ouverture et Dialogue: Mélanges offerts à Wolfgang Leiner* (1988).

MARY K. LAWRENCE is an independent scholar. Her contribution, coauthored with her spouse, is her first publication.

WOLFGANG LEINER is professor of Romance Languages and Literatures at the University of Tübingen and professor emeritus of the University of Washington where he was professor of Romance and Comparative Literature from 1963 to 1978. He has published extensively on French literature and is the editor of two journals: *Oeuvres et Critiques* and *Papers on French Seventeenth-Century Literature/Biblio 17*.

JOHN D. LYONS is professor of French at the University of Virginia. In addition to many articles and three edited books, he has authored *A Theatre of Disguise: Studies in French Baroque Drama* (1978), *The Listening Voice: An Essay on the Rhetoric of Saint Amant* (1982), and *Exemplum: The Rhetoric of Example in Early Modern France and Italy* (1989).

NANCY K. MILLER is distinguished professor of English at Lehman College and the Graduate Center, CUNY. She is the author of *The Heroine's Text: Readings in the French and English Novel, 1722–1782* (1980), *Subject to Change: Reading Feminist Writing* (1988), and *Getting Personal: Feminist Occasions and Other Autobiographical Acts* (1991). She is the editor of *The Poetics of Gender* (1986), and coeditor with Joan DeJean of *Displacements: Women, Tradition, Literatures in French* (1990).

STEVEN RENDALL is professor of Romance Languages at the University of Oregon and editor of *Comparative Literature*. He is the author of numerous articles on French literature and critical theory and of *Distinguo: Reading Montaigne Differently* (1992).

MARIE-ODILE SWEETSER is professor of French at the University of Illinois at Chicago. She has written extensively on all the major authors of the French classical period. Among her many publications are *Les Conceptions dramatiques de Corneille d'après ses écrits* (1962), *La Dramaturgie de Corneille* (1977), and *La Fontaine* (1987).

JANE MARIE TODD is currently visiting assistant professor at the University of Oregon. She has published articles on Derrida, Freud, Rousseau, and feminist theory. Her *Autobiographics in Freud and Derrida* was published in 1990.

General Index

Index to *La Princesse de Clèves*

anonymous publication, seventeenth-century background for, 41, 42, 43, 43–44

appearance versus reality, theme of, 54, 77, 78, 90–91, 146, 158, 202, 238

author's foreword, 58

autoeroticism, 30

bildungsroman, status as, 175, 179–80, 209, 252–53

Cartesian architecture of, 119

Catholic ethos, *see* ideologies reflected in, Catholicism

Catholic references, their absence, 8, 139–41, 141n11, 153, 167–69, 211

ceremonial events, 88

chain of responsibility for the Prince's death, 130

characters: Catherine de Médicis/the Queen, 61, 91, 196–97, 213; Chartres, Mme de, 22, 73–74, 75, 78–80, 97n14, 101n21, 109–10, 143, 145, 146, 147–48, 154, 158–60, 174–75, 197–98, 199, 202, 210–11, 213, 214n9, 214–15, 219, 233, 235, 236–41, 247, 252; Chartres, Vidame de, 61, 62, 77, 91, 92, 132, 137, 166, 168, 201, 206; Chevalier de Guise, 73, 74, 112, 178; Clèves, Prince de, 63, 64, 72–73, 79, 91, 91n6, 94, 111–12, 115, 116–17, 118, 123, 127, 131–32, 137, 145, 148, 161, 162, 163, 168, 178, 184, 187, 202, 203, 204, 206, 212–13, 214–15, 219, 230, 231, 239, 240, 242; Diane de Poitiers, 76–77, 77–78n8, 78, 94, 95, 136n6, 137, 197–

98, 203, 204; Henri II/the King, 76–77, 91, 92, 94, 101, 136n6, 137, 151–52, 204, 213; Nemours, Duc de, 28, 29, 30, 31, 61, 63, 70, 73, 74, 75, 78, 79, 82, 88, 91, 92, 94, 95–96, 97, 100–101, 107, 108, 109, 110, 112, 113, 115, 117, 118, 122, 123, 128, 129, 130, 131, 134, 135, 148, 153, 163–64, 168, 170–71, 171–72, 178–79, 184, 186, 188–89, 190, 201, 204, 205, 206, 239, 242–43, 253; Orleans, Duc d', 80; Prince's spy, 82, 117, 128, 133, 137, 228, 231–32; Reine Dauphine, 61, 62, 63, 64, 75, 77, 107, 114, 131, 132, 161, 205, 206, 227, 231, 243; Saint-André, Maréchal de, 72, 90, 107, 109; Tournon, Mme de, 52, 95, 146, 148–50, 161, 203

court versus country, theme of, 78, 96, 163, 216

crisis of novel, 122–23

critical heritage: seventeenth century: contemporary reactions, 1–2, 3–4, 17, 98, 130; Bussy-Rabutin critique, 1–2; Valincour's *Lettres à Mme la Marquise * * * sur le sujet de "La Princesse de Clèves,"* 2–4, 47, 48, 49, 51–54, 55, 57, 60, 67–68, 130, 134n4, 209; Charnes's *Conversation sur la critique de "La Princesse de Clèves,"* 4, 47, 49, 57; Fontenelle's praise, 2, 137; eighteenth century, 5–7; nineteenth and early twentieth centuries, 7–8, 23, 168, 169; mid-twentieth century to today, 9–12

death versus splendor of life at court, theme of, 150–52

An Inimitable Example: The Case for the Princesse de Clèves was composed in 11/12.5 Garamond #3 by Brevis Press, Bethany Connecticut; printed and bound by John Deyell Co., Ltd., Lindsay, Ontario; and designed by Kachergis Book Design, Pittsboro, North Carolina.

DEMCO